ADVANCE PRAISE

"*Inhuman Traffick* is a boundary-busting epic in graphic history form. The story of the crew and passengers of the *Neirsée* was a dramatic transatlantic saga, transformed into a richly-textured narrative through Blaufarb's meticulous research and Clarke's vivid images. They weave together a history of international law and political relations with intimate descriptions of personal suffering and fortitude. In the process, Blaufarb conveys the lessons historians have learned over the last century about the operation and the human experiences of the Atlantic slave trade that raise provocative questions for the reader."

TREVOR GETZ *author of* Abina and the Important Men

"Rafe Blaufarb and Liz Clarke's stirring work will introduce students to the conflicts over slavery and show them the precariousness of freedom in the Atlantic world. The narrative of the slaver *Neirsée*, its captives, and its pursuers opens a revealing window onto individual lives and sweeping historical processes. The authors brilliantly convey the craft of the historian and the artist as they seek to comprehend and to represent the past."

CHRISTOPHER SCHMIDT-NOWARA *Tufts University*

"Rafe Balufarb's *Inhuman Traffick* takes the emerging form of the graphic history to an impressive new level of excellence. It presents a complex and critical history that adds new layers to our understanding of the history of the global slave trade in the age of abolition in the form of a swashbuckling, rollicking saga that jumps deftly from European capitals to the West Coast of Africa to the slave plantations of the Caribbean islands. The book brings international politics and high diplomacy down to the level of the individual lives impacted; centers the voices and experiences of groups who are often overlooked in historical surveys; and powerfully highlights the role of enslaved Africans in their own liberation. There is an impressive level of detail—everything from the footwear of the African Krumen to the buttons on the coats of the European politicians is rendered with perfect accuracy. The story has something for everyone—high seas combat, legal drama, and running through the middle, a love story. The beautiful and moving illustrations and the powerful and gripping dialogue will render students, scholars and the general reader captivated. This will be perfect for use in courses on Atlantic and Caribbean History and the History of Slavery. The author's thoughtful reflections on his creation of the graphic history; the sustained reflection within the graphic history of how the archival record for this incident at the heart of the book was created and preserved; and the inclusion of the original text will also make it suitable for use in Methods Courses. Very highly recommended—I can't wait to use it in my own classes!"

NICOLA FOOTE *Florida Gulf Coast University*

"How wonderful and rare that an accurate historical tale of such richness and complexity has been related with all the verve of a graphic novel. Liz Clarke has done a remarkable job of giving life to Rafe Blaufarb's narrative of the *Neirsée* affair, a compelling chapter in the story of how Britain's Royal Navy helped end the traffic in human flesh. Readers will encounter a host of key players in the drama: antislavery activists, African Krumen, obstreperous colonial officials, international diplomats, and the enslaved African who struggled against an entrenched and inhumane system. The scholarly apparatus supporting the narrative is excellent, offering readers a compelling introduction to the topic and meaningful exercises for exploring it further. My students will delight to have *Inhuman Traffick* added to their reading list."

PATRICK RAEL *Bowdoin College*

"In uncovering the *Neirsée* affair, Blaufarb has done far more than bring to light a largely unknown episode in the suppression of the Atlantic slave trade. In cooperation with Liz Clarke he has produced a multifaceted perspective on the complexity of the the Atlantic world in the early nineteenth century—particularly in highlighting the hierarchies of sovereignty which determined the fate of so many whose lives were transformed by the slave trade."

JONATHAN REYNOLDS *Northern Kentucky University*

"*Inhuman Traffick*'s painstaking attention to the production of historical documents and their capacity to engender change—often great distances from where they are authored—has profound pedagogical value for professional historians and students of international and transatlantic history. The fleeting presence of Sarah, the sole female character in this history, confirms the gendered nature of power in the transatlantic slave trade. Her disappearance from the written record, as well as that of the Krumen and African craftsmen, portray how the gaps and silences in the documented historical record multiply exponentially around women, Africans, and people of African descent. Blaufarb adroitly problematizes the inherent authority of the written word, as well as the narrow range of people who held a monopoly over communication technologies in the early nineteenth-century transatlantic.

SARAH ZIMMERMAN *Western Washington University*

"Through a gripping tale of intrigue, violence, and tragedy on the high seas, *Inhuman Traffick* reveals the complexity of the geographic, political, social, and cultural space that is the nineteenth century Atlantic. From the island of Fernando Po, to the French colonial plantations of Guadeloupe, to the freed slave haven of Sierra Leone and the machinations of the British naval office, this text brings to vivid life the different populations that together constitute this world. *Inhuman Traffick*'s dedication to exposing the moral and diplomatic quandaries of abolition makes it particularly useful text for all interested in exploring both the possibilities and the pitfalls of international justice mechanisms."

ABENA AMPOFOA ASARE *Stony Brook University*

"The real achievement of *Inhuman Traffick* is not the clear summation of what is generally known about transatlantic slaving and its legal abolition, but its openness about the production and presentation of a 'graphic' history and in telling a panoramic story with as many layers, currents, and peoples that came to constitute the 'Atlantic world,' the author's real main character."

KWASI KONADU *Borough of Manhattan Community College*

"This cutting-edge graphic history represents Atlantic history at its finest. Thoroughly researched and beautifully illustrated, *Inhuman Traffick* brings to life the drama of the abolition era, offering scholars, teachers and students an opportunity to assess the complex political and social worlds created by the campaign to suppress the transatlantic slave trade."

PHILIP MISEVICH *St. John's University*

"The history of slavery is fraught with pain and ineffable sadness. Any pedagogical means that promotes knowledge about the unspeakable cruelty we humans perpetrated upon each other has profound implications for our world today, especially since we all share African origins. Graphic history may hold some of the balm to heal many of the festering wounds of bondage and Jim Crow. *Inhuman Traffick* successfully applies historical creativity, essential context, and skillful imagery to written British and French primary sources, many of which are traditionally reproduced here. Rafe Blaufarb's lively script and Liz Clarke's graphic art will not only awaken historical consciousness and empathy in students so gripped by technology and imagery of the twenty-first century, but will also introduce them to historical methodology and scholarship to promote their critical thinking. The innovative pedagogy of *Inhuman Traffick* successfully supports more traditional presentations of the Atlantic slave trade."

KEN WILBURN *East Carolina University*

"The product of painstaking archival research, *Inhuman Traffick* tells the gripping story of 280 Africans who were forcibly transported across the notorious Middle Passage to be sold into Caribbean slavery, of the British and African sailors who attempted to liberate them, and of an ensuing diplomatic crisis between Britain and France. Liz Clarke's graphic illustrations are beautiful, arresting and unforgettable. The images of Thomas George and his wife Sarah, separated by the brutality of the slave trade, are particularly haunting. Meanwhile Rafe Blaufarb presents a rich trove of primary documents and crucial contextual information to enable students and other readers to do, and to understand, what historians do."

RONALD SCHECHTER *author of* Mendoza the Jew: Boxing, Manliness, and Nationalism: A Graphic History

"Rafe Blaufarb meticulously tells the story of the *Neirsée*, which embarked on one of the most intriguing transatlantic slaving voyages. A compelling story that is replete with useful visual illustrations, *Inhuman Traffic* caps off with thought-provoking questions to facilitate comprehension and deep reflection of life in the nineteenth-century Atlantic world. Blaufarb contextualizes all this with the most up-to-date information that exists about the transatlantic slave trade. This book is a must-read for all those interested in nineteenth-century Atlantic history."

UGO NWOKEJI *University of California, Berkeley*

"Rafe Blaufarb's *Inhuman Traffick* explores two issues of great importance in world history—the transatlantic slave trade and abolitionism. Revolving around the little known *Neirsée* incident, the book introduces us to the world of clandestine slavers bent on delivering their human cargo, the British Royal Navy determined to stop them and the Krumen, Africans who assisted the British in the struggle against slave trade. This is a well-crafted book that tells a captivating story with creativity and compassion. In *Inhuman Traffick,* students can see a master historian plying his craft, creating secondary source information based on original sources. The book's innovative approach of mixing graphic novel, primary texts and historical analysis is fresh and engaging and will undoubtedly appeal to readers. Beautiful illustrations, engrossing narrative, excellent primary sources and keen historical analysis: what else can one want!?"

ALEXANDER MIKABERIDZE *Louisiana State University in Shreveport*

INHUMAN TRAFFICK

THE INTERNATIONAL STRUGGLE AGAINST THE TRANSATLANTIC SLAVE TRADE

A GRAPHIC HISTORY

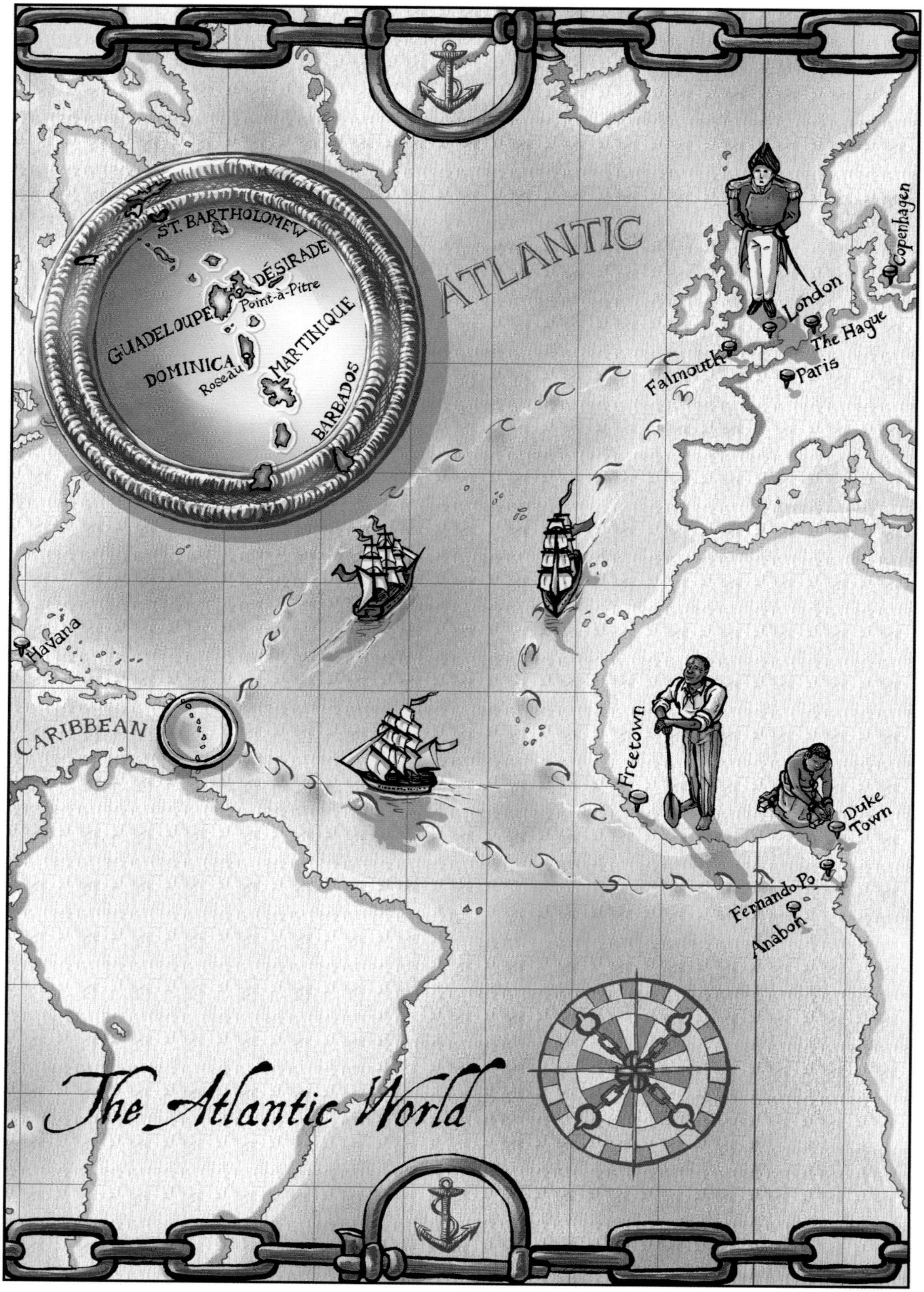

The Atlantic World
ATLANTIC
CARIBBEAN
ST. BARTHOLOMEW
DÉSIRADE
Point-à-Pitre
GUADELOUPE
DOMINICA
Roseau
MARTINIQUE
BARBADOS
Havana
London
Copenhagen
The Hague
Falmouth
Paris
Freetown
Duke Town
Fernando Po
Anabon

INHUMAN TRAFFICK

THE INTERNATIONAL STRUGGLE AGAINST THE TRANSATLANTIC SLAVE TRADE

A GRAPHIC HISTORY

RAFE BLAUFARB

LIZ CLARKE

New York   Oxford

OXFORD UNIVERSITY PRESS

Oxford University Press is a department of the University of Oxford.
It furthers the University's objective of excellence in research,
scholarship, and education by publishing worldwide.

Oxford   New York
Auckland   Cape Town   Dar es Salaam   Hong Kong   Karachi
Kuala Lumpur   Madrid   Melbourne   Mexico City   Nairobi
New Delhi   Shanghai   Taipei   Toronto

With offices in
Argentina   Austria   Brazil   Chile   Czech Republic   France   Greece
Guatemala   Hungary   Italy   Japan   Poland   Portugal   Singapore
South Korea   Switzerland   Thailand   Turkey   Ukraine   Vietnam

For titles covered by Section 112 of the US Higher Education
Opportunity Act, please visit www.oup.com/us/he for the latest
information about pricing and alternate formats.

Published in the United States of America by
Oxford University Press
198 Madison Avenue, New York, NY 10016
http://www.oup.com

Oxford is a registered trade mark of Oxford University Press.

Library of Congress Cataloging-in-Publication Data
Blaufarb, Rafe.
   Inhuman traffick : the international struggle against the transatlantic slave
trade : a graphic history / Rafe Blaufarb, Liz Clarke.
      pages cm
   Includes bibliographical references.
   ISBN 978-0-19-933407-0 (pbk. : alk. paper)   1. Slave trade—Africa, West—
History. 2. Slave trade—America—History. I. Clarke, Liz (Illustrator) II. Title.
   HT1332.B56 2015
   306.3'62—dc23
                                                                        2014013436

Printing number: 9 8 7 6 5 4 3 2 1

Printed in the United States of America
on acid-free paper

A page from the Constitution of the Unites States is reproduced courtesy
of the National Archives and Records Administration.

To Sarah

CONTENTS

MAPS AND FIGURES

MAPS

TABLES

FIGURES

PREFACE

THE MAKING OF *INHUMAN TRAFFICK*

I learned of the *Neirsée* affair by accident in the fall of 2011, at the start of a year's leave in London. I was doing archival research at the British National Archives for a book on the maritime history of the Latin American Wars of Independence. I had begun by looking at what I had anticipated to be one of the richest sources—the correspondence of the commander of the Royal Navy's West Indian Station. As the world's hegemonic mercantile and naval power, Great Britain kept a close eye, through naval forces deployed across the globe, of whatever was happening on the high seas. I had assumed (correctly) that the doings of Latin American insurgent **privateers** in the seas near the rich European plantation colonies of the Caribbean would be of special concern to them.

Having worked my way through the documents from 1815 to 1828, I ordered the box of letters for 1829 (Admiralty, 1 280). In it I found Admiral Fleming's dispatches of February 18 and March 13, 1829 (Documents 13 and 18). They not only described the incident but also forwarded to the Admiralty the depositions of Master's Assistant Davies (Document 6), the Sierra Leoneans (Document 9), and the Krumen (Document 10). These last two depositions offered a rare eyewitness glimpse into the personal experience of enslavement and liberation. I transcribed all these documents verbatim, intending to include one of them in a primary source reader on the revolutionary Atlantic I had contracted to write for Oxford University Press. But I had no intention at the time of digging any deeper into the affair.

In early June 2012 I contacted Charles Cavaliere, my editor at Oxford, to tell him about a future project I wanted to pursue: a detailed history of the first two years of the West African Squadron's operations, 1819–1821. As luck would have it, he was going to be in London later that month, so we were able to have a face-to-face meeting. This took place on June 13 at the Athenaeum, the London club that had been founded two hundred years earlier by none other than John Wilson Croker, the long-serving First Secretary of the Admiralty who appears in this graphic history. It was in well-stuffed leather armchairs under Croker's bust that I pitched my idea to Charles. It was clear that he was not interested, for halfway through my pitch, he interrupted to ask if I had seen *Abina*, the graphic history he had just produced. I had not, nor did I know what a graphic history was. He gave me a copy of Trevor Getz's *Abina and the Important Men* and asked me to take a look and see if I had any subjects suited to that format. I did: the *Neirsée* incident.

Charles liked the idea, particularly because (as he wrote), "the themes it touches upon are so central to so many world history courses—slavery, empire, the Atlantic, the Caribbean etc." He encouraged me to write a formal book proposal. After returning to my teaching duties in the United States in the fall of 2012, I began to do so. Making the proposal required conceptualizing the overall structure of the work and then scripting a sample portion of the graphic narrative. For this, I chose to focus on the landing of the Africans on Guadeloupe and their experience of slavery.

Here is the script for the second page of the proposal sample I submitted:

Page 2
Cell 1

Image: Panorama of slaves on the beach, in chains, herded together, guarded by whites with torches and weapons. It is still dark night, but the scene is backlit by the torches, bonfire, and moonlight. If possible, show as part of the panorama the group of free Africans and Krumen, grouped slightly apart from the rest of the captives.

Text Type: none

Cell 2

Image: Dawn is breaking (7 AM). The chained captives have been formed into a long column, which is being marched inland by the guards.

Text Type: text box

Text: By 7 AM the disembarkation has been completed, and the captives are marched inland.

Cell 3

Image: They arrive at their destination, a sugar plantation three miles inland. Panorama of column of captives arriving on the grounds of the plantation, which features many buildings and is surrounded by sugar cane fields.

Text Type: text box

Text: Several hours later, they arrive at their destination—a sugar plantation three miles from the coast.

Cell 4

Image: Sarah is forcibly separated from the free Africans and led off with the slaves into a large building (a sugar boiling room), She is screaming and crying. Her husband, Thomas George, is also crying out, protesting, struggling against his chains.

Text Type: text box and two speech boxes

Text: Text box: Sarah is separated from her husband.; Sarah's speech box "No!"; Thomas George's speech box "Sarah!"

Cell 5

Image: Interior of large sugar boiling room. Close-up of Sarah in despair, in the midst of the 280 slaves.

Text Type: thought bubble

Text: Sarah: "Will I ever see my husband again?"

Cell 6

Image: Interior of small loft adjoining the boiling room. Close-up of Sarah's husband, Thomas George, in midst of the free Africans and Krumen, looking through a small interior window down onto Sarah in the boiling room, surrounded by the slaves.

Text Type: thought bubble

Text: Thomas George: "What are they going to do to my wife?"

Once the script was complete, I emailed it to Liz Clarke, the talented South African artist who had done the illustrations for *Abina and the Important Men* and was then working on a second volume in the series, Ron Schechter's *Mendoza the Jew*. Liz fortunately found time within her busy schedule to illustrate the sample script.

But before putting pen to paper, she peppered me with questions that made me realize for the first time how different this project was from the writing of a traditional history text. It required me to visualize things that were not explicitly described in the sources—things that historians rarely concerned themselves with. Her most difficult question concerned the footwear of the **Kru** sailors. Would they have worn shoes or not? Liz needed to know in order to draw her illustrations, but this kind of information rarely, if ever, turns up in historical documents, especially the kind of governmental dispatches I had at hand. As I tried to find an answer for Liz, I encountered another unexpected challenge—the issue of African footwear (and clothing in general) turned out to be highly politicized. Depictions of Africans barefoot are sometimes denounced as racist on the grounds that they suggest Africans are primitive. At the same time, to portray Africans in European-style shoes implies to some critics a disparagement of or discomfort with indigenous African culture. What were Liz and I to do? How were we to portray our subjects in ways that were both historically accurate and nondemeaning? Luckily in this case, the eminent British naval historian, Nicholas Rodger, came to the rescue. In response to my query about the footwear of Kru sailors, he pointed out that *no* sailors in the 1820s wore shoes while on shipboard. The Kru and European crewmembers, therefore, would all be shoeless. In this case, a shared professional identity, "sailor," was more important than national or racial differences.

[See the facing page for the completed proposal page derived from the script above.]

Liz and I finished the proposal at the end of September and turned it in to Charles. He sent it to seven expert reviewers, whose comments I appreciated: Trevor Getz, San Francisco State University; Ibrahim Hamza, Virginia Commonwealth University; Patrick Rael, Bowdoin College; Nicola Foote, Florida Gulf Coast University; Jonathan T. Reynolds, Northern Kentucky University; Matthew Hassett, University of North Carolina–Wilmington; Ousman M. Kobo, The Ohio State University; and Arthur Abraham, Virginia State University. By January 2013 they had all returned their assessments to Charles. Their verdict was unanimously positive, but all had thoughtful and constructive suggestions for improving the project. We took these suggestions to heart and tried to incorporate them in the final book. For example, one reviewer thought it important that the graphic narrative make explicit the hardships of the Middle Passage. This reviewer also emphasized how important it was in the "Historical Context" section to situate the *Neirsée* affair in relation to "British abolitionism and imperialism, the ongoing slave economy of the Americas, and also the complexity of the African relationships to the Atlantic world," especially "the ongoing slave trade in Africa and role of slavery in Africa." Hopefully, the final product is better because of this reviewer's feedback. On a couple of occasions, however, we had to grapple with their suggestions. For example, one reviewer appreciated that the French characters in the sample graphic narrative spoke French (with English subtitles provided), while another worried that this "linguistic switching" might "prove distracting for students." Reviewers sometimes offer contradictory advice and, when they do, it is up to the writer to decide. In the end, I decided to have all the characters speak English, in large part for the purely practical reason of not obscuring Liz's

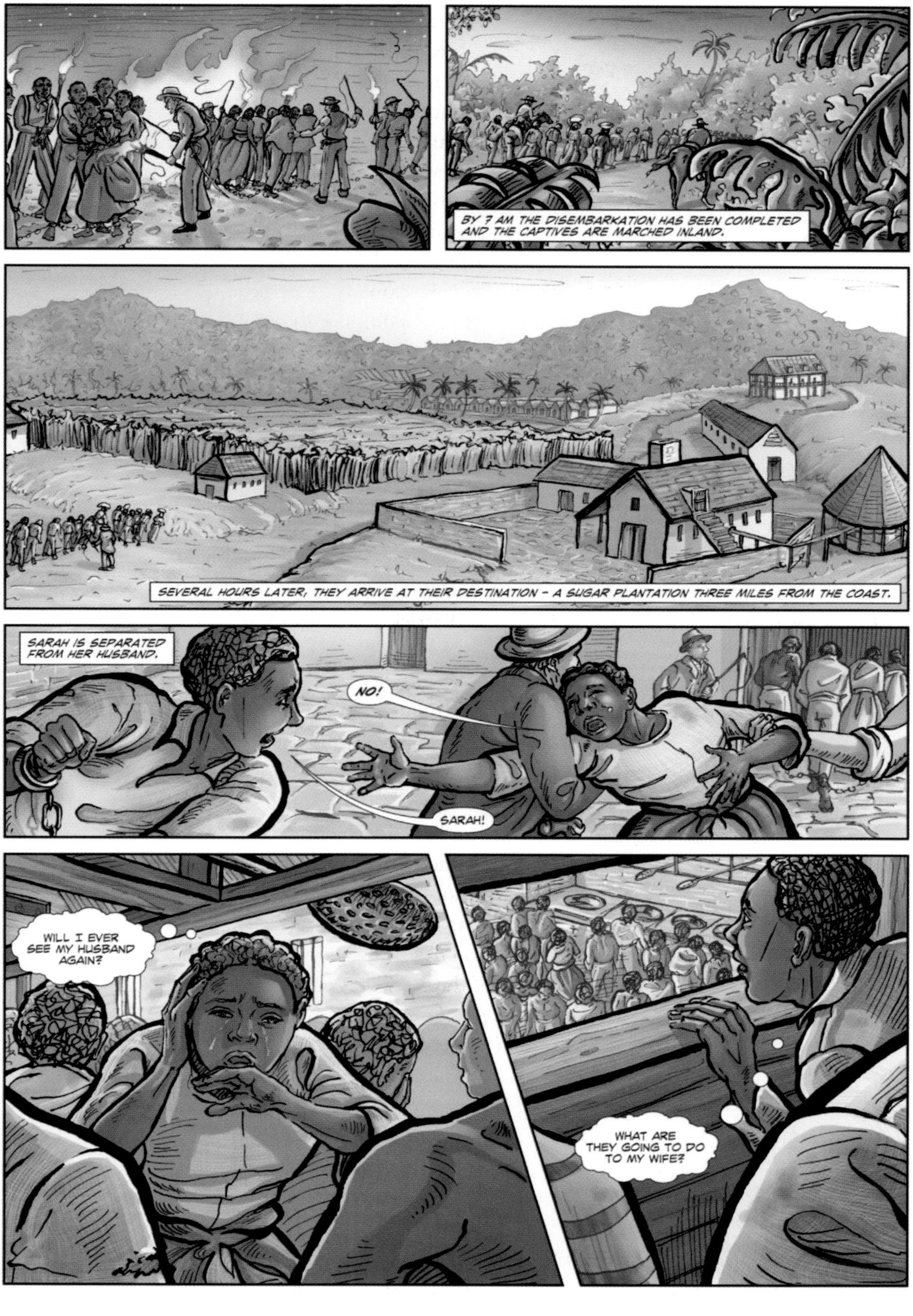
BY 7 AM THE DISEMBARKATION HAS BEEN COMPLETED AND THE CAPTIVES ARE MARCHED INLAND.
SEVERAL HOURS LATER, THEY ARRIVE AT THEIR DESTINATION – A SUGAR PLANTATION THREE MILES FROM THE COAST.
SARAH IS SEPARATED FROM HER HUSBAND.
NO!
SARAH!
WILL I EVER SEE MY HUSBAND AGAIN?
WHAT ARE THEY GOING TO DO TO MY WIFE?

artwork with too many speech bubbles. Other reviewers liked some of our original ideas. One was particularly enthused that the graphic narrative was going to show the itineraries of the documents themselves as they moved across the Atlantic world (see Map 6).

In February I signed a formal contract with Oxford University Press. Now the real work began. I had to write a complete script and provide a full set of primary documents, but all I had were two of Fleming's dispatches and the depositions. These were interesting enough, but clearly did not tell the whole story of the *Neirsée*. How had the slave ship been captured by the H.M.S. *Eden*? What happened to the Krumen and the Sierra Leoneans after they had been cast ashore upon Dominica? Whatever became of Sarah? Were the slavers ever caught? What did the French think of the affair? Did it have any broader diplomatic repercussions? I did not know if there were any additional documents that could answer these questions, but I had to go back to the archives to see. So I returned to Europe in the summer of 2013.

The highlights of this research trip were two-week stays in London and Paris and a weeklong visit to Aix-en-Provence. I did my London research exclusively at the National Archives. There, I obtained digital photographs of the following documents:

Admiralty (ADM) series:
- all of the relevant correspondence of Admiral Fleming;
- all of Captain Owen's correspondence;
- all of the surviving ships' logs and muster books for the vessels concerned;
- all of the existing correspondence of the junior naval officers involved.

Colonial Office (CO) series:
- all of the relevant correspondence of the governor of Dominica;
- ditto for Sierra Leone;
- ditto for Fernando Po.

Foreign Office (FO) series:
- all of the relevant materials from the British embassy to France;
- ditto for the minor powers (Denmark, Holland, and Sweden);
- all of the relevant material from the Foreign Office department in charge of slave trade matters.

The amount of material generated by the British on the *Neirsée* affair was overwhelming, particularly the correspondence of Captain Owen, who literally wrote thousands of pages of dispatches during his brief command at Fernando Po. I would not have been able to manage it all, had it not been for the help of both my wife and my research assistant, the soon-to-be

Dr. Bryan Banks. My visit to London also gave me the opportunity to pick the brains of Professors Nicholas Rodger and Andrew Lambert, the two leading historians of the Royal Navy.

After London, I moved on to Paris, where I worked at two archives, the Service Historique de la Défense (the Historical Service of the Defense Ministry) and the Archives des Affaires étrangères (Foreign Affairs Archives). The naval records at the Historical Service of the Defense Ministry, while providing insight into the French antislavery efforts of the late 1820s, made no reference to the *Neirsée* affair. The Foreign Affairs Archives, however, had a full dossier containing not only much of the correspondence between Portalis, Rothsay, Aberdeen, and Polignac (most of which I had already obtained in London) but also internal correspondence between Hyde de Neuville, the colonial minister, and Portalis at Foreign Affairs. This gave me my first taste of the French government's perspective on the matter and also revealed some difference of opinion between the naval/colonial and diplomatic branches of the French government. Paris, however, was not nearly as helpful as Aix-en-Provence, home to France's rich (but woefully catalogued, organized, and run) Overseas Archives. In these, I eventually found the letter books of the governor of Guadeloupe, the Baron des Rotours, which at last gave me a sense of how the French authorities in the Caribbean dealt with the affair. These provided a necessary counterpoint to Fleming's correspondence. I finished all this research in mid-July. In all, I had about 10,000 photos, a more-than-ample basis for the book. Indeed, in the months to come, my biggest problem became figuring out what to cut—something historians dislike doing.

The next step was to write the script. I had already begun sketching a basic outline while in Europe, but I did not shift into high gear until returning to the United States on August 13. For the next three weeks I worked nonstop on the script, driven by the knowledge that Liz had only a narrow window of opportunity (September–February) in which she could work on the project. At the same time, I made an initial selection of archival documents for the "Primary Sources" section. It soon became clear that scriptwriting and document selection were entangled challenges. I wanted the script and documents to correspond to each other. This meant that I had to eliminate documents that did not directly advance the narrative or send it veering off on tangents. Similarly, I had to cut from the script episodes based on documents that I could not include because of space constraints. Examples of what ended up on the cutting room floor include Captain Deare's trip to St. Bartholomew to discover what had become of the *Neirsée* and Admiral Fleming's angry correspondence with the co-governors of that island when he learned that they had not facilitated Deare's mission. Space constraints forced me to leave out a number of documents, such as excerpts from ships' log books, that would have added color but were not necessary to move the story forward. I eliminated others for excessive repetition, a particular characteristic of the ambassadorial communications that usually reproduced verbatim the phrasing of ministerial directives. Finally, to save space for more substantive content, I decided to cut the lengthy salutations and closing formalities that preceded and ended all the letters. I did, however, retain these in Document 1, to give a feeling for the formality of the documents.

At the start of the project, I had been concerned about not having enough documents for a narrative. I need not have worried. In the end, there was only space for a fraction of the documents I found. Yet, while there were plenty of primary sources, they were inadequate in some ways. Except for the depositions, they did not directly describe the characters' personal experiences. A novelist, screenplay writer, or poet would use imagination to fill in this gap. But as a historian, I did not feel comfortable straying too far from what the sources said. Because of this, the graphic history does not focus on the relationship between Thomas George and Sarah, an aspect of the story around which a movie might be structured. Nor does it focus on the experience of a single person (perhaps one of the original *Neirsée* captives), a narrative strategy pioneered by Alex Haley in his pathbreaking novel *Roots* (1976) and extended by Toni Morrison in *Beloved* (1987). To zoom in on one individual would have narrowed the wide-angled perspective on the Atlantic world opened up by the *Neirsée* incident. Moreover, in poring over the documentary record, I felt that the incident's center of gravity—its people, places, and issues—was not fixed, but rather shifted as the plot developed. To capture this, I drew inspiration from film and designed the narrative as a zoom out, moving from the personal to the colonial/regional and finally to the international level. The graphic narrative begins off the coast of Africa and then moves over the ocean to Guadeloupe, providing a close-up view of the retaking of the *Neirsée* and enslavement of its passengers. The frame then widens to encompass the colonial Caribbean and the attempts of the local European authorities there to deal with the incident. In the final act, the scene expands still further and shifts to Europe to recount the *Neirsée* affair's international diplomatic repercussions. My intention was to bring to light the Atlantic world itself, in all of its complex and interrelated human, spatial, and temporal dimensions.

This was a big, abstract goal. But writing the script also demanded a degree of highly detailed, almost miniscule, technical work. To give Liz a product she could work from, I had to translate my ideas for the plot flow, images, and dialogue into a particular format. First, the narrative had to be broken into a series of discrete snapshots that would form the frames or cells of the graphic narrative. For each cell, I had to specify the visual image to be portrayed, the type of text to be included (speech or narrative), and the context of the text itself. I did this by early September 2013, although I continued to make changes to the script for the next six weeks or so. In all, the script contains over 350 cells. This example, for pages 85–86, shows you what it looked like. Since this scene formed part of the original proposal, it also gives you a sense of some of the changes Liz and I had made for the final version. I've left unchanged the comments I made to help guide Liz as she visualized the scene.

Cell 126

Image: Panorama of the ship anchored off the beach at Guadeloupe; there is a large bonfire on the beach, men milling around, and at least 12 large rowboats drawn up on the sand.

Text Type: text box

Text: 11 PM. The ship anchored near the small town of Saint-François. On the beach, the slavers' agents were waiting to disembark the ship's human cargo.

Cell 127

Image: The rowboats from the shore, with white men on board, rowing out to the slave ship. A leader in one of the rowboats is crying out:

Text Type: speech box

Text: Leader in rowboat: "Faster, we've got to land them before dawn!"

Cell 128

Image: Slaves being loaded off the ship onto the boats; boats that have been already loaded on the way back to the shore; perhaps some of the boats have already arrived back at the shore with slaves. Some of the slavers in the rowboats are yelling:

Text Type: three speech boxes

Text: "Come on!"; "Move on down!"; and "Hurry up!"

Cell 129

Image: Panorama of slaves on the beach, in chains, herded together, guarded by whites with torches and weapons. It is still dark night, but the scene is backlit by the torches, bonfire, and moonlight. If possible, show as part of the panorama the group of KRUMEN and FREE AFRICANS, grouped slightly apart from the rest of the captives.

Text Type: none

Cell 130

Image: Dawn is breaking (7 AM). The chained captives have been formed into a long column, which is being marched inland by the guards.

Text Type: text box

Text: By 7 AM the disembarkation was completed, and the captives began to be marched inland.

Cell 131

Image: They arrive at their destination, a sugar plantation three miles inland. Panorama of column of captives arriving on the grounds of the plantation, which features many buildings and is surrounded by sugar cane fields.

Text Type: text box

Text: Several hours later, they arrived at their destination—a sugar plantation three miles from the coast.

Cell 132

TO PORTRAY THESE WRENCHING SCENES FOCUSED ON THE SEPARATION OF THOMAS AND SARAH, WORDS FALL SHORT. I THINK THE IMAGES HAVE TO SPEAK FOR THEMSELVES. I HAVE TWO IDEAS TO HELP CONVEY VISUALLY WHAT CAN'T BE EXPRESSED VERBALLY. (1) USE "TRAUMATICALLY"-SHAPED CELL BORDERS (FOR EXAMPLE, JAGGED EDGES, WHICH MIGHT INDICATE A RIPPING APART); (2) INSTEAD OF DEPICTING THE PLANTATION SURROUNDINGS, AS IN THE OTHER IMAGES, PERHAPS USE A BLACK BACKGROUND—SO THERE IS NOTHING BUT THOMAS, SARAH, AND THEIR PAIN IN THE IMAGE.

FOR AN EMOTIONAL PARALLEL, THINK ABOUT THE CONCENTRATION CAMPS—THOSE DESIGNATED FOR THE GAS CHAMBERS TO THE RIGHT, THOSE WHO WILL LIVE ANOTHER DAY TO THE LEFT. SARAH IS GOING TO THE RIGHT (DOOM AND HOPELESSNESS, FEAR), THOMAS IS GOING TO THE LEFT (FEAR AS WELL, BUT SOME HOPE, AS WELL AS SOME GUILT BECAUSE HE'S GOING TO A BETTER FATE THAN HIS WIFE).

Image: SARAH is forcibly separated from the free Africans and led off with the slaves into a large building (a sugar boiling room). She is screaming and crying—panicked horror. Her husband, THOMAS GEORGE, is also crying out, protesting, struggling against his chains—combination of anger, horror, and fear.

Text Type: none

Cell 133

Image: Interior of large sugar boiling room. Close-up of SARAH in absolute despair, despondency, and dejection, total loss, in the midst of the 280 slaves.

Text Type: none

Cell 134

Image: Interior of small loft adjoining the boiling room. Close-up of Sarah's husband, Thomas George, in midst of the free Africans and Krumen, looking through a small interior window down onto Sarah in the boiling room, surrounded by the slaves. IT IS CLEAR TO THOMAS THAT SARAH HAS BEEN DISTINGUISHED FROM THE FREE AFRICANS AND PLACED WITH THE "SLAVES" WHO ARE CLEARLY DESTINED FOR SALE AND SLAVERY WITH NO HOPE OF BEING SAVED. IN ADDITION TO FEELING THE DEEPEST DESPAIR AT THEIR SEPARATION, THOMAS MIGHT BE FEELING SOME GUILT TOO, SINCE HE IS BEGINNING TO SENSE THAT HE IS NOT BEING ASSIMILATED TO THE GENERAL MASS OF SLAVES, WHILE HIS WIFE IS. . . . HE MAY BE GUILTILY COMING TO REALIZE THAT HE'S GOT A CHANCE OF GETTING OUT OF THIS SITUATION, WHILE HIS WIFE IS DOOMED.

Text Type: none

As you can see from Cells 132–134, we eliminated the verbal expressions of dismay uttered by Sarah and Thomas in the proposal sample. I never felt comfortable with the words I had originally put in their mouths. Their utterances seemed flat, a completely inadequate reflection of their interior upheaval. Several reviewers felt the same way. Reviewer four put it succinctly: the dialogue lacked "visceral appeal." Clearly we had to find another way of getting at Sarah's and Thomas's anguish. But how to put the experience of enslavement and forcible, probably permanent, separation from a loved one into words? The works of Alex Haley and Toni Morrison, not to mention the personal accounts of people like Solomon Northup who actually experienced enslavement (his remarkable story is powerfully depicted in the 2013 film *Twelve Years a Slave*), show that it is possible to convey a sense of such trauma through writing. But these writers had thousands of words and hundreds of pages in which to do so. Even if I had their extraordinary gifts and insight, I still had just a few speech bubbles to work with. There was simply no way that a handful of words could distill Sarah's and Thomas's emotions. It was at this point I recalled the adage, "a picture is worth a thousand words," and asked Liz to do the heavy lifting. As an author, stepping aside and shutting up seemed to be the most effective way of expressing the inexpressible.

My reliance on Liz to convey things that words—or at least my words—could not express underlines the collaborative nature of our endeavor. For the most part, historical writing is a solitary activity, but this was far different. During our eighteen-month collaboration, we have had an intense dialogue. To draw her illustrations, Liz needed to know what people, places, and things looked like: William Wilberforce, a Guadeloupean sugar plantation, Old Calabar, a palm oil house, a British naval uniform, and many, many more. To provide her with answers, my research assistant Caleb Greinke and myself spent dozens of hours in the university library and on the internet. Frequently, this proved inadequate, and I had to turn to various experts in various fields for guidance. I have already mentioned the two British naval historians, Professors Rodger and Lambert, whose help was invaluable. Others in Britain—Dr. Jennifer Daley, a specialist in naval uniforms, and Peter Grindal, a retired officer of the Royal Navy—provided further assistance. Colleagues in France—Cécile Vidal and Myriam Cottias in particular—kindly answered questions related to West Africa and Guadeloupe. It was the community of American-based historians specializing in African history and the transatlantic slave trade, however, who gave me the most sustained, invaluable aid. Unlike most academic historians, who are fiercely individualistic and often jealous of their preserves, these scholars have an exceptional tradition of cooperation. This has undoubtedly been reinforced by their great achievement, the Trans-Atlantic Slave Trade Database, directed by David Eltis—a monument to what collective effort can achieve. Dr. Philip Misevich has been particularly unstinting with his time and has been uncommonly patient with my often naïve questions. Others who have given me invaluable assistance include Rebecca Hartkopf Schloss, Sean Hawkins, Benjamin Lawrance, Lisa Lindsay, Joe Miller, Ugo Nwokeji, Chris Schmidt-Nowara, and Randy Sparks. They all had the grace to admit an outsider into their world and guide his steps. I hope that I have been able to give something worthwhile back.

Working from our images and information, Liz produced black-and-white sketches. When she finished a batch (anywhere from three to six pages), she emailed them to Charles and myself to review. On occasion we wanted to change details or correct small errors that I had let slip into the script. For the most part, however, the sketches were perfect. Once we approved them, Liz set to work coloring them. I was amazed with what they looked like—I had never seen my work in visual form before. I am grateful to Liz for rendering it so brilliantly and to Charles for having the vision to pursue this kind of historical work.

ABOUT THE AUTHOR

Rafe Blaufarb (Ph.D., University of Michigan) is Ben Weider Eminent Scholar Chair and Director of the Institute on Napoleon and the French Revolution in the History Department at Florida State University. He is the author of books and articles on French history as well as several articles on other topics, including Atlantic and Latin American history.

ABOUT THE ILLUSTRATOR

Liz Clarke is an illustrator based in Cape Town, South Africa. Her artwork has appeared in magazines, games, and books, including *Abina and the Important Men* by Trevor R. Getz and *Mendoza the Jew* by Ronald Schechter, both published by Oxford University Press.

PART I
THE HISTORICAL CONTEXT

It is an unjust and inhuman traffick, degrading to the character of

man and most disgraceful to the character of the British nation.

—*Lord Holland speaking to the House of Lords (24 June 1806)*

From the early 1500s until 1867, the slave trade from Africa to the Americas carried 10.7 million captives across the Atlantic, two-thirds of them making the journey after 1750.[1] Nearly two million more died during the horrendous crossing, known as the Middle Passage. This massive, involuntary deportation was one of the largest migrations in history. At its height in the mid-eighteenth century, six out of seven migrants to the Americas were from Africa. African women accounted for fourteen out of fifteen females who crossed over during that same period. Dwarfing European migration during the same period, the transportation of enslaved Africans to the Americas profoundly shaped the composition of the New World's population. The economic impact of these migrants was decisive. Although they participated in almost every occupation, even that of soldier, the vast majority were employed on the Brazilian and Caribbean plantations that dominated the colonial American economy. Without their cultural, social, and economic influence, the history of the Americas would have followed a radically different path.

The impact of the transatlantic slave trade was probably not as great in Africa as it was in America. Long-established African practices of enslavement and slave trading were able to meet European demand, even though that demand rose to unprecedented levels by the late seventeenth century. This is not to minimize the impact on individuals and communities that suffered from and participated in enslavement and the transatlantic trade. But changes in Africa were incremental and geographically uneven. In the regions from which captives were taken and in coastal centers where they were marketed to European traders, the impact was especially profound.

---

1 *Substance of the Debate on a Resolution for Abolishing the Slave Trade* (London: Phillips and Fardon, 1806), 141.

In these areas the transatlantic slave trade affected demographic patterns, gender and age balance, gender norms, political and social organization, the economy, and the meaning of slavery itself. This was true not only of those groups targeted for enslavement but frequently of others as well. For example, the far-flung community of Aro traders who ran the slave markets of the Bight of Biafra progressively abandoned its mercantile ethos for a martial conception of status and masculinity. In other coastal centers, **Eurafrican** elites arose, exerting political influence through their control of the trade (see Map 4).

The abolition of the transatlantic slave trade (initiated by Britain in 1807) may have had as great an impact on Africa as the trade itself. By making available cheap labor for internal use, it helped spur economic innovation and growth in nineteenth-century Africa. Slaves who would have been taken to the Americas were now employed in Africa cultivating lucrative export crops—especially palm oil—demanded by industrializing Europe. At the close of the nineteenth century, however, the European powers seized upon internal African slavery as a pretext for direct intervention and, ultimately, occupation. The entwined legacies of European imperialism and internal slavery continue to influence the international relations and domestic politics of African countries today.

THE ATLANTIC ENVIRONMENT

For the first hundred years or so, Portuguese merchants were the main European participants in the transatlantic slave trade. From ports in their American colony, Brazil, they could catch the bottom of the counterclockwise currents and winds of the South Atlantic for rapid passage to West Central Africa. There, after purchasing slaves and, critically, provisions to feed them, the Portuguese merchants would return, using the currents and winds of the northern leg of the cycle to speed their voyage. Although the scale of the Portuguese trade was initially smaller than the older, trans-Saharan trade between West and North Africa, it grew steadily, ultimately accounting for nearly half of all those caught up in the transatlantic slave trade. The majority were destined to labor on Brazilian sugar and coffee plantations. Portugal was also the main supplier of slaves to Spanish America.

In the middle of the seventeenth century, northern European countries began to imitate the Portuguese and develop sugar and coffee plantations in their Caribbean colonies. And like the Portuguese, they sought slaves from Africa to provide labor. But the established Portuguese presence in the West Central African slave markets gave the northern Europeans an incentive to develop a new, additional source of supply by building a different circuit of trade. They found that the climactic conditions north of the equator worked in their favor. It allowed northern European slave traders to depart from their home countries and sail with the currents and winds to reach the West African coast. Many continued on, catching the Guinea current to reach the larger markets of the Gold Coast and the Bights of Benin and Biafra (see Map 1). Having acquired their

EUROPE
NORTH AMERICA
WESTERLIES
ATLANTIC OCEAN
AFRICA
NORTH EAST TRADES
SOUTH AMERICA
SOUTH EAST TRADES
ATLANTIC OCEAN
WESTERLIES
N
W
E
S
0 km
1700
0 miles
1700
Wind Patterns and Ocean Currents of the Atlantic
Ocean currents
Winds

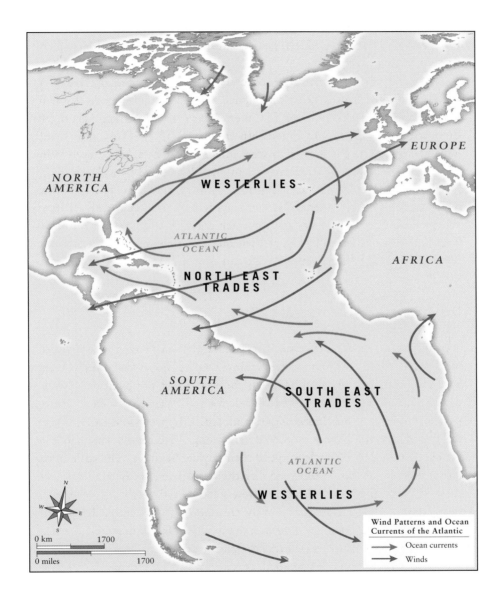

Map 1 Wind Patterns and Ocean Currents of the Atlantic. This map shows the distinctive weather systems of the north and south Atlantic. These patterns shaped the flow of people, goods, and information across the Atlantic world.

Source: Eltis & Richardson, *Atlas of the Transatlantic Slave Trade*, Yale University Press, ©2010. Used with permission.

human cargoes, they would head to the Caribbean, again helped along by the cycle of winds and currents. They would sell their slaves there and then return to northern Europe, taking advantage yet again from this cycle. The British soon came to dominate this trade, although many other countries—France, the Netherlands, Denmark, Sweden, and, eventually, the United States—also participated.

Environmental factors thus played a critical role in structuring the transatlantic slave trade. The cyclical patterns of winds and currents in the South and North Atlantic, respectively, demarcated two distinct routes, the first a Portuguese one mostly originating from and destined for Brazil, the second a northern European (but largely British) one beginning in Europe and intended for the Caribbean. The distinctive environments of the South and North Atlantic, moreover, also determined the regions of Africa from which slaves would be obtained, as well as the regions of America to which they would be taken. Thus, captives taken from West Central Africa formed the vast majority of Brazil's slave population, while those from West Africa and the Gulf of Guinea constituted the lion's share in the Caribbean (although about one-quarter came from Central Africa). British North America (and later the United States) played a minor part in this economy, receiving less than 5 percent of captives carried from Africa to the Americas.

THE SLAVE TRADES OF AFRICA

From the discussion so far, which has emphasized the interaction of American, African, and European influences within a specific environmental context, it should be clear that the transatlantic slave trade was a collaborative endeavor. It involved people, some willing and many more coerced, from all four continents. Without the demand of European plantation owners in the Americas, the transatlantic slave trade never would have existed. But the Africans and Eurafricans involved in the trade—whether as rulers, merchants, soldiers, mariners, peasants, or captives—played a decisive role in determining how the trade would operate and who would be swept up in it.

Beginning in the 1440s, Europeans occasionally raided the African interior for slaves. Those who survived realized that such activities were not appreciated and that those targeted by them were capable of effective, armed resistance. Instead, the Europeans turned to African merchants who were entirely willing to do business—provided it was on their terms.

African merchants controlled the supply side of the transatlantic slave trade. Although the oceanic dimension of this new economy was unfamiliar to them, they were well versed in slave trading. Slavery had long existed in Africa. Drawn primarily from the ranks of criminals, debtors, outcasts, and war prisoners, African slaves had been sold to Africans and non-Africans since classical antiquity. After 700 C.E., the Muslim Mediterranean and Arabia assumed the place Rome previously occupied in this relatively small-scale trade, as they continued to acquire African slaves through long-distance trading networks stretching across the Sahara Desert. African merchants would draw upon existing practices of domestic enslavement and interregional slave trading to meet the new European demand after 1500.

Since they controlled the sources of supply, African merchants could demand in exchange specific types of goods. These varied widely, both in kind and provenance. Although Europeans could procure some of these goods at home, notably firearms, metal goods, furniture, and the like, they had to range far and wide to obtain what the African merchants primarily demanded. These included Indian textiles (the most important trade item), Indonesian cowry shells, American rum and tobacco, and even gold and ivory from other parts of Africa. Because of the exacting cosmopolitan demands of the African merchants, the transatlantic slave trade had the effect of linking more closely the economies of the globe.

African merchants had the upper hand in another way: they largely determined who would be offered for sale as slaves. Although European slave traders and planters preferred male slaves from certain regions, who were judged to be more compliant, disciplined, and hard-working, they ultimately had to take whoever the African merchants offered. Consequently, African actors played a pivotal role in determining the regional origins, gender balance, and age distribution of the American slave population.

WHO WERE THE CAPTIVES?

African merchants often sought captives from regions relatively close to the ports from which they did business. Reducing the distance they had to travel to reach the point of sale lowered the merchants' costs and raised profits. But an even more important factor than proximity to the coast in determining the African geography of the transatlantic slave trade was the presence (or absence) of institutions that could guarantee the security of markets and enforce credit arrangements. In many areas, these facilities were provided by states such as Kongo, Segu, Futa Jallon, Dahomey, and Asante (see Map 2). In other areas, these functions were carried out by nonstate actors with state-like powers (notably the administration of justice) essential to the functioning of large-scale international commerce. An

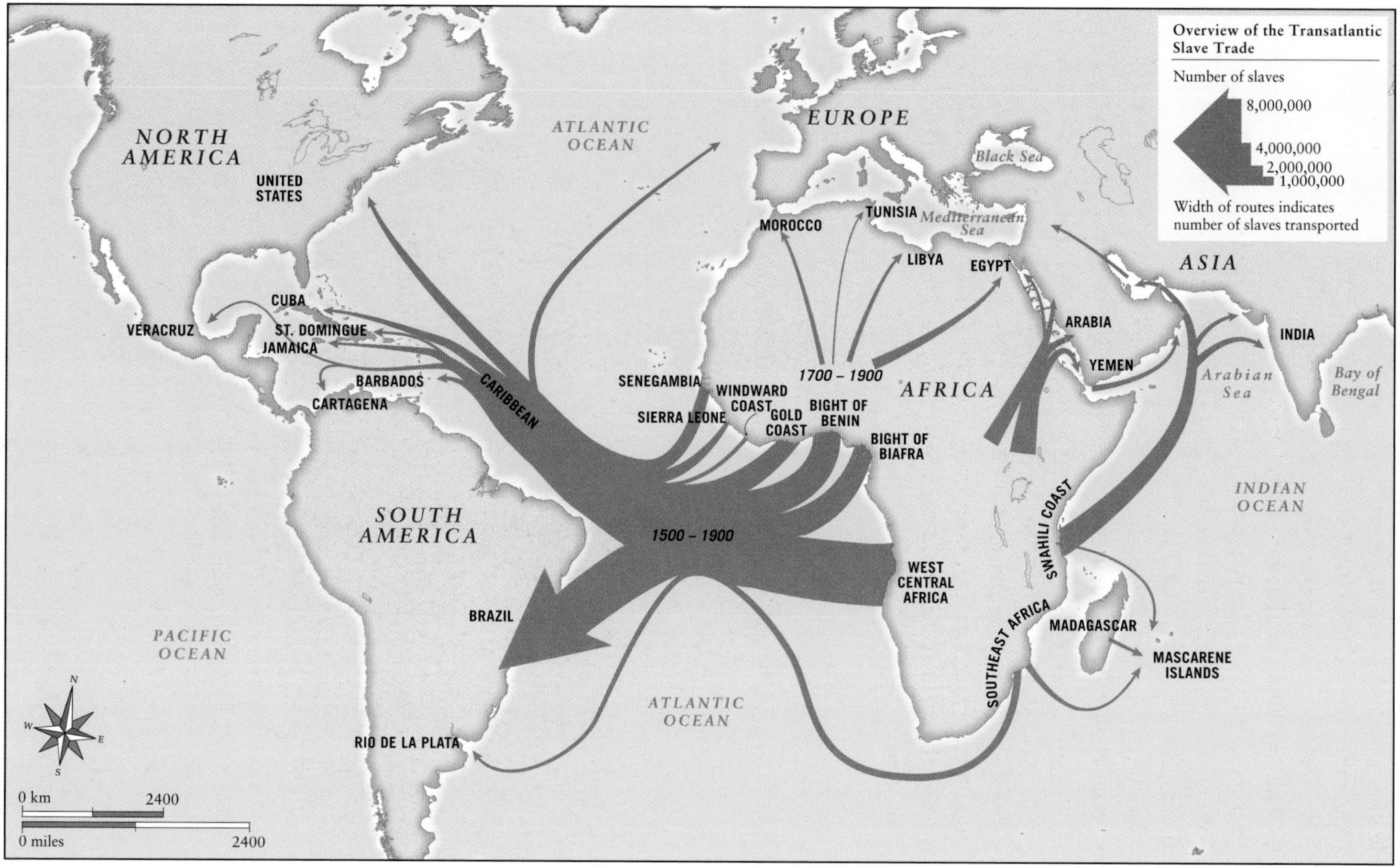
Overview of the Transatlantic Slave Trade
Number of slaves
8,000,000
4,000,000
2,000,000
1,000,000
Width of routes indicates number of slaves transported
NORTH AMERICA
UNITED STATES
ATLANTIC OCEAN
EUROPE
Black Sea
Mediterranean Sea
MOROCCO
TUNISIA
LIBYA
EGYPT
ASIA
ARABIA
YEMEN
INDIA
Arabian Sea
Bay of Bengal
CUBA
VERACRUZ
ST. DOMINGUE
JAMAICA
BARBADOS
CARTAGENA
CARIBBEAN
SENEGAMBIA
WINDWARD COAST
SIERRA LEONE
GOLD COAST
BIGHT OF BENIN
BIGHT OF BIAFRA
1700 – 1900
AFRICA
SWAHILI COAST
INDIAN OCEAN
SOUTH AMERICA
1500 – 1900
WEST CENTRAL AFRICA
BRAZIL
SOUTHEAST AFRICA
MADAGASCAR
MASCARENE ISLANDS
PACIFIC OCEAN
ATLANTIC OCEAN
RIO DE LA PLATA
N
W
E
S
0 km
2400
0 miles
2400

Map 2 Overview of the Transatlantic Slave Trade

Source: Eltis & Richardson, *Atlas of the Transatlantic Slave Trade*, Yale University Press, ©2010. Used with permission.

example can be found in the Bight of Biafra, where the above-mentioned Aro trading network had legal mechanisms for dispute resolution, contract fulfillment, and debt enforcement in their slave-trading ports of Bonny, New Calabar, and Old Calabar (see Map 3).

The main point here is that two crucial factors determining the regional origins of captives were the African merchants' pursuit of profit and the political geography of Africa itself.

Internal African market forces shaped the age distribution of those sold into the transatlantic slave system. Slavery in sub-Saharan Africa placed a premium on children because they could be more easily integrated with the families who purchased them. Responding to this domestic market preference, African merchants tended to sell child captives to other Africans. As a result, the percentage of children sold into transatlantic slavery was rather small, although it increased throughout the eighteenth and nineteenth centuries.

OLD CALABAR FACTORIES, NEAR DUKE TOWN.

Figure 1. Old Calabar (ca. 1870–1880s).

Source: http://en.wikipedia.org/wiki/Akwa_Akpa.

AFRICA
ATLANTIC OCEAN
CROCK TOWN
CROF'S RIVER
Swamp
Duke's Plantation
Low Trees
High Trees
CROSS RIVER CRECK
OLD TOWN
TOM ROBIN'S TOWN
DUKE'S TOWN OR OLD CALLEBAR
HENSHAW'S TOWN
KING QUA'S TOWN
Swamp covered with Trees
SEVEN FATHOM'S POINT
A Corrected Draught of OLD CALLEBAR RIVER From the Breakers To Creek Town
Sand dry at Ebb
TOBACCO HEAD
TOBACCO LAND
JAMES'S ISLAND
PARROT ISLAND
RIO DEL REY
FISH TOWN
Qua River
BACKASSEY
DELROY PT.
Runby Land
High Land of Carrarroons
TOM SHOTTS TOWN
Big Tree
TOM SHOTTS PT.
EAST HEAD
Lowland covered with Trees
N
S
E
W
0 km
24
0 miles
24

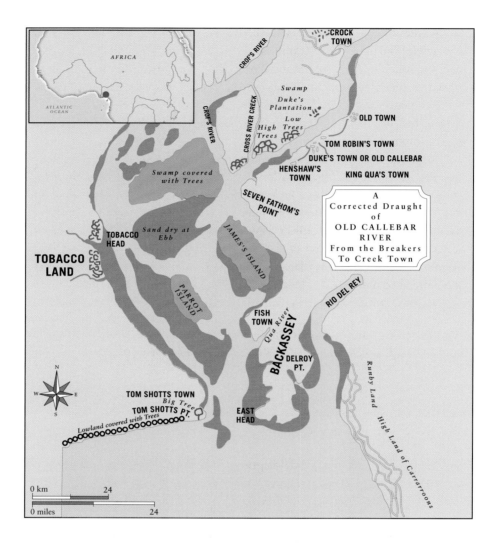

Map 3 Old Calabar (c. 1820)

TABLE 1. AGE OF SLAVES CARRIED FROM AFRICA TO THE CARIBBEAN, 1545–1864.

	1545–1700	1701–1807	1808–1864
Children	10.9%	23.1%	30.9%
Adults	89.1%	76.9%	69.1%

Source: The Trans-Atlantic Slave Trade Database:
http://www.slavevoyages.org/tast/index.faces

Market forces connected with the trans-Saharan slave trade influenced the gender balance of the transatlantic slave population. Two-thirds of all captives sold into the transatlantic slave system were men. Although this happened to suit the plantation owners in America, their preferences actually had little influence on the gender composition of the captives. Two factors determined this composition. First, North African buyers tended to prefer women slaves whom they desired for domestic as well as sexual services. As a result, a disproportionate share of female captives was directed toward the trans-Saharan rather than the transatlantic trade. A second factor, which influenced all regions, even those little affected by the trans-Saharan trade, was even more important. Women in most African societies were the primary agriculturalists. Since the bulk of food production depended upon their labor and organization, they were considered more indispensable than men to the communities in which they lived. Additionally, many African societies were **matrilineal** or **matrilocal**. The skewed gender composition of those sold into the transatlantic slave system reflected these African realities.

TABLE 2. GENDER OF SLAVES CARRIED FROM AFRICA TO THE CARIBBEAN, 1545–1864.

	1545–1700	1701–1807	1808–1864
Females	42.0%	35.6%	33.9%
Males	58.0%	64.4%	66.1%

Source: The Trans-Atlantic Slave Trade Database:

http://www.slavevoyages.org/tast/index.faces

As with all such general descriptions of economic, social, and cultural conditions across a continent as vast and diverse as Africa, these characterizations must be tempered by a recognition of the wide range of variation from region to region. The region from which the captives in this illustrated history were most likely taken, the Bight of Biafra, was one area in which the predominance of male captives was not so pronounced. A major reason why women from this region were more likely to be sold into transatlantic slavery than in other parts of Africa is that the males there had a central role in agriculture. In fact, they alone had the honor of cultivating the yam, the main food crop. This made Biafran men more indispensable than their counterparts in other regions. In addition, male war prisoners in this region were generally beheaded, rather than enslaved. This further reduced the proportion of males available to the transatlantic slave market. The relative lack of adult males, in turn, raised the proportion of children in the captive population drawn from the region. Though an exception to the general age and gender mix, Biafra illustrates the more important point that local African factors were decisive in determining the composition of the population sent into the transatlantic slave trade.

Although African merchants controlled the supply of captives for the transatlantic slave trade, it must be emphasized that the growing demand for plantation labor ultimately drove this market. Explosive American demand in the eighteenth century placed great strain on the internal African slave market. This pressure altered existing practices of enslavement, perhaps accounting for the rising proportion of women and children carried across the Atlantic during the last century of the trade. The complex interplay between economic forces of supply and demand, on the one hand, and cultural norms in Europe, the Americas, and especially Africa, on the other, ultimately determined the composition of the transatlantic slave trade (see Map 4).

EUROPE
Mediterranean Sea
MIDDLE EAST
Sahara
Red Sea
Gulf of Aden
AFRICA
SENEGAMBIA
SIERRA LEONE
WINDWARD COAST
GOLD COAST
BIGHT OF BENIN
BIGHT OF BIAFRA
ATLANTIC OCEAN
INDIAN OCEAN
WEST CENTRAL AFRICA
SOUTHEAST AFRICA
MADAGASCAR
Kalahari Desert
Regions from which Slave-Trade Voyages Departed Africa, 1501-1867
Number of slaves
5,000,000
2,000,000
1,000,000
500,000
N
W
E
S
0 km
1200
0 miles
1200

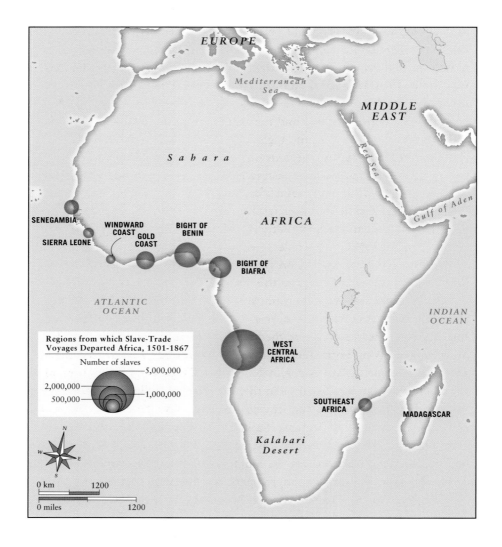

Map 4 Regions from Which Slave-Trade Voyages Departed Africa, 1501–1867

Source: Eltis & Richardson, *Atlas of the Transatlantic Slave Trade*, Yale University Press, ©2010. Used with permission.

TEMPORALITIES OF THE TRADE

African factors also influenced the pace and annual rhythm of the trade. Usually a year passed from the moment an individual entered into the circuits of the trade until his/her arrival in the Americas. Only one to three months of that time were spent crossing the ocean. The rest was spent marching toward a coastal slave market, often carrying goods for sale, and then waiting. Sometimes captives were sold from person to person along their route or were even sold permanently into internal African slavery. As the coffles of slaves arrived on the coast, European slave traders would purchase them bit by bit, gradually completing their cargo. Known as **coasting**, this process could be lengthy and was thus detested by the European merchants. The wait on the coast, which could take up to six months in regions with smaller Atlantic slave markets like Upper Guinea, was costly, for slaves acquired during this interval had to be fed and the ship's crew had to be paid and nourished. Moreover, coasting could be deadly. Since both the slaves and the crew were generally confined on the ship, mortality could be quite high, especially if an epidemic broke out among them. Despite these serious disadvantages, European slave traders had to accept the hazards of coasting because it was imposed upon them by the operation of the internal African slave market.

The patterns of African agriculture had a profound impact on the timing of European slaving ventures. Whether setting out from Brazil or northern Europe, slave traders generally attempted to time their departure so that their arrival on the African coast would coincide with the local harvest. In the region this graphic history treats, the Bight of Biafra, the principal crop, the yam, was harvested between July and October. European merchants—overwhelmingly British in this region before 1807—preferred to arrive there in June or July, spend the next few months purchasing both slaves and newly harvested yams to feed them, and then sail for the Americas in November. Departing at this time allowed the slave traders to arrive in the Caribbean for the December start of the sugar and coffee harvest. It was then that slaves fetched the highest prices in the markets of Jamaica, Saint-Domingue, and the other plantation colonies of the area. In one way, however, this temporal rhythm was unfavorable to the Europeans. In equatorial Africa, the harvest months coincided with the rainy season, the period of the year that saw the highest mortality among slave-ship crews. But, in the calculation of ship owners and investors, the deaths of a few European sailors was a small price to pay for guaranteeing a supply of cheap yams for the voyage to the Americas. In other regions of Africa, European traders also sought to coordinate their voyages with the local harvests, whether the crops being harvested were millet, manioc, rice, or sorghum. Supplying the captives with sufficient quantities of familiar foodstuffs was seen as essential to their health—and thus their arrival in good condition for the slave markets of the Americas.

THE MIDDLE PASSAGE

The most notorious aspect of the transatlantic slave trade was the Middle Passage. Although it could take anywhere from one to three months, depending on the African port of departure and the American port of arrival, the voyage was always frightening, crowded, dirty—and often deadly. Being taken, often violently, from one's home, marched to the coast, imprisoned in a dark, dank ship's hold with similarly traumatized captives, and taken onto the rough seas for an unknown period of time was undeniably harrowing. But it may not have been the utterly atomizing, disorienting experience often portrayed in film and literature. Captives on some slave ships may have come from the same region, perhaps even the same village. For them, the Middle Passage may not have been a total plunge into the unknown. In other cases, though, African factors such as a slowdown in the market, increased demand for agricultural labor, and varied regional patterns of procurement led to much greater diversity of captives. Whether made in the company of acquaintances or strangers, however, the crossing to America was always dehumanizing.

The profit motive dictated that conditions aboard the vessel were cramped for everybody, but more so for the captives than the crew. But the same desire for profit imposed some limits, however slight, on crowding. Although we now know that the principal factor determining death rates was the length of the voyage, slave traders at the time believed that excessive packing was the main cause of mortality. In their view, crowding too many captives into a vessel defeated the basic purpose of the endeavor—to bring a maximum number of reasonably healthy slaves to American markets. But the profitability of a slaving voyage also depended on volume. By the eighteenth century, slave traders of all nations had arrived more or less independently at what they believed was the optimal balance. This was to allot five to seven square feet of deck space and one ton of the ship's displacements to each individual. It was thought that less space would damage the captives' health, while more would unnecessarily reduce the numbers that could be transported—which is to say, profits.

This is not to say that conditions aboard slave ships were good. The cramped conditions, long periods of confinement, poor (if not inadequate) food and water, mental stress, and harsh treatment favored outbreaks of disease and increased their lethality. The most common diseases were gastrointestinal, especially dysentery, which caused diarrhea and exacerbated the dehydration (probably the leading cause of death) provoked by the minimal amounts of water the captives were provided. Smallpox, measles, malaria, parasitical infections, fevers, ophthalmic ailments, and open wounds were also frequent. The likelihood that a ship would experience an outbreak of disease during the Middle Passage seems to have been linked to epidemiological conditions at its port of departure. Perhaps the most unhealthy port in the entire transatlantic slave trade was Old Calabar, the one where the slave ship in this graphic history acquired its human commodities. The length of the voyage also seems to have increased the level of mortality by increasing the chance of disease and shipwreck, putting strain on water and food supplies, prolonging the terrible conditions, and raising the suicide rate among the captives.

A final cause of mortality with special significance for the transatlantic slave trade was shipboard insurrection. Uprisings occurred on about 10 percent of all slave ships. Unlike in the famous case of the *Amistad*, these were usually unsuccessful, resulting in the death of captives rather than their liberation. In the history of the trade, probably 100,000 captives lost their lives in failed shipboard insurrections.

Yet, while rarely successful, the insurrections had a significant economic impact. The threat of insurrection drove up the cost of slaving voyages in several ways. First, it required more crew members and specialized equipment than any other kind of commercial voyage. Even more important, maritime insurers demanded higher premiums for slave ships because of the risk of uprisings. These security and insurance precautions together represented 18 percent of the cost of a typical slaving voyage. Without this added cost, European merchants would have been able to carry perhaps one million additional captives from Africa during the eighteenth century. Insurrections may have shaped the transatlantic slave trade in another way. Although Upper Guinea was the region closest to both Europe and America, it was also the region with the highest rate of insurrection. This perhaps is why it sent fewer captives to the Americas than any of the other main Atlantic slave-trading areas. In contrast, the region with the lowest rate of insurrection, West Central Africa, sent the most. These are suggestive correlations.

Mortality during the Middle Passage varied widely from ship to ship. The best outcome, a rapid "healthy" passage, could see mortality rates as "low" as 6 percent—still a much higher death rate than in any normal village in Africa, Europe, or the Americas. In the worst case scenario, such as a truly devastating outbreak of disease or a shipwreck, all of the captives and crew could be lost. Over time, the average rate of mortality fell, from 25 percent in the early years of the trade to 14 percent in the eighteenth century. However, these averages conceal great variation. Three quarters of voyages experienced mortality below the mean, while the remaining one-quarter suffered much higher death rates—generally from epidemic

Figure 2. Rebellion on a Slave Ship.

Source: http://www.brh.org.uk/gallery/slavery.html. Bristol Radical History Group.

disease, accident, and insurrection. The crews of the slave ships suffered too. Their average mortality rate was 11 percent.

Underlying these bland figures was the horrific experience of the Middle Passage. A monotonous daily routine structured the rhythm of shipboard existence. Although the exact details varied from ship to ship, usually based on its national origin, the typical British schedule is representative. The captives were given two meals and one pint of water a day. The first meal took place in the morning. In preparation, the captives would be taken on deck, chained together, and shackled to special rings in the deck—precautions against insurrection and suicide. Some of the crew would distribute food, while others stood at arms. As mentioned above, what the captives received to eat depended upon the part of Africa from which the vessel had left. Once the meal had been finished, the captives would be made to sing and dance on the deck. The reason for this was not only to provide "entertainment" for the crew but also to preserve muscle tone. Captives who refused to participate or who did so without a convincing show of enthusiasm were flogged. During this activity, crew members would descend into the hold, clean it, remove dead bodies, and throw them overboard. As an additional health precaution, the crew would wash the mouths of the captives with vinegar. A second meal was distributed in the afternoon, after which the captives were confined in the hold until the next morning.

Between meals, the captives were granted varying degrees of freedom to move about the ship. On many voyages, especially from regions associated with resistance, the captives might remain shackled even after being returned to the hold after the morning meal. On voyages from regions reputed for docility, however, the captives might be allowed to stay on the deck. In most instances, however, the male captives would be returned to the hold, while only the women and children would remain on deck. It is perhaps because of the greater freedom of movement of women and children that revolts were more common on vessels where they formed a higher proportion of the captives. On the other hand, their proximity to the crew may have made them more vulnerable to sexual assault—a frequent occurrence in the Middle Passage and on the far side of the Atlantic.

IN AMERICA

Upon arriving in America, the captives might have to endure shipboard quarantine—perhaps suffering more deaths—before disembarking. Once ashore, they would be sold at slave markets near the port or, less commonly, transshipped for sale in other parts of the Americas. In either case, the captives would have to travel again, usually on foot, to their final destination— nine times out of ten a sugar plantation. These repeated movements, coupled with the distances captives had to march in Africa to reach the ports, make it difficult to trace the precise African origins and American destinations of the 10.7 million survivors of the Middle Passage (see Map 5).

This has bearing on the question of whether African cultures were transplanted intact to America. For many years, it was thought that the experience of enslavement, sale, the Middle Passage, and resale resulted in such mixing of people from disparate parts of Africa that languages, religions, and identities were quickly lost. More recently, however, some historians have argued that African identities were able to weather the passage to America. Since the slave populations of the European colonies in the Americas usually came from just a few principal regions, this is a plausible idea. But it has been difficult to prove statistically because of the great movement of captives both before embarkation in Africa and after disembarkation in the Americas. A further complicating factor is that all that remains of the identities of captives taken three or four centuries ago is what European merchants, planters, and bureaucrats noted in their records. The terms they used to describe the captives—for example, "Coromantees," "Gambians," or "Angolans"—generally referred to the ports, rivers, and interior regions from which a particular shipload of captives originated. They thus reflect geographical notions that made sense to Europeans, not the familial, cultural, religious, or political categories with which the captives associated themselves. These methodological challenges and the limitations of the written sources may mean that we will never be able to answer definitively the question of how African identities informed New World cultures. The truth probably lies somewhere between the extremes of cultural dislocation and transatlantic continuity.

NORTH AMERICA
ATLANTIC OCEAN
NORTHERN U.S.
CHESAPEAKE
MISSISSIPPI/ FLORIDA
CAROLINAS/GEORGIA
SPANISH MAINLAND
The Caribbean
Cuba
St. Domingue
Virgin Islands
St. Kitts
Jamaica
Antigua
Puerto Rico
Guadeloupe
Dutch Caribbean
Dominica
Montserrat, Nevis
Martinique
St. Vincent
Barbados
Grenada
Trinidad/tobago
BRITISH GUIANA
DUTCH GUIANA
FRENCH GUIANA
NORTHEAST BRAZIL
PERNAMBUCO
SOUTH AMERICA
BAHIA
ATLANTIC OCEAN
PACIFIC OCEAN
SOUTHEAST BRAZIL
N
W
E
S
RIO DE LA PLATA
American Destinations of Transatlantic Slave Trade, 1501-1867
Number of slaves
2,000,000
1,000,000
500,000
100,000
0 km
2400
0 miles
2400

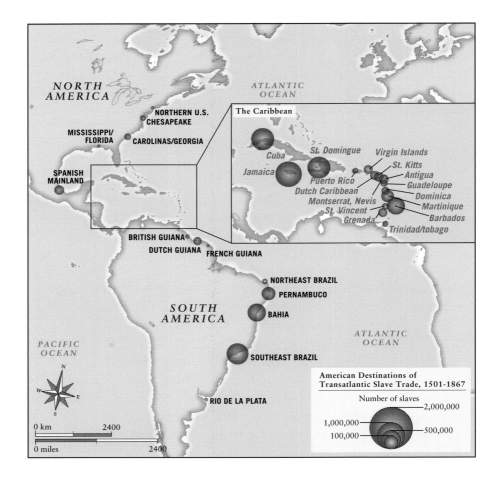

Map 5 American Destinations of Transatlantic Slave Trade, 1501–1867

Source: Eltis & Richardson, *Atlas of the Transatlantic Slave Trade*, Yale University Press, ©2010. Used with permission.

THE ORIGINS OF ABOLITIONISM

By the late 1780s, the trade had reached new heights, carrying 80,000 enslaved Africans annually to the Americas to meet the labor needs of the plantation economy. Britain led the way, its fleet of slave ships supplying not only its own establishments but of those of the other European colonial powers as well. The money kept rolling in, with no end in sight. Yet, within two decades the British transatlantic slave trade would be brought to a sudden, definitive end by a homegrown abolitionist movement. How did British abolitionism triumph?

Although Denmark was actually the first European country to abolish the transatlantic slave trade (announced in 1792, effective in 1803), the end of that country's miniscule trade had little impact. British abolitionism, however, dramatically altered societal and governmental attitudes—first toward the slave trade and then toward slavery itself. Change was not immediate, but the rise of British abolitionism in the 1780s marked the beginning of the end of a particularly inhuman era.

Abolitionist critiques of slavery and slave trading originated in the mid-eighteenth century, in the writings of **Enlightenment** philosophers such as Montesquieu, Smith, and Rousseau. In continental Europe, their ideas won the support of part of the intellectual elite but were dismissed or ignored by almost everyone else. In Great Britain, however, things were different. First **Quakers** and then a wide range of evangelical and non-evangelical protestant denominations embraced these philosophical critiques of slavery and added to them a strong religious element. They then diffused the potent new blend to a mass audience through their network of churches. This was the broad social base to which British abolitionist leaders would appeal.

In 1787 a group of religious leaders and politicians, the majority Quakers, founded the Society for Effecting the Abolition of the Slave Trade to organize a mass political campaign against the institution. Its leaders—Thomas Clarkson, Granville Sharpe, William Wilberforce, and others—decided to set aside temporarily the issue of slavery itself, which they also viewed as a great evil. This was a strategic choice. Pragmatically, they believed that to attack slavery directly would make enemies of the colonial planters, a group they considered too powerful to defeat at present. The slave traders, however, seemed less formidable. Morally, the abolitionists believed that the transatlantic slave trade, especially the Middle Passage, was the cruelest part of the entire slave system and that, if ended, slavery itself would falter. Having resolved to do battle with the slave traders, the Society moved into action. It encouraged the formation of antislavery clubs (ultimately more than 1,000), organized massive petition drives garnering hundreds of thousands of signatures, and engaged in high-level lobbying

TABLE 3. STATISTICAL OVERVIEW OF THE TRANSATLANTIC SLAVE TRADE.

	SPAIN / URUGUAY	PORTUGAL / BRAZIL	GREAT BRITAIN	NETHERLANDS	U.S.A.	FRANCE	DENMARK / BALTIC	TOTALS
1501–1510	950	950	0	0	0	0	0	1,900
1511–1520	4,404	5,041	0	0	0	0	0	9,444
1521–1530	5,495	5,495	0	0	0	0	0	10,990
1531–1540	7,197	7,204	0	0	0	0	0	14,402
1541–1550	13,693	13,697	0	0	0	0	0	27,390
1551–1560	2,823	2,826	94	0	0	0	0	5,742
1561–1570	18,760	20,374	1,591	0	0	0	0	40,725
1571–1580	13,040	16,350	0	0	0	66	0	29,456
1581–1590	23,695	32,959	237	0	0	0	0	56,891
1591–1600	29,906	49,295	0	1,365	0	0	0	80,566
1601–1610	25,332	65,716	0	878	0	0	0	91,926
1611–1620	30,979	117,003	0	951	0	0	0	148,932
1621–1630	36,170	146,857	141	326	0	0	0	183,494
1631–1640	25,089	88,278	381	6,452	0	0	0	120,199
1641–1650	10,240	51,275	33,173	24,951	824	1,827	1,053	123,342
1651–1660	10,389	91,236	26,720	25,983	0	706	653	155,687
1661–1670	1,778	109,188	67,469	48,592	0	2,512	0	229,539
1671–1680	4,001	92,660	71,689	43,953	623	9,149	316	222,391
1681–1690	2,293	86,613	112,193	40,482	974	14,280	3,729	260,564

Period								Total
1691–1700	0	162,368	116,495	27,363	1,730	9,961	21,640	339,557
1701–1710	0	175,140	151,877	35,589	120	27,196	4,319	394,241
1711–1720	0	200,583	167,409	22,465	2,021	60,279	651	453,408
1721–1730	0	209,128	226,192	31,793	5,364	74,353	1,563	548,392
1731–1740	0	205,206	243,929	29,457	17,504	100,730	1,178	598,003
1741–1750	0	221,086	175,232	37,607	12,272	117,477	2,915	566,589
1751–1760	284	215,934	255,346	41,044	23,066	99,127	8,157	642,958
1761–1770	3,955	212,655	360,785	59,797	37,444	138,216	6,109	818,960
1771–1780	0	210,497	301,323	47,712	24,838	164,756	6,542	755,667
1781–1790	510	254,899	277,276	16,775	16,331	283,897	18,304	867,993
1791–1800	5,905	307,875	385,928	7,775	50,344	72,983	17,597	848,407
1801–1810	13,419	393,392	283,959	1,605	103,922	10,942	16,316	823,554
1811–1820	124,236	516,854	0	734	5,276	38,744	0	685,843
1821–1830	105,847	594,421	0	687	2,197	152,595	0	855,747
1831–1840	245,849	438,826	0	0	0	1,609	0	686,284
1841–1850	79,464	517,078	0	0	0	0	0	596,542
1851–1860	161,633	9,309	0	0	476	0	0	171,418
1861–1866	54,191	0	0	0	0	0	0	54,191
Totals	1,061,524	5,848,265	3,259,440	554,336	305,326	1,381,404	111,041	12,521,336

Source: The Trans-Atlantic Slave Trade Database:

http://www.slavevoyages.org/tast/assessment/estimates.faces

within Parliament itself. Within a year or two, the abolition of the transatlantic slave trade had become a prominent national political cause.

Early historians of the abolitionist movement saw the noble efforts of the Society's leaders, the so-called Saints, as the key to the movement's rise and triumph. Their dedication and moral authority convinced the nation to put aside its economic self-interest (for Britain was then the world's leading slave-trading power) in order to pursue what a leading scholar considered one of the "three or four perfectly virtuous acts recorded in the history of nations."[2] By the mid-twentieth century, however, some historians began to question this moral interpretation of abolitionism's causes and motives. Recognizing that abolitionism occurred concurrently with rising capitalism and industrialization, they argued that the abolition of slavery

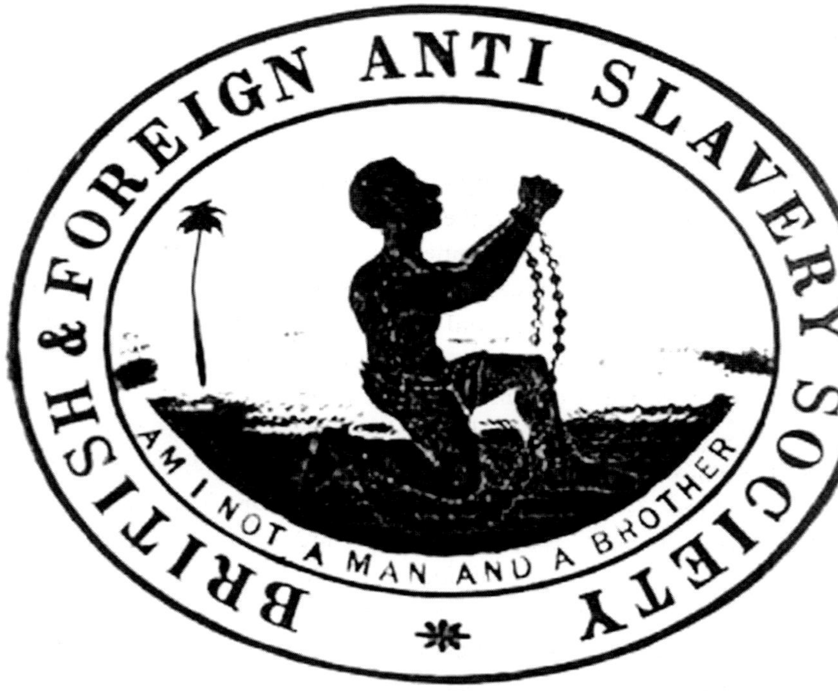
BRITISH & FOREIGN ANTI SLAVERY SOCIETY
AM I NOT A MAN AND A BROTHER

Figure 3. Am I Not a Man and a Brother (popular symbol of the abolitionist movement).

Source: http://www.bbc.co.uk/history/british/abolition/abolition_tools_gallery_06.shtml. BBC History—British History in Depth.

2 W. E. H. Lecky, quoted in David Brion Davis, *The Rise and Fall of Slavery in the World* (New York: Oxford University Press, 2006), 234.

was dictated by economic necessity. In the emerging modern economy, they asserted, slavery was less efficient than wage labor. The abolitionists' moral arguments, therefore, were pretexts for what was really a hardheaded economic calculation. In the last quarter of the twentieth century, however, this interpretation has been questioned. Research has shown that the plantation economy was not in decline, that slavery was actually more profitable than wage labor, and, thus, that there was no economic rationale for abolition. It is now generally thought that British abolitionism derived from humanitarian and religious commitment, not economic self-interest. But instead of focusing on the movement's leaders, historians now emphasize the unprecedented degree of mass participation in the abolitionist campaigns. This has led to a new appreciation of the significance of abolitionism: it was a founding moment in the birth of modern politics and a critical element of British national self-definition.

ABOLITION IN 1807

From the foundation of the Society in 1787 to the abolition of the British transatlantic slave trade in 1807, the first twenty years of the abolitionist movement were shaped by the momentous events occurring in Revolutionary and Napoleonic France. Between 1788 and 1792, the abolitionist movement grew in strength and seemed poised to achieve its goals. This coincided with the beginning of the French Revolution, whose initial burst of optimistic idealism may have inspired British abolitionists. But in 1792 the Revolution took a radical turn. Parisian mobs overthrew the king, Louis XVI, who was executed shortly thereafter. During this same period, a huge slave uprising broke out in France's principal Caribbean colony, Saint-Domingue, and threatened to engulf the whole island. To regain a semblance of authority, local French officials abolished slavery there in 1793, a decision ratified by the French government and extended to all French colonies the following year. All this terrified American slave-owners, as well as moderates in Britain who might have supported abolition before but now associated it with revolution. Moreover, by 1794 Great Britain was locked in a tough war with Revolutionary France, a war that seemed to be going badly. In this context, all calls for change appeared as pro-French sedition. Against these adverse winds, the abolitionist movement could make no headway. It subsided for more than a decade.

When it reemerged after 1805, the situation had changed. The previous year, the French had given up their final attempt to regain control over Saint-Domingue. Renamed Haiti, the new republic of self-liberated former slaves declared its independence in 1804. For the British, the French defeat meant the end of serious competition in the world sugar market. In the 1780s, Saint-Domingue had been the world's largest and most efficient producer of sugar—an economic rival against which the British colonies had no chance. With the prospect of France regaining control of Saint-Domingue now gone, Britain no longer had to fear that the French might gain economic advantage from the abolition of the transatlantic slave trade. Although it scared planters, Haitian independence had eliminated Britain's principal colonial competitor. Another event contributed to the growing sense of British well-being: the destruction of the main French fleet at the Battle of Trafalgar (1805). This not only freed Britain from the fear of invasion but also gave it unchallenged global dominance on the high seas. Confident in the nation's power, sure of the righteousness of its cause, and encouraged by the newly roused mass abolitionist movement, Parliament outlawed British participation in the transatlantic slave trade in mid-1807. It went into force on 1 January 1808.

Compliance was remarkable. Although the Royal Navy, still busy fighting Napoleon, was unable to spare many resources for anti-slave-trade patrols off the coast of West Africa, those areas where British slavers had predominated—notably in the Gulf of Guinea—saw the trade vanish almost overnight. British naval dominance prevented France from moving into the vacuum. Only Britain's allies, Portugal and Spain, were able to continue the transatlantic slave trade. As a result, the numbers of Africans taken to America during the period 1807–1815 declined significantly.

INTERNATIONALIZING ABOLITIONISM

Britain emerged victorious in 1815 from the Napoleonic Wars and the War of 1812 against the United States. Triumphant—and again spurred by a massive petition drive—the British government resolved to spend its peacetime dividend on gaining international support for ending the entire transatlantic slave trade. At the **Congress of Vienna**, the postwar peace conference, British diplomats flexed their diplomatic muscle to wrest a condemnation of the trade from their French, Portuguese, Dutch, Spanish, German, and Scandinavian colleagues. In a rousing statement, it denounced the slave trade as "repugnant to the principles of humanity and universal morality." But since the declaration contained no provisions for enforcement, it remained a dead letter.

The years immediately following the return of peace saw an influx of slave traders, mostly Iberian and French, into the regions that had been dominated by the British before 1807. The volume of the trade began to rise again toward the levels of the 1780s. Realizing that the declaration had been ineffective and that antislaving laws passed independently by certain countries, notably France, were not being enforced, the British government renewed its international efforts against the trade. It now took a new approach: to secure abolition through bilateral treaties with the major slave-trading countries. This new diplomatic drive was pushed along by a combination of factors. One of these seems to have been self-interest. Having unilaterally abolished the trade, the British did not want colonial rivals to thrive at the expense of their own colonies, now bereft of new infusions of slave labor. The other reasons were familiar: genuine moral commitment among important British politicians and continued pressure from the abolitionist movement, which had just formed an insider lobbying group, the African Institution, to accompany its mass mobilization.

Abolition treaties were signed with the Netherlands, Spain, and Portugal in 1817. The Netherlands agreed to end its transatlantic slave trade immediately. Spain, however, only agreed to phased abolition (to go into effect in 1820) and extracted a 400,000£ payment from Britain. The Portuguese drove an even harder bargain. For 300,000£, they agreed to end their trade only north of the equator. Given that the Portuguese, who had become the world's largest slave-trading nation after British abolition in 1807, had always obtained most of their human commodities south of the equator, this condition greatly reduced the impact of the treaty.

The treaties did, however, establish an enforcement procedure accepted by all three countries. The signatories agreed to let each other's warships stop and search each other's ships if suspected of having slaves on board. Given British naval supremacy, this meant in practice that the Royal Navy would be able to act as a kind of police force, ensuring the compliance of the Dutch, Spanish, and Portuguese. If slaves were found on board, the suspected vessel could be detained for judgment. To rule on the legality of seizures, **Courts of Mixed Commission**, composed of magistrates from the signatory nations, were set up at Sierra Leone, Rio de Janeiro, Havana, and Surinam. Additional locations were added during the course of the nineteenth century. This was one of the first examples of an international effort to adjudicate violations of human rights. Although far from perfect, they suggest the importance Europeans had come to attach to diplomatic endeavors after 1815, following more than twenty years of war, revolution, and upheaval. The creation of international legal mechanisms to combat the transatlantic slave trade was one of the most striking accomplishments of this golden age of diplomacy.

The Courts of Mixed Commission were the first internation human rights tribunals in history.

However, the British initiative was not entirely successful. The two countries with whom Britain had just been at war—France and the United States—refused to enter into any bilateral agreement. To accord British warships the right of search was politically unacceptable to them, especially since this had been an issue in their recently terminated conflicts. But France did agree to end its own trade and enforce the ban with its own naval vessels. Although its initial efforts were so ineffective that many in Britain suspected the French government of duplicity, it progressively toughened its antislaving laws and devoted substantial naval resources to self-policing. The United States, which had already abolished the transatlantic slave trade in the same year as Britain, also promised to use its own navy to police itself. The American navy, however, never maintained a large or consistent presence off the African coast. Nonetheless, neither French nor American slavers played a leading role in the transatlantic slave trade after 1807. However, their refusal to grant the right of search meant that British warships could not legally detain vessels flying French or American flags even if suspected of—or positively known to be—engaging in the trade. This fact was not lost on those who continued to pursue slave trading after 1817.

THE WEST AFRICAN SQUADRON

To enforce the treaties, Britain established a permanent antislaving squadron on the West African coast in 1819. Under its first commander, Sir George R. Collier, it mustered seven vessels. At its height several decades later, it would grow to thirty-six ships, more than 10 percent of the Royal Navy at that time. British naval action to suppress the transatlantic slave trade thus represented a major military commitment. From its creation to disbandment in 1860, the West African squadron absorbed nearly 2 percent of the British government's annual revenue and cost the lives of 5,000 naval personnel, mostly from disease. The cost of Britain's naval campaign against the trade is even greater if the complementary efforts in the Caribbean and off the coast of Brazil are taken into account.

Most of the squadron's vessels were small. This was not a disadvantage, for the sandbars and treacherous surf of the West African coast made it impossible for larger vessels to enter the rivers to which the illicit trade had migrated. Most of the Royal Navy's actions were carried out in small, open craft that could approach slave ships silently and take them by surprise.

Tenders were also widely used. These were small, fast craft that the Royal Navy officers purchased with their own funds to support their operations. Typically, a regular Royal Navy warship would make a show of inspecting a slaving center, essentially acting as a decoy for its lurking tender, which would take the unsuspecting slavers by surprise once the warship had ostensibly departed.

The West Africa squadron depended upon local mariners, known as the **Kru. Krumen,** as they were called, made up about one-third of the squadron's personnel. The history and origins of the Kru are not well-known. They seem to have been a cluster of small societies living in the area of the present-day Ivory Coast and Liberia. The origin of their name is unclear, but one plausible explanation attributes it to their tradition of naval service. British officers liked recruiting them because of their skill, especially at the inshore navigation so essential to the war against the slavers, bravery, habits of discipline and hard work, and relative immunity to West African diseases. Typically, British officers enlisted groups of Kru sailors through the intermediary of a headman. He would negotiate the terms of the group's contract, taking part of their pay in exchange, and guarantee its good conduct. The European sailors with whom the Kru worked gave them distinctive names—Bottle-of-Beer, Soda Water, or Jack-Frying-Pan are common examples. Whether these names reflected a sense of camaraderie among the European and African sailors or were expressions of disdain is unclear. Krumen would serve on Royal Navy vessels for no more than a few years, then return to their home villages to establish families with their earnings. Without the contribution of Kru seamen, the West African squadron would have been much less effective.

EFFECTS OF INTERDICTION

British diplomatic and naval efforts had a significant impact on the transatlantic slave trade. The most important was to shift the bulk of the trade south of the equator. Since the Portuguese had refused to renounce slaving in this area, massive deportations from West Central Africa to Brazil continued unimpeded. Volume may have even increased to meet the growing demands of Brazil, whose plantation economy was expanding to fill the gap created by the Haitian Revolution. Similar growth in the Cuban economy also induced the Spanish to begin seeking slaves in the same region. Thus, British interdiction efforts had the unintended consequence of making the transatlantic slave trade revert to its original national and geographic pattern: Iberian and subequatorial.

The southward shift was neither immediate nor complete. Illegal traders of many nations moved into the areas north of the equator whose
transatlantic slaving economies had been dominated by the British before
1807. The presence of the West Africa squadron's patrols in this area,
however, forced them to change their methods. They abandoned the practice of coasting, which required slave ships to linger for months while collecting their human cargoes. Waiting so long with incriminating captives
aboard meant near-certain capture. To speed up loading and departure
time, the African and Eurafrican merchants now began to gather entire
cargoes of captives in stockades ashore. When a deal had been concluded,
they would be loaded with all haste. Then the vessel would depart immediately for the Americas. This change had several subsidiary effects. The
long waiting periods, during which the African merchants had to feed
their captives, increased the cost slave traders had to pay. It may have also
driven up initial mortality because conditions in the stockades were un-
sanitary and exposed the captives to coastal diseases, especially virulent
in the Gulf of Guinea. On the other hand, the rapid loading and departure
of slave ships reduced the duration of shipboard confinement the captives
had to endure.

European slave traders had always used violence, but after 1807 they
seem to have become even more aggressive. This heightened violence was
undoubtedly driven by the slavers' growing desperation. Before 1807, they
had enjoyed the same legal protections as other oceangoing merchants. But
British abolition and the bilateral treaties criminalized the transatlantic
slave trade. When accosted by the Royal Navy, they did not hesitate to use
all the force at their disposal—cannon, firearms, and cutlasses—to avoid
capture. Nor was the Royal Navy the only threat facing the slavers. As
criminals, they found themselves vulnerable to attack by pirates, privateers, and other slavers. If attacked, slavers had nowhere to turn for protection or redress, since they were involved in an illegal activity themselves.
The slavers thus armed themselves more heavily than before, frequently to
the point of outgunning the Royal Navy boats they encountered. Alone in
dangerous waters, engaged in an inherently violent pursuit, and hunted by
law-enforcers and criminals alike, the slavers can be compared to present-
day drug smugglers. They were simultaneously perpetrators and victims of
extreme violence.

What happened when the West African squadron seized a suspected
slave ship? First, a **prize crew** of sailors from the squadron would take
charge of the captured vessel. The captives would remain aboard, albeit
with more freedom of movement. So would the slaver's crew. Then the
vessel would be sailed to Freetown, Sierra Leone, for judgment by the
Court of Mixed Commission. The length of the voyage varied, depending

upon the location of the seizure, but could last up to two months. Consequently, mortality could be as great as during the Middle Passage. Upon arrival at Freetown, the captives remained confined on board until the Court issued its ruling. Since the bilateral treaties gave neither the British nor the Court jurisdiction over the crew of the slave ship, however, they were allowed to go free. After three or four weeks, the Court announced its decision. If the court upheld the seizure—the outcome in 484 of 513 cases—the captured vessel was sold at auction, and the proceeds shared between the captors (as prize money) and the Court, which used the revenue to fund its operations. As for the captives, they were finally released from the ship and given plots of land around Freetown. Over time, these became self-sufficient villages. In all some 60,000 **recaptives** (as they were called at the time) settled near Freetown. The British also captured many slave ships in the West Indies, liberating some 55,000 captives and giving them land in various Caribbean colonies. For its part, the U.S. Navy freed 5,000 captives from slave ships and resettled them in the American-backed African country of Liberia, which, like Sierra Leone, had been founded as a home for liberated slaves. The fate of captives aboard ships taken to the Courts of Mixed Commission at Havana and Rio de Janeiro, however, was far bleaker. Even when the Courts ruled for liberation, the recaptives were neither given land nor allowed freedom of movement, but instead they were condemned to forms of government indenture barely distinguishable from slavery itself.

BEYOND THE 1817 TREATIES

Infrequently, the Courts of Mixed Commission ruled captures illegal. In this case, the ship and its human cargo were returned to the slave traders to do with as they pleased, and the British naval officer responsible for the detention would have to pay them damages. This placed the captains of the West Africa squadron in a bind: should they let a known slaver go if it was displaying a French or American flag, or act and risk the expense of an illegal seizure? The squadron's frustration at the ease with which slavers could hide their activities under false flags and papers rapidly communicated itself to the British government. British diplomats constantly pressured the United States and France to agree to the mutual right of search in order to end the abuse of their respective flags. The United States absolutely refused, although it did send ships to the African coast from time to time and agreed to strengthen its antislaving laws. It enforced these laws diligently, making it very difficult for illicit slave traders to sell their human cargoes in America. But in the place of the transatlantic slave trade there arose a new trade within the United States itself: the sale of slaves from the Upper South to the booming cotton plantations of the Deep South. Between 1808 and 1861, one million people of African descent were forcibly relocated as a result of this internal trade. Per capita, this represented a much greater forced migration than the transatlantic slave trade itself.

France responded similarly to British pressure, strengthening its antislaving laws and establishing a permanent naval squadron off the coast of Senegambia, north of the main British patrol zones of Sierra Leone, the Windward Coast, and the Gulf of Guinea. But the French government steadfastly refused to accept the right of search, which it viewed as an affront to its sovereignty. Moreover, it appears that some of the colonial and naval officials responsible for enforcing French antislaving laws turned a blind eye to or were even complicit with the slavers. Perhaps because of this laxity, France was the third-largest participant (after Portugal and Spain) in the transatlantic slave trade after 1807.

In 1830, however, a liberal revolution brought to power a new constitutional monarch, Louis Philippe. A member of France's leading abolitionist club, the Society for Christian Morality, the new king readily agreed to the right of search. This was enshrined in the Convention of 1831. Louis Philippe followed this up with new efforts to patrol the coast of West Africa. By the mid-1840s, France's naval presence there was nearly as great as Britain's. During the period 1807–1867, the French navy's number of captures was second only to that of Britain.

Despite these promising developments of the 1830s and 1840s, Britain's international campaign was dealt a setback when Portugal's principal colony, Brazil, declared independence in 1822 and repudiated the bilateral treaty of 1817. Since almost all Portuguese slaving voyages had originated in Brazil, the withdrawal of Brazil from the 1817 arrangement meant that Britain had to go back to the drawing board. Under intense British pressure, Brazil signed a treaty in 1826, promising to abolish its transatlantic slave trade in 1830, to agree to the right of search, and to accept the jurisdiction of the Courts of Mixed Commission. But when 1830 arrived, the Brazilian authorities did nothing to enforce the treaty. With the sugar and coffee economy of Brazil expanding to fill the void left behind by the Haitian Revolution, there was every economic reason for them not to do so. Moreover, few Brazilians held moral sentiments in favor of abolition. Brazilian noncompliance was well-known to the British, but further diplomatic pressure did nothing to change it. In 1845 Brazil went a step further by repudiating the 1826 treaty, throwing aside all pretense of cooperation with the international crusade against the transatlantic slave trade. For the British, this was the last straw. Orders were sent to the Royal Navy, directing it to seize all Brazilian vessels suspected of slaving. The Navy obeyed these orders with enthusiasm and even ventured into Brazilian territorial waters to seize slave ships in its ports. During these same years, British abolitionists were busy within Brazil itself, building domestic support for abolition. The potent combination of coercion and public opinion finally forced the Brazilian government to abolish the trade in 1850 and, more importantly, to actually enforce the ban. The last slave ship arrived in Brazil in 1851.

This left Spain as the only major participant left in the transatlantic slave trade. Although most of its American possessions had broken away during the Latin American Wars of Independence (1810–1826), it still retained Cuba and Puerto Rico. Like Brazil, these two plantation colonies had been experiencing rapid economic growth since the 1790s. And as in Brazil, economic expansion meant growing demand for slaves. Although a signatory to the 1817 treaty, Spain did not want to cut off the main source of fresh labor for its two richest colonies. But unlike Brazil, Spain did not dare to defy the British openly. Instead, it pursued a devious course, ostensibly going along with British initiatives and signing new treaties, but quietly abstaining from enforcing them. The British government was aware of this duplicity, but it hesitated to intervene forcibly as it had with Brazil. The reason for its hesitation was that it wanted to avoid stoking tensions with the United States, which viewed Cuba as falling within its own sphere of influence. To send naval forces to the island, less than one hundred miles from American shores, would have entailed risks the British did not want to run. This situation changed dramatically, however, with the U.S. Civil War. Eager to win favor with Great Britain to keep it from aiding the Confederacy, in 1862 the Lincoln administration offered to set up joint Anglo-American anti-slave-trade patrols off the Cuban coast. With the prospect of American intervention against British interference gone, Spain capitulated and began to enforce the treaties effectively. In 1867 a lone slave ship arrived in Cuba, probably the last in the history of the transatlantic trade.

RESULTS OF BRITISH ABOLITIONISM

Despite the Royal Navy's efforts, most illicit slavers avoided capture. Although the Navy freed about 175,000 captives, this represented only 6 percent of the total number taken to America after 1807. Certainly this is not an insignificant result, especially for those individuals saved from slavery, but it barely made a dent in the overall volume of the trade. Ultimately, the transatlantic slave traded ended only when the governments that had tolerated or even surreptitiously encouraged it made genuine efforts to suppress it. Once they did, the end came very quickly.

What explains these policy shifts in countries like Brazil and Spain, whose slavery-based plantation economies were booming at the moment they ended the trade? This is a complex question that involves a wide range of economic, cultural, and political factors. It is clear, however, that public opinion was turning against all aspects of slavery by the mid-nineteenth century, even in places like Cuba. The reasons for this moral evolution, as with all such changes, are extremely difficult to identify. A more tangible cause for the change is British diplomatic policy. Although the British government's international drive against the slave trade had not, on its own, done much to sway Brazilian or Spanish policy before 1850, it became much more effective thereafter. In part, this reflected those governments' responses to growing domestic unease with the transatlantic slave trade. But the application of force by Great Britain, as in the case of Brazil, or its threat, as with Cuba, cannot be discounted. In the final analysis, a number of factors together played a role in ending the transatlantic slave trade, including changing global economic conditions; the exploitation of new sources of cheap, coercible labor in India, China, and even the poorer parts of Europe; shifts in public opinion; and British diplomatic and military pressure.

While it had little impact on the volume of the trade, the Royal Navy's antislaving campaign did have important transformative effects. First, it broke nearly a century of British dominance of the trade and shifted its geographic locus south of the equator. This shift transformed the cultural composition of the Africans taken as slaves to the Americas after 1807 and thus influenced the character of American society, especially in Brazil and Cuba. British efforts against the trade had another effect on the population of the Americas. It reversed the proportion of African to European immigrants from four to one before 1820 to one to four in the decades that followed. Finally, the political and moral movement against the transatlantic slave trade provided Great Britain with an apprenticeship in modern mass politics and established an example emulated elsewhere, notably by the abolitionists of the antebellum United States. That the Royal Navy failed to end the transatlantic slave trade is tragically clear. That British abolitionism in all of its moral, diplomatic, and military dimensions had a significant impact on that trade is no less evident. Should any doubt remain, one need only indulge in a bit of counterfactual speculation by imagining what would have happened had there been no moral shift, no mass movement, no diplomatic offensive, and no naval campaign against the transatlantic slave trade.

HOW THE END OF THE TRANSATLANTIC SLAVE TRADE AFFECTED AFRICAN SOCIETY

The ending of the transatlantic slave trade thus had profound effects—perhaps nowhere more so than on slavery in Africa itself. Traditionally within Africa, acquiring slaves was a way of adding status and power to one's lineage. This was especially true of rulers and aristocrats, for whom acquiring a retinue of slave administrators, soldiers, and servants increased their political strength. Slavery also played a role in credit (with debtors offering their creditors themselves or family members as "pawns") and in social regulation (with certain types of criminals or outcasts condemned to enslavement). It even had a religious function in some areas, with slaves being dedicated to shrines or sacrificed at funerals. Neither demand in the Muslim world for slaves nor that of the Portuguese in the sixteenth and early seventeenth centuries were strong enough to alter this conception of slavery. But with the explosion in American demand after 1650, African slavery began to change from a familial, cultural, social, and even religious institution into an increasingly economic one.

This shift was gradual and uneven. It was most evident in the coastal centers of the transatlantic slave trade. There, in the eighteenth century, African and Eurafrican elites began to retain captives for their own use instead of selling them to European slave traders. These local slaves were used to grow food for the port communities, provisions for the transatlantic slave trade, and, eventually, lucrative export crops. This practice of using slaves as a primary source of agricultural labor—which suggests a new understanding of slavery as an economic rather than a political or social institution—spread slowly and spottily inland from the coastal slave-trading centers. The growing demand for slaves for the transatlantic trade, coupled with this new African understanding of slaves as economic resources, drove up their value. The result was to intensify enslavement (albeit still largely by traditional methods), sharpen the traditionally porous line between slave status and other forms of personal dependency, and probably exacerbate conflict and instability.

The transatlantic slave trade transformed slavery into a central economic institution in some coastal enclaves. More far-reaching transformation occurred only after 1807 with the abolition of that trade. Imposed unilaterally by European powers, abolition left people in Africa—from rulers and merchant elites to farmers and slaves themselves—to respond to the change. In some areas, such as those linked to the trans-Saharan slave trade or those whose geographic features permitted the transatlantic trade to continue illicitly, there was little immediate impact. But in those regions most affected by the measure, particularly those most exposed to the Royal Navy's interdiction efforts, continuing the transatlantic slave trade covertly was not feasible. Yet captives continued to arrive from the interior in large numbers. The combination of oversupply and greatly reduced demand drove down the price of slaves. This hastened the transformation of slavery into a source of large-scale agricultural labor in two ways. First, the price drop made the already-risky transatlantic trade less profitable and, thus, even less attractive. Second, it made slaves so affordable that aristocrats and merchants found that it made financial sense to purchase large numbers for use in agriculture. In some instances, the price was so low that even people from more modest social strata, such as farmers, could acquire one or two slaves as laborers.

The shift toward agricultural slavery was encouraged by the emergence at this very moment of new opportunities to produce export crops. During the first half of the nineteenth century European industrialization took off. Industrial machinery required lubrication, which, it turned out, could be provided by palm and peanut oil. In much of coastal West Africa, the former slave-trading elites quickly adapted to this economic opening by shifting the glut of unsaleable slaves into the production of palm oil on large plantations. Within a short time, the abolition of the transatlantic slave trade had transformed African slavery and society more radically than had three hundred years of the trade itself. Halting the flow of captives from Africa to America had paradoxically led to the rise in Africa itself of a way of understanding slavery (as an economic institution) and a mode of production (plantation slave labor) that had previously existed only in the Americas.

EMANCIPATION IN AMERICA AND AFRICA

The abolition of the slave trade after 1807 thus gave African slavery a new raison d'être—and possibly even a new lease on life. This leads us to the central irony of the movement to abolish the transatlantic slave trade: it did not immediately affect—and in some cases it actually reinforced—slavery itself. Back in the 1780s, the British abolitionists had taken the strategic decision to decouple the issue of the trade from that of slavery. But once the international campaign against the trade was well-established, they then turned their attention to the evil of slavery itself. Through their efforts, Great Britain emancipated the slaves in its Caribbean colonies in 1833. France followed suit in 1848, only after a bloody revolution brought to power a republican government. In the case of the United States, emancipation only came in the 1860s, following a brutal civil war. After this, other countries followed suit: the Netherlands (1863), Puerto Rico (1873), Cuba (1886), and finally Brazil (1888). In all these cases, emancipation was never clear cut. Instead, the end of slavery was usually followed not by freedom, but by a period of forced labor, known euphemistically under terms such as **apprenticeship** and **indenture,** justified as necessary to ease former slaves into their new condition of liberty. Even after this period of servitude, relations of dependency persisted. Emancipation allowed former slaves to renegotiate their relationship with their former masters, but rarely from a position of strength. In the place of slavery came **debt peonage**, sharecropping, subsistence-level wage labor, and other forms of subordination, often backed by the power of the state. Former slaves and their descendants continued to suffer all manner of liabilities—racial discrimination, exclusions, violent intimidation, political disenfranchisement, and different types of segregation. Although the formal legal status of slavery was abolished, emancipation did not end economic dependency, social marginalization, or political subordination.

Although it came somewhat later than in the Americas, emancipation in Africa followed a similar pattern. The European colonial powers did not begin to enact emancipation laws for their African possessions until the 1870s. At that time, these holdings were largely restricted to narrow coastal areas, so the laws had no impact on most of the continent. Even within the European possessions, the laws were not always enforced. This laxity stemmed in part from the colonial governments' lack of resources, but just as often colonial officials hesitated to undermine the institution of slavery. The European powers were only able to govern their African possessions with the help of intermediaries—local rulers, aristocrats, and merchants—whose power depended to a great extent on their ownership of slaves. To undermine slavery, colonial officials understood, would weaken the very social elites upon whose cooperation effective European rule depended. Faced with the choice between enforcing the laws against slavery demanded by metropolitan public opinion and the need to maintain the power of local elites, colonial officials often turned a blind eye or equivocated. In one striking case, France even relinquished direct control over parts of West Africa to preserve slavery there. French influence, it was reasoned, could be more effectively maintained by indirect rule through the medium of contented, slave-owning elites.

British emancipation in West Africa reveals yet another aspect of this ambiguous process. Drawing on precedents from colonial India, the British emancipation laws categorically ended the legal status of slavery but did not authorize the colonial administration to initiate action to free slaves. This was left up to the slaves themselves. Some remained unaware of the law and did not act. Others, who lacked economic possibilities, also did nothing. But most slaves acted upon the law. Some took legal action before a British court to obtain their freedom, but this was relatively rare. Many more ran away, particularly if they had families within reach. Even more frequently, slaves used the law as leverage to renegotiate their relations with their masters, seeking, for example, to gain land of their own.[3]

Masters found themselves in a difficult position. Many would have preferred maintaining slavery. But as they had grown increasingly dependent upon the British, few dared to flaunt the emancipation law. Although some tried to evade the law, most ended up establishing new relationships with their former slaves. These arrangements often resembled forms of dependency, such as **sharecropping**, common in the postemancipation Americas. Although emancipation in Africa was a process conducted by Africans themselves, with little direct European participation, it tended to perpetuate economic subordination, social discrimination, and political disenfranchisement—just as in the Americas. Wherever slavery once existed, its legacy still weighs heavily.

In the last decade of the nineteenth century, the European powers occupied most of Africa and imposed direct rule. One of the justifications they advanced was the moral imperative of eradicating slavery. In a certain sense, therefore, the partition of Africa was the final expression of the moral crusade that had begun in the 1780s. Yet, direct European control still did not end slavery in Africa. Deeply entangled with social, economic, and even religious practices, slavery had to be approached with care. It was only gradually dismantled during the course of the twentieth century. As late as the 1960s, slave trading from Africa to the Arabian Peninsula was still taking place, and incidents of slavery still appear occasionally not only in Africa, but all across the world—including the United States—today.

---

3 For a superb treatment of African slavery and European imperialism, see Trevor R. Getz and Liz Clarke, *Abina and the Important Men: A Graphic History* (New York: Oxford University Press, 2012).

THE *NEIRSÉE* INCIDENT IN A TRANSATLANTIC CONTEXT

1828 was a banner year for the West African Squadron. The Royal Navy captured more slave-trading vessels that year (thirty-four) than ever before. Nine of the captures were made by William Fitzwilliam Owen, captain of the H.M.S. *Eden*, and his men. This surpassed even the eight captures made by the Squadron's flagship, the H.M.S. *Sybille* under Commodore Collier, and its famous tender, the *Black Joke*, the most celebrated British slaver-chaser of the age. Owen had arrived in West Africa the year before, with orders to establish a base on the island of Fernando Po in the Bight of Biafra. Although his primary mission was to prepare facilities for the projected transfer of the Court of Mixed Commission from Freetown, Fernando Po's proximity to the slave-trading centers of Bonny, New Calabar, and Old Calabar offered an opportunity Owen could not resist. A veteran of the long wars against France and accustomed to independent command (he had led extended surveying expeditions along unknown coasts in the years after Waterloo), Owen sent his forces to the coast. Led by intrepid young officers such as Lieutenant Badgeley, they pursued the slavers up-river to their entrepôts, taking them by surprise and overpowering them in hand-to-hand combat despite inferior numbers.

One of the captured ships was the *Neirsée*. It was taken by Badgeley on 23 November 1828 near Old Calabar. Like other slave ships its crew was motley, its flags various, and its national identity unclear. Following the standard procedure, Owen prepared to send the *Neirsée* to Freetown for adjudication. Since his forces were stretched so thin by their many activities, he had to give command of its prize crew to an unusually junior officer, Midshipman James Davies. On 2 December 1828, Davies set sail for Sierra Leone with the *Neirsée*. On board were the 7 Europeans and 5 Krumen under his command, 18 slavers, and the 309 captives who had been found on board when the ship was seized. There were also 6 craftsmen from Sierra Leone who had been hired by Owen and were now returning home, having finished their contracts. One of them, Thomas George, was accompanied by his wife, Sarah.

So far, the *Neirsée* incident had unfolded in typical fashion. But when a storm separated it from its escort, the situation changed dramatically. The slavers overpowered the prize crew, regained control of the ship, and steered a course to the Caribbean. They arrived after a month's voyage. Although they landed the Europeans at the British colony of Dominica, they disembarked the African passengers—not just the 280 survivors of the original captives, but the surviving Krumen and Sierra Leoneans as well—in French Guadeloupe and sold them into slavery. The enslavement of the Krumen, active-duty Royal Navy personnel, and the Sierra Leoneans, British subjects, prompted British authorities to intervene. Informed of what had occurred by Davies, the governor of Dominica demanded the release of the British African subjects. He also informed Admiral Fleming, the British naval commander in the West Indies. Fleming sailed to Guadeloupe, deployed warships, and exchanged heated correspondence with the governor of Guadeloupe, the Baron des Rotours, that threatened to transform the incident into an international crisis. One of Fleming's officers, Captain Deare, even landed on Guadeloupe—without authorization—to look for the captives. Although Fleming's methods infuriated French colonial authorities, the British African captives were soon released, with the exception of Sarah.

When informed of the incident in late March 1829, British diplomats applied pressure of their own. Although they soon learned that the British African subjects had been released, they continued to press the incident to insist that, so long as France refused to join the international effort against transatlantic slave trading, slavers would use its flag for protection. French diplomats hit back, pointing out that Captain Owen had acted illegally in seizing the (presumably) French-flagged *Neirsée*, and demanded an official explanation. When this arrived at the end of August 1829, it satisfied them because Owen stated that he had only seized the *Neirsée* because he had believed it to be Dutch. By this point, both governments had grown concerned about the mounting tension between Fleming and Rotours and were eager to nip it in the bud. They worked out a compromise: the admiral and governor would be reined in, the British would consider themselves satisfied by the release of their African subjects, and the French would accept Owen's explanation and overlook Deare's violation of their territory. Lost in the shuffle were the 280 captives and Sarah. Despite Thomas George's efforts, which were actively seconded by the British naval authorities in the West Indies, she was never found. Ultimately he and the other British African subjects gave up and returned home.

Although it ended in neither war nor diplomatic breakthrough, and although its ambiguous finale left tragic loose ends, the *Neirsée* affair is nonetheless important. It opens a panoramic view on the spatial, temporal, and human dimensions of the Atlantic world in the early nineteenth century. The affair spanned a vast geographical space: coastal West Africa, the Caribbean, Europe, and the waters in between. This was a natural space of rivers, islands, winds, and waves, as well as a human space of stockades, wharfs, decks, ship holds, roads, huts, plantations, villages, cities, and palaces. It was a diverse space hundreds of thousands of miles in extent. Yet, while vast, it was a connected space, albeit one in which people, goods, and information only traveled as fast as the sailing vessels that formed its circulatory and nervous system. An illustration: the last person to know what had happened to the *Neirsée* was the man at its origin, Captain Owen, who only learned of it more than six months later, in a dispatch from Europe.

Enormous, connected, and slow, these features of the Atlantic world make the *Neirsée* affair difficult to reconstruct and recount as a narrative. The affair ultimately involved several government ministries in five European countries (Britain, France, Denmark, Holland, and Sweden) and their respective colonies in West Africa and the Caribbean. An even greater challenge in imposing narrative structure on the incident arose from the spatial and temporal context of the Atlantic world. Instead of a single chain of events, the *Neirsée* incident consisted of distinct episodes played out on different stages (ships, beaches, plantations, government offices, etc.), all of which took place more or less simultaneously in different parts of the Atlantic world. The various protagonists were well aware of this. To keep their colleagues abreast of what was going on, they sent frequent dispatches to all concerned. The volume of this correspondence was daunting; in fact, one sometimes wonders how naval officers like Owen and Fleming had time to do anything else than sit at their writing desks. The flurry of dispatches traveling back and forth across the Atlantic was so dense, overlapping, and often redundant that writers often opened their communications with a summary of what they had received, as well as to what they were responding. To further clarify the criss-crossing, simultaneous streams of communication, official regulations required all dispatches to be numbered sequentially (see Map 6).

As if that were not enough, colonial and naval officials in their distant postings were also required to send back to Europe logs of the communication flow.

A challenge at the time to keep this straight, it is even more difficult for a historian today to untangle this web of communications. Map 6 offers a simplified spatial and chronological outline of the *Neirsée* incident as it took shape in the Atlantic context.

Communications and transport in the Caribbean was simpler, mainly because most of the action took place in Dominica and Guadeloupe, adjacent islands separated by less than a day's travel time (see Map 7).

The *Neirsée* affair is a story with a cast of hundreds, with different episodes taking place simultaneously in different parts of the world and its actors only dimly and tardily aware of the overall shape of the drama they were enacting. The graphic narrative that follows attempts to capture this. I hope that this will not be confusing, but rather will bring to life a new character, the real main character of the story—the Atlantic world itself.

WEST INDIES TO EU
ATLANTIC
OCEAN
Havanna
EUROPE TO
Guadeloupe
Désirade
Trinidad
Suriname
N
W
E
S
0 km
850
0 miles
850

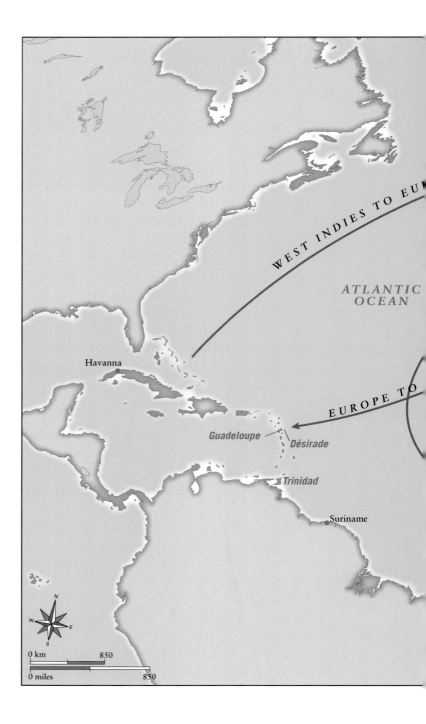

Map 6 Atlantic Communication Itineraries

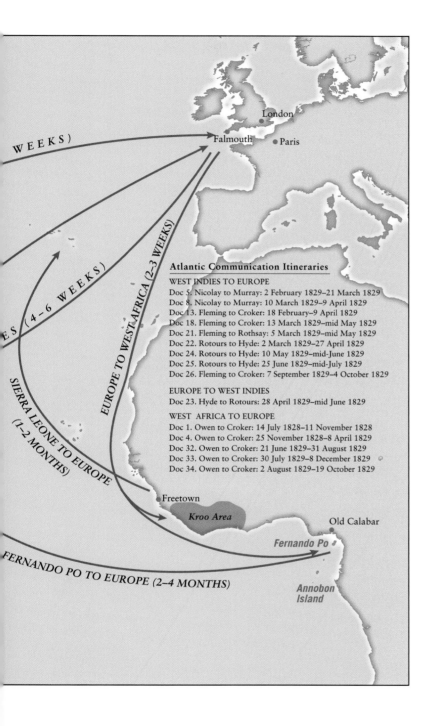

WEEKS)

ES (4–6 WEEKS)

SIERRA LEONE TO EUROPE
(1–2 MONTHS)

EUROPE TO WEST AFRICA (2–3 WEEKS)

FERNANDO PO TO EUROPE (2–4 MONTHS)

London

Falmouth • Paris

Atlantic Communication Itineraries

WEST INDIES TO EUROPE
Doc 5. Nicolay to Murray: 2 February 1829–21 March 1829
Doc 8. Nicolay to Murray: 10 March 1829–9 April 1829
Doc 13. Fleming to Croker: 18 February–9 April 1829
Doc 18. Fleming to Croker: 13 March 1829–mid May 1829
Doc 21. Fleming to Rothsay: 5 March 1829–mid May 1829
Doc 22. Rotours to Hyde: 2 March 1829–27 April 1829
Doc 24. Rotours to Hyde: 10 May 1829–mid-June 1829
Doc 25. Rotours to Hyde: 25 June 1829–mid-July 1829
Doc 26. Fleming to Croker: 7 September 1829–4 October 1829

EUROPE TO WEST INDIES
Doc 23. Hyde to Rotours: 28 April 1829–mid June 1829

WEST AFRICA TO EUROPE
Doc 1. Owen to Croker: 14 July 1828–11 November 1828
Doc 4. Owen to Croker: 25 November 1828–8 April 1829
Doc 32. Owen to Croker: 21 June 1829–31 August 1829
Doc 33. Owen to Croker: 30 July 1829–8 December 1829
Doc 34. Owen to Croker: 2 August 1829–19 October 1829

Freetown

Kroo Area

Old Calabar

Fernando Po

*Annobon
Island*

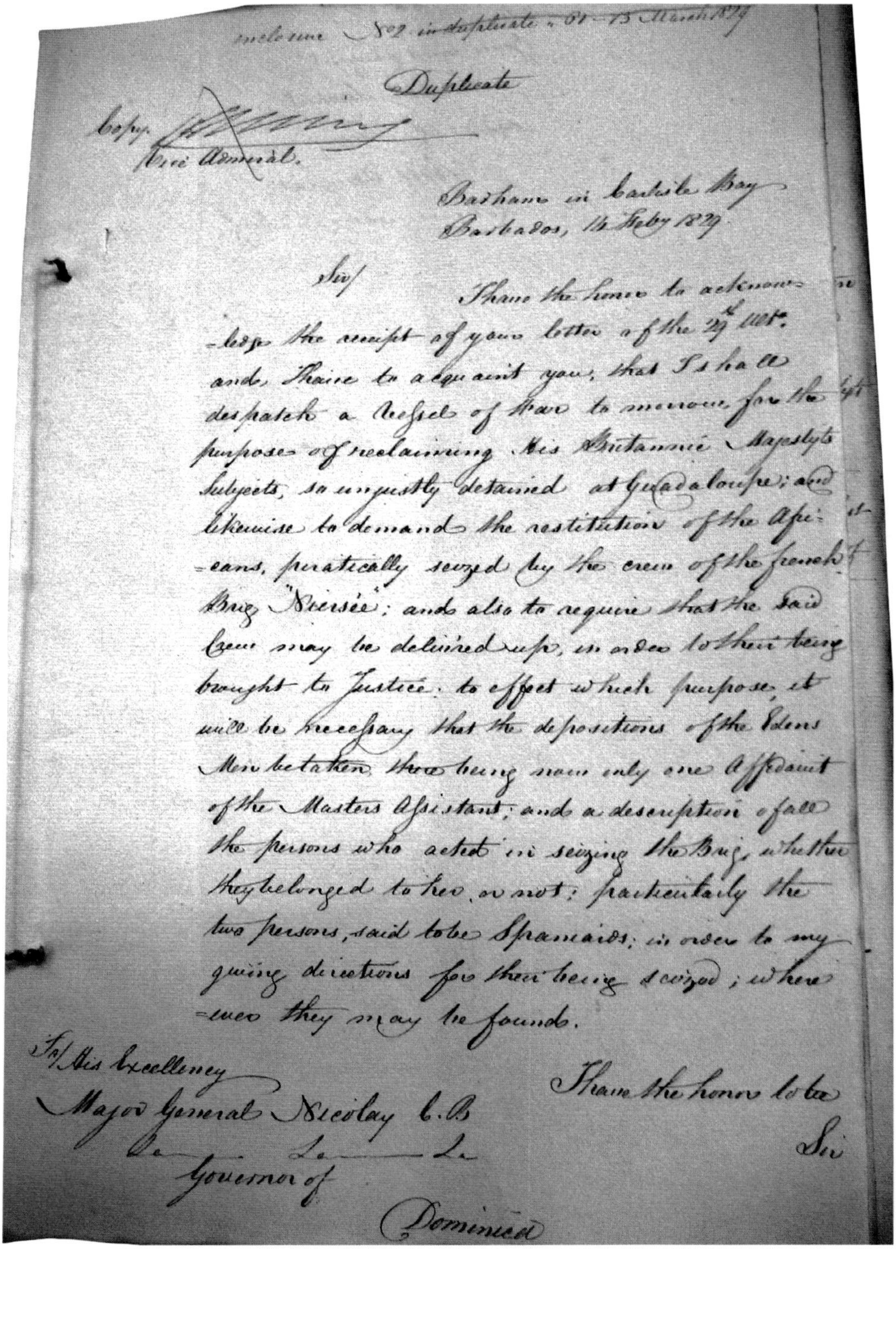

Figure 4. Admiral Fleming to Governor Nicolay (14 February 1829).

Source: The National Archives, ADM 1 280.

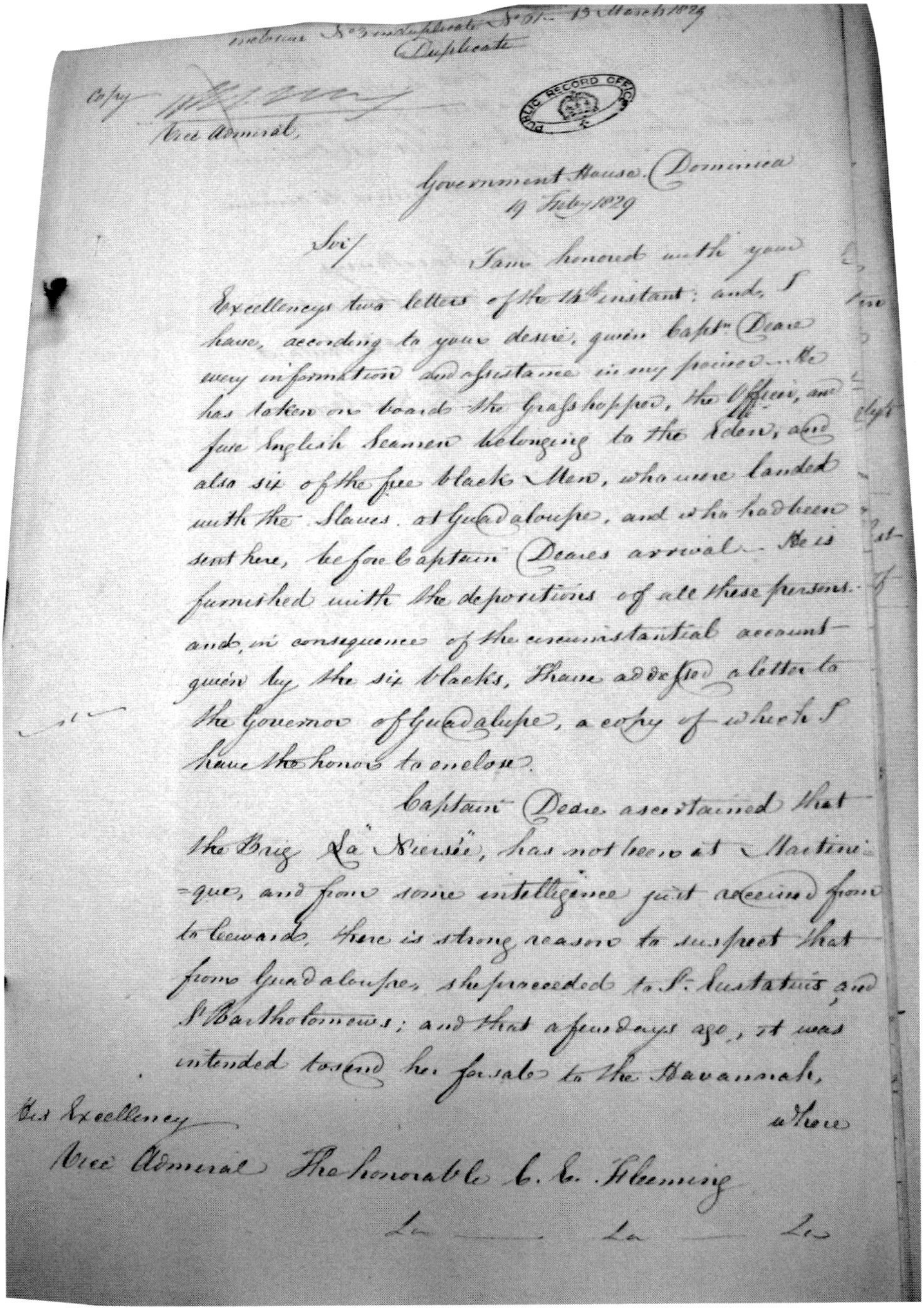

Figure 5. Governor Nicolay to Admiral Fleming (19 February 1829).

Source: The National Archives, ADM 1 280.

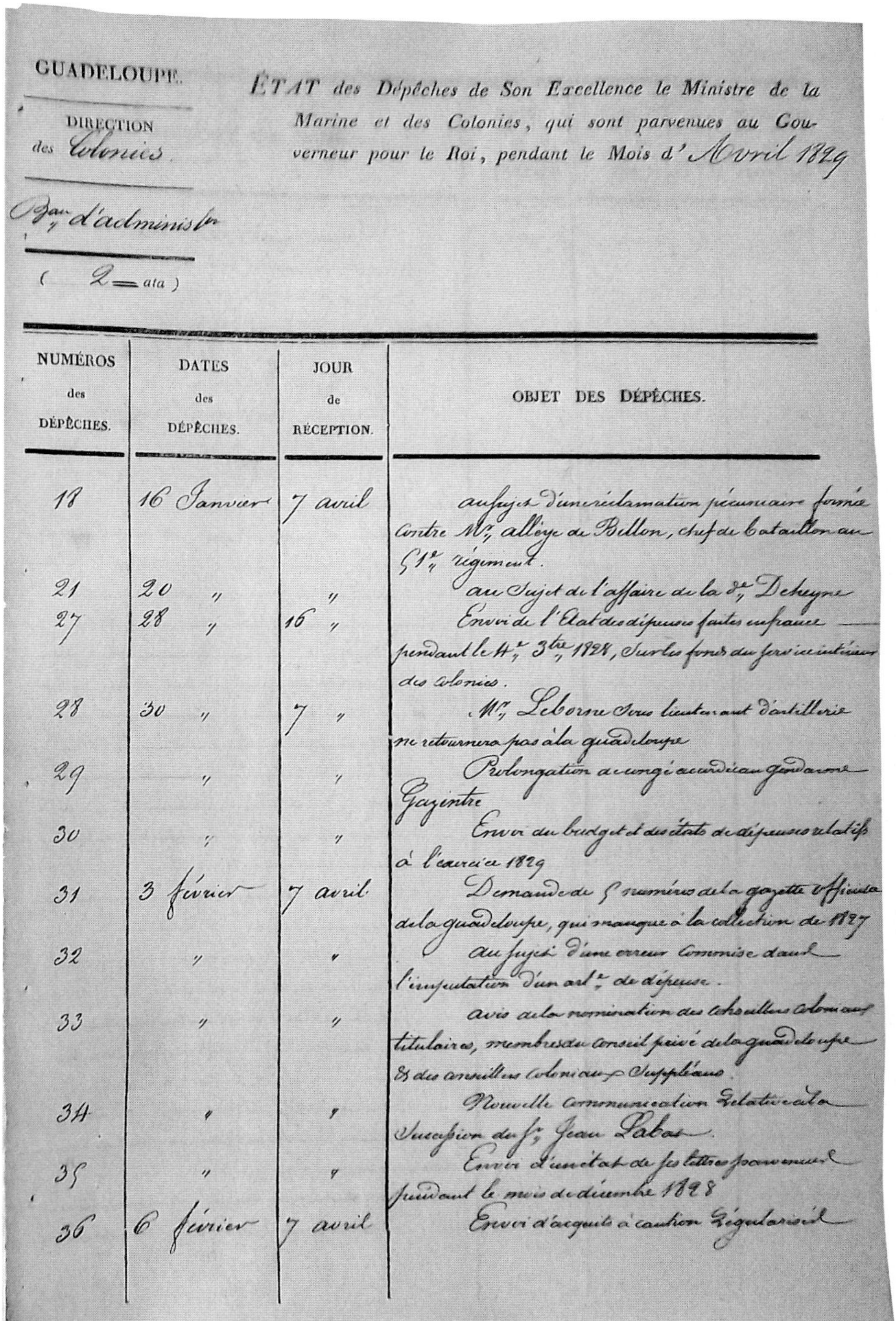

Figure 6. The Baron des Rotours' Monthly Log of Dispatches Received in April 1829.

Source: Archives Nationales d'Outre Mer, Fonds Ministériel, Série Géographique, *GUA/CORR/78.

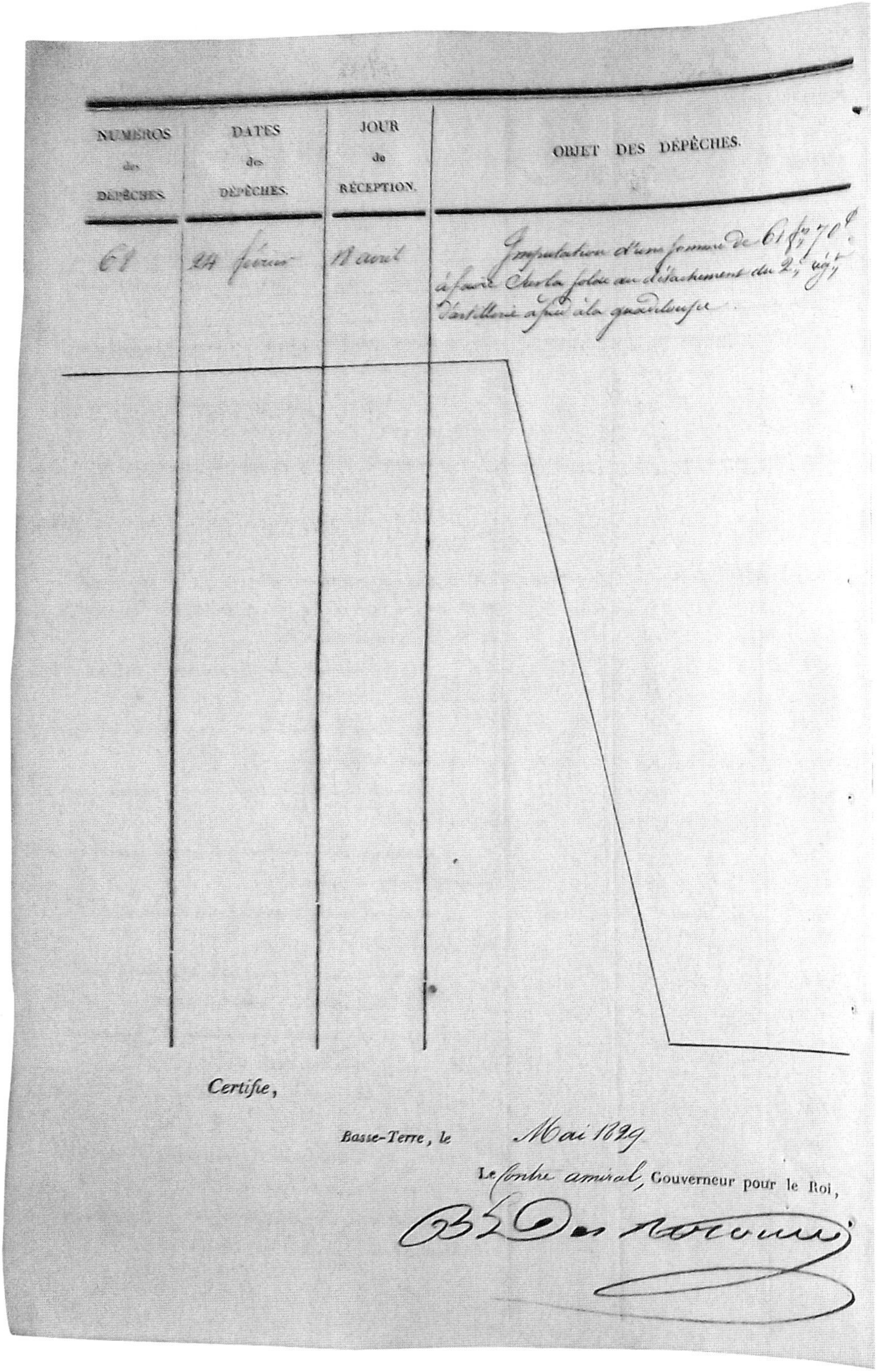

NUMÉROS des DÉPÊCHES.	DATES des DÉPÊCHES.	JOUR de RÉCEPTION.	OBJET DES DÉPÊCHES.
61	24 février	18 avril	Imputation d'une somme de 61f 70c à faire état la solde au détachement du 2e régt d'artillerie à pied à la Guadeloupe.

Certifie,

Basse-Terre, le Mai 1829

Le Contre amiral, Gouverneur pour le Roi,

Bon Des Rotours

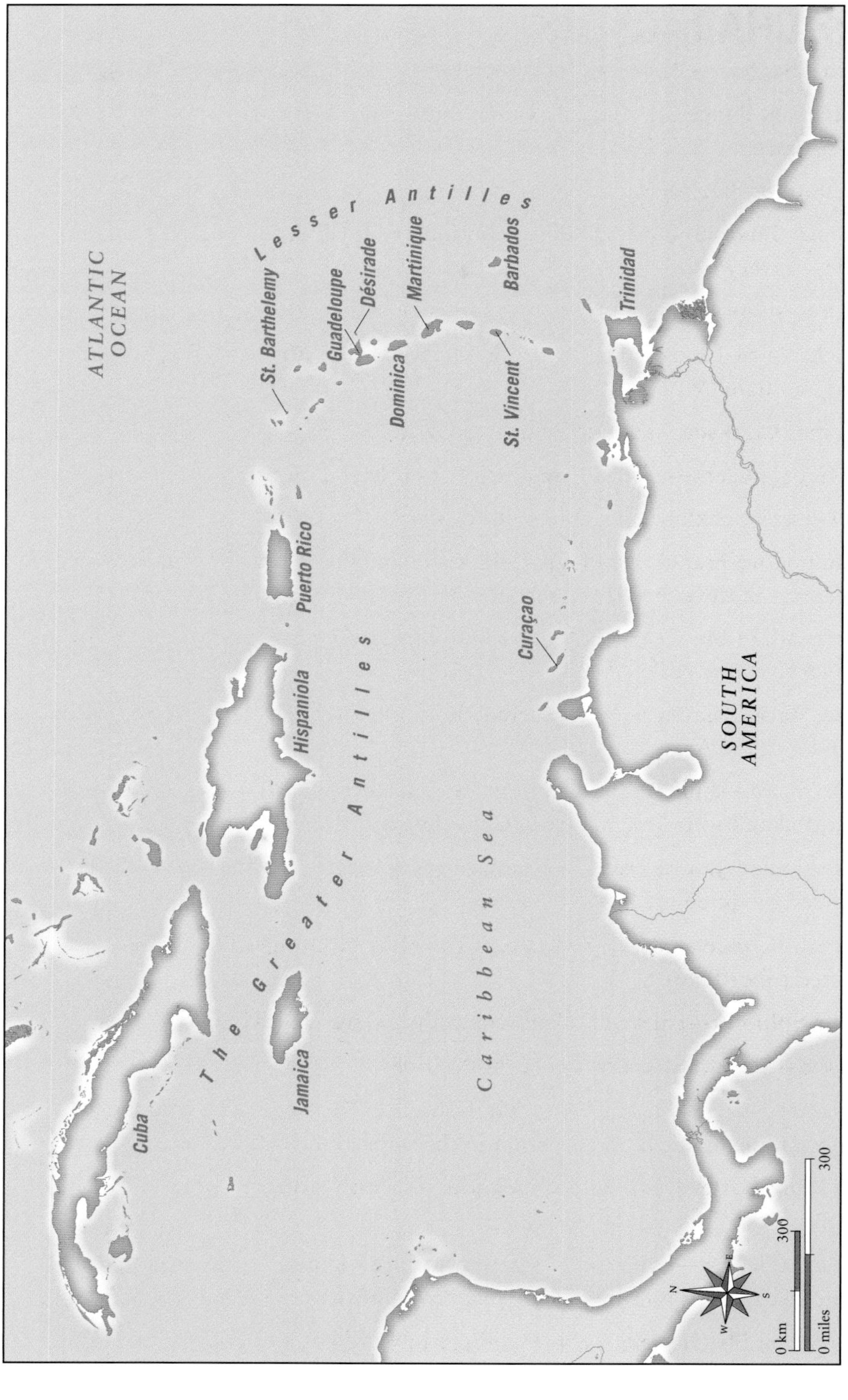
ATLANTIC OCEAN
Lesser Antilles
St. Barthelemy
Guadeloupe
Désirade
Dominica
Martinique
Barbados
St. Vincent
Trinidad
Puerto Rico
Hispaniola
The Greater Antilles
Cuba
Jamaica
Caribbean Sea
Curaçao
SOUTH AMERICA
0 km 300
0 miles 300
N
S
E
W

Map 7 The Caribbean

CAST OF CHARACTERS

Lord Aberdeen—British Foreign Secretary

Lieutenant Badgeley—Captain Owen's intrepid subordinate who captured the *Neirsée*

The Earl of Brecknock—a Lord Commissioner of the Admiralty

Thomas Buxton—leading British abolitionist politician who called for an end to slavery itself

Lord Castlereagh—British Foreign Minister in the 1810s

The Duke of Clarence—the Lord High Admiral and future King of England, William IV

Thomas Clarkson—leading British abolitionist

Sir George Clerk—a Lord Commissioner of the Admiralty

Sir George Cockburn—a Lord Commissioner of the Admiralty

Commodore Francis Augustus Collier—commander of the West African Squadron in the late 1820s, when the *Neirsée* incident occurred

Commodore Sir George Collier—first commander of the West African Squadron in the early 1820s

John Wilson Croker—First Secretary of the Admiralty, historian, and founder of the Athenaeum

Jack Davies—skilled craftsman from Sierra Leone; passenger on the *Neirsée*; captured and sold into slavery in Guadeloupe

Midshipman James Davies—young subordinate of Captain Owen; commanded the prize crew of the *Neirsée*

Captain Charles Deare—Captain of the H.M.S. *Grasshopper*; Fleming's trusted subordinate

Duke Ephraim—ruler of Duketown; leading slave-trader in Old Calabar

Feraud—Slave trader, captain of the *Neirsée*

Ferdinand VII—King of Spain who signed 1817 treaty with Britain formally ending Spanish participation in the transatlantic slave trade

Admiral Charles Fleming—commander of British naval forces in the West Indies

Thomas George—skilled craftsman from Sierra Leone; a passenger on the *Neirsée*; captured and sold into slavery in Guadeloupe; husband of Sarah

Lieutenant Hagan—Sir George Collier's intrepid subordinate

Sir Henry Hotham—a Lord Commissioner of the Admiralty

Baron Hyde de Neuville—French Minister of the Navy and the Colonies

Midshipman Robert Inman—member of the West African Squadron, brutally killed and mutilated by slave traders in 1820

Kru—a West African group that specialized in naval service, especially on vessels of the Royal Navy's West African Squadron

Ben Liverpool—skilled craftsman from Sierra Leone; passenger on the *Neirsée*; captured and sold into slavery in Guadeloupe

Louis-Philippe—King of France after the Revolution of 1830

Lieutenant Mayne—Captain Deare's subordinate and French translator

Viscount Melville—a Lord Commissioner of the Admiralty

Joseph Michael—skilled craftsman from Sierra Leone; passenger on the *Neirsée*; captured and sold into slavery in Guadeloupe

Sir George Murray—Secretary of State for War and the Colonies

Governor Nicolay—Governor of Dominica

Captain William Fitzwilliam Owen—captain of the H.M.S. *Eden* and superintendant of Fernando Po; commanded the forces that captured the *Neirsée*

Prince Polignac—French ambassador to Britain and then French Foreign Minister

Joseph-Marie Portalis—French Foreign Minister

James Rawson—skilled craftsman from Sierra Leone; passenger on the *Neirsée*; captured and sold into slavery in Guadeloupe

Richard—Second Captain of the *Neirsée*; led the retaking of the *Neirsée*

Henry Ricketts—Governor of Sierra Leone

Lord Stuart de Rothsay—British ambassador to France

Admiral, Baron des Rotours—Governor of Guadeloupe

Sarah—a woman settled in Sierra Leone after being liberated from a slave ship by the British; passenger on the *Neirsée*; captured and sold into slavery in Guadeloupe; wife of Thomas George

Sergente—Guadeloupean planter who purchased the Sierra Leoneans and Krumen

Granville Sharp—leading British abolitionist

General Vatable—commander of French ground forces in Guadeloupe

Villaret de Joyeuse—French naval officer; commanded France's West African Squadron in the late 1820s

William Wilberforce—leading British abolitionist; spearheaded Parliamentary campaign that led to the passage of the 1807 abolition law

Prince Will—Kru sailor of the *Neirsée* prize crew; captured and sold into slavery in Guadeloupe

Yellow Will—Kru sailor of the *Neirsée* prize crew; captured and sold into slavery in Guadeloupe

Dick Wilson—Kru sailor of the *Neirsée* prize crew; captured and sold into slavery in Guadeloupe

PART II
THE GRAPHIC
HISTORY

CHAPTER 1
INTERNATIONAL EFFORTS AGAINST THE TRANSATLANTIC SLAVE TRADE

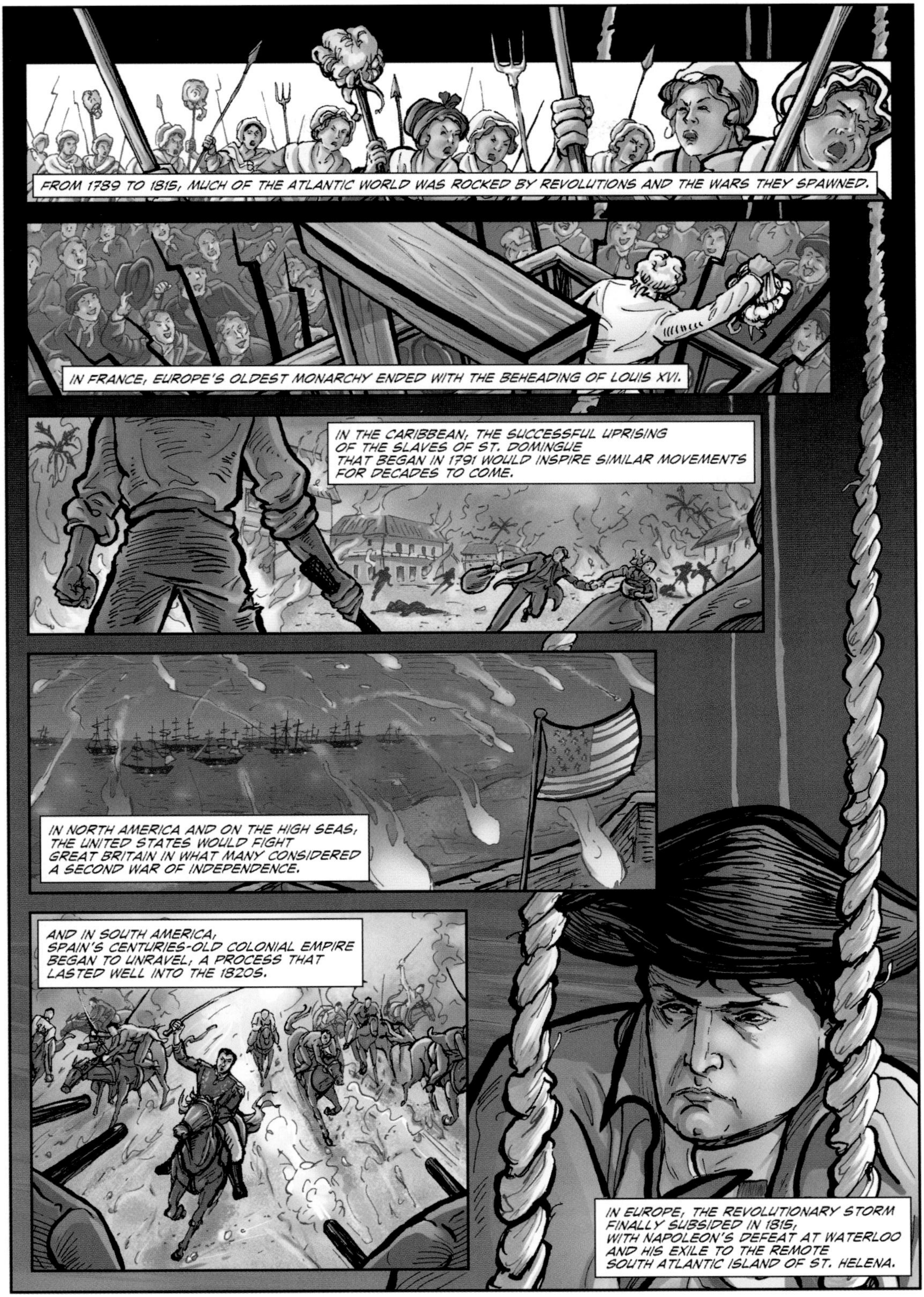
FROM 1789 TO 1815, MUCH OF THE ATLANTIC WORLD WAS ROCKED BY REVOLUTIONS AND THE WARS THEY SPAWNED.
IN FRANCE, EUROPE'S OLDEST MONARCHY ENDED WITH THE BEHEADING OF LOUIS XVI.
IN THE CARIBBEAN, THE SUCCESSFUL UPRISING OF THE SLAVES OF ST. DOMINGUE THAT BEGAN IN 1791 WOULD INSPIRE SIMILAR MOVEMENTS FOR DECADES TO COME.
IN NORTH AMERICA AND ON THE HIGH SEAS, THE UNITED STATES WOULD FIGHT GREAT BRITAIN IN WHAT MANY CONSIDERED A SECOND WAR OF INDEPENDENCE.
AND IN SOUTH AMERICA, SPAIN'S CENTURIES-OLD COLONIAL EMPIRE BEGAN TO UNRAVEL, A PROCESS THAT LASTED WELL INTO THE 1820S.
IN EUROPE, THE REVOLUTIONARY STORM FINALLY SUBSIDED IN 1815, WITH NAPOLEON'S DEFEAT AT WATERLOO AND HIS EXILE TO THE REMOTE SOUTH ATLANTIC ISLAND OF ST. HELENA.

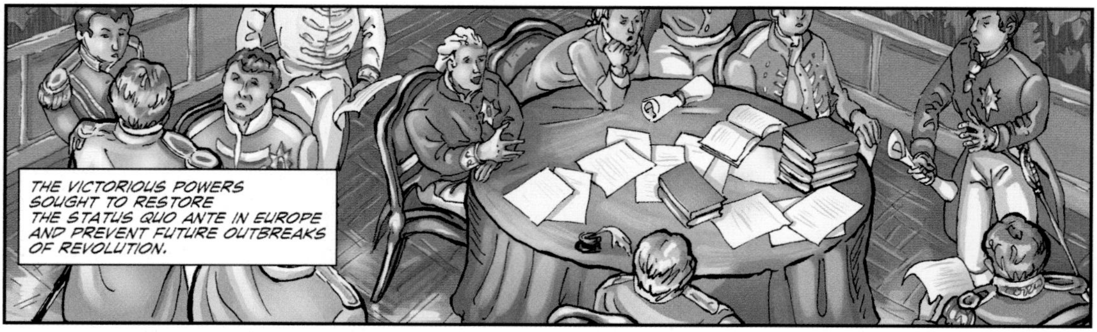
THE VICTORIOUS POWERS SOUGHT TO RESTORE THE STATUS QUO ANTE IN EUROPE AND PREVENT FUTURE OUTBREAKS OF REVOLUTION.

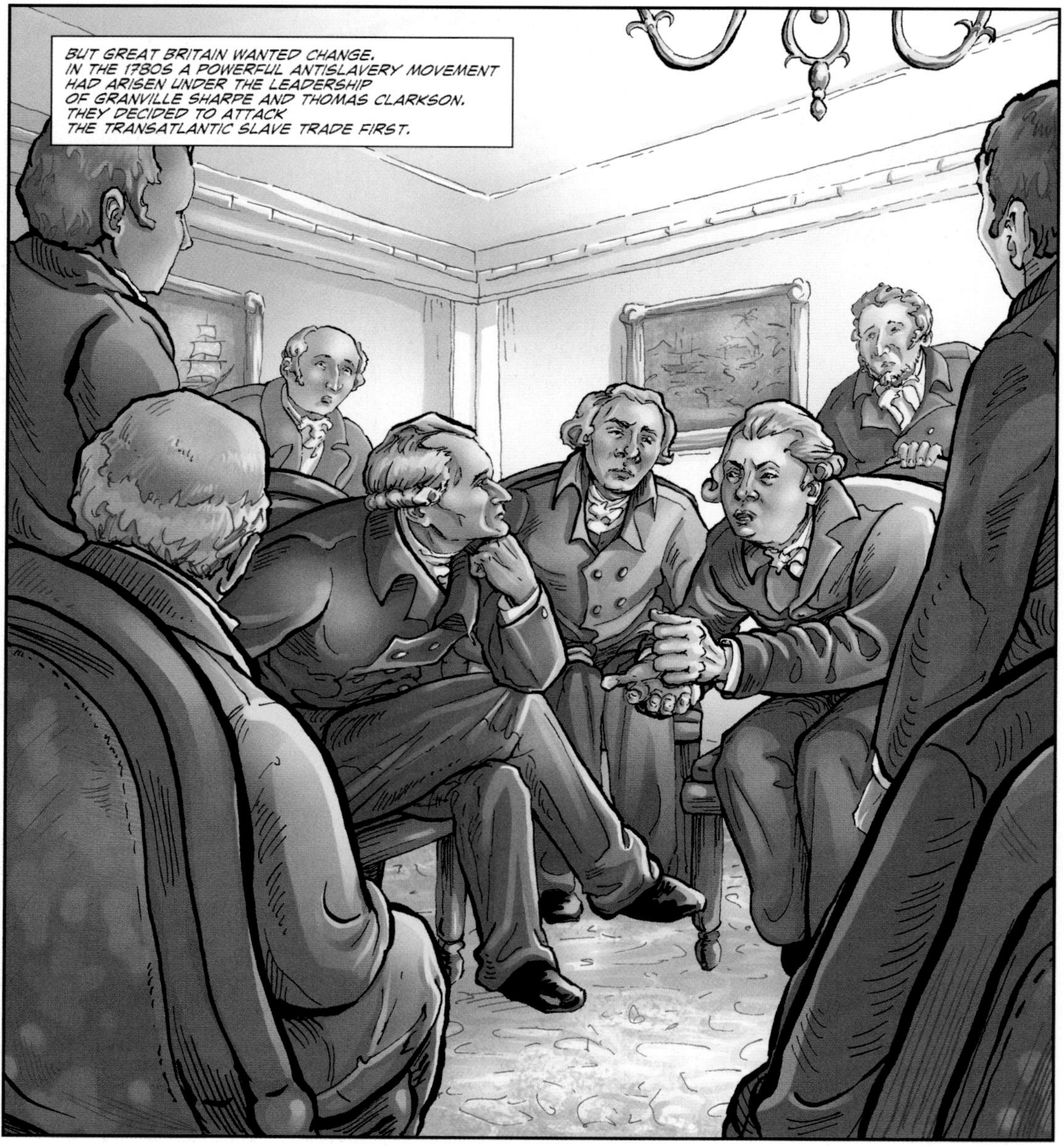
BUT GREAT BRITAIN WANTED CHANGE. IN THE 1780S A POWERFUL ANTISLAVERY MOVEMENT HAD ARISEN UNDER THE LEADERSHIP OF GRANVILLE SHARPE AND THOMAS CLARKSON. THEY DECIDED TO ATTACK THE TRANSATLANTIC SLAVE TRADE FIRST.

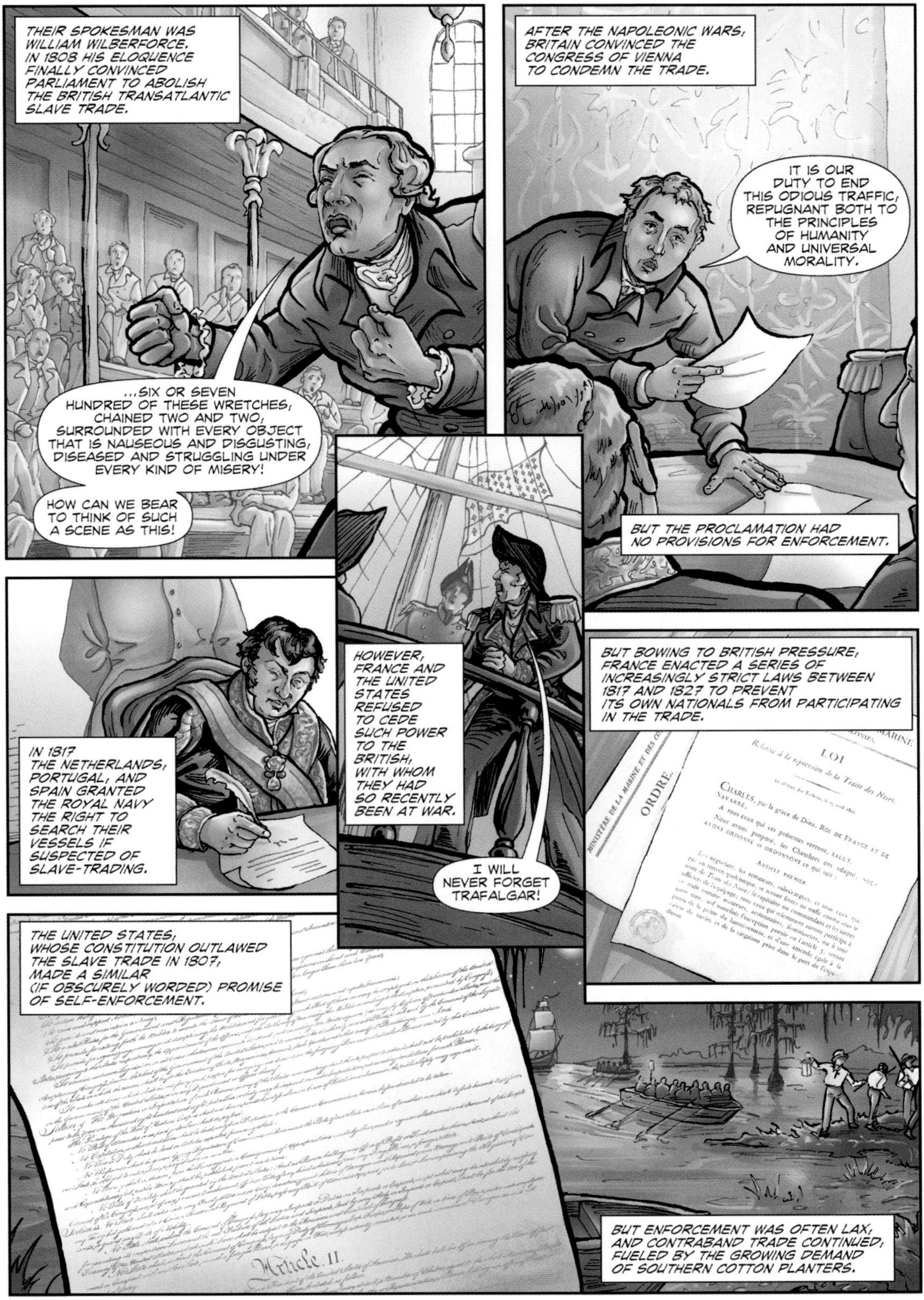
THEIR SPOKESMAN WAS WILLIAM WILBERFORCE. IN 1808 HIS ELOQUENCE FINALLY CONVINCED PARLIAMENT TO ABOLISH THE BRITISH TRANSATLANTIC SLAVE TRADE.
...SIX OR SEVEN HUNDRED OF THESE WRETCHES, CHAINED TWO AND TWO, SURROUNDED WITH EVERY OBJECT THAT IS NAUSEOUS AND DISGUSTING, DISEASED AND STRUGGLING UNDER EVERY KIND OF MISERY!
HOW CAN WE BEAR TO THINK OF SUCH A SCENE AS THIS!
AFTER THE NAPOLEONIC WARS, BRITAIN CONVINCED THE CONGRESS OF VIENNA TO CONDEMN THE TRADE.
IT IS OUR DUTY TO END THIS ODIOUS TRAFFIC, REPUGNANT BOTH TO THE PRINCIPLES OF HUMANITY AND UNIVERSAL MORALITY.
BUT THE PROCLAMATION HAD NO PROVISIONS FOR ENFORCEMENT.
IN 1817 THE NETHERLANDS, PORTUGAL, AND SPAIN GRANTED THE ROYAL NAVY THE RIGHT TO SEARCH THEIR VESSELS IF SUSPECTED OF SLAVE-TRADING.
HOWEVER, FRANCE AND THE UNITED STATES REFUSED TO CEDE SUCH POWER TO THE BRITISH, WITH WHOM THEY HAD SO RECENTLY BEEN AT WAR.
I WILL NEVER FORGET TRAFALGAR!
BUT BOWING TO BRITISH PRESSURE, FRANCE ENACTED A SERIES OF INCREASINGLY STRICT LAWS BETWEEN 1817 AND 1827 TO PREVENT ITS OWN NATIONALS FROM PARTICIPATING IN THE TRADE.
LOI
ORDRE.
THE UNITED STATES, WHOSE CONSTITUTION OUTLAWED THE SLAVE TRADE IN 1807, MADE A SIMILAR (IF OBSCURELY WORDED) PROMISE OF SELF-ENFORCEMENT.
Article. II.
BUT ENFORCEMENT WAS OFTEN LAX, AND CONTRABAND TRADE CONTINUED, FUELED BY THE GROWING DEMAND OF SOUTHERN COTTON PLANTERS.

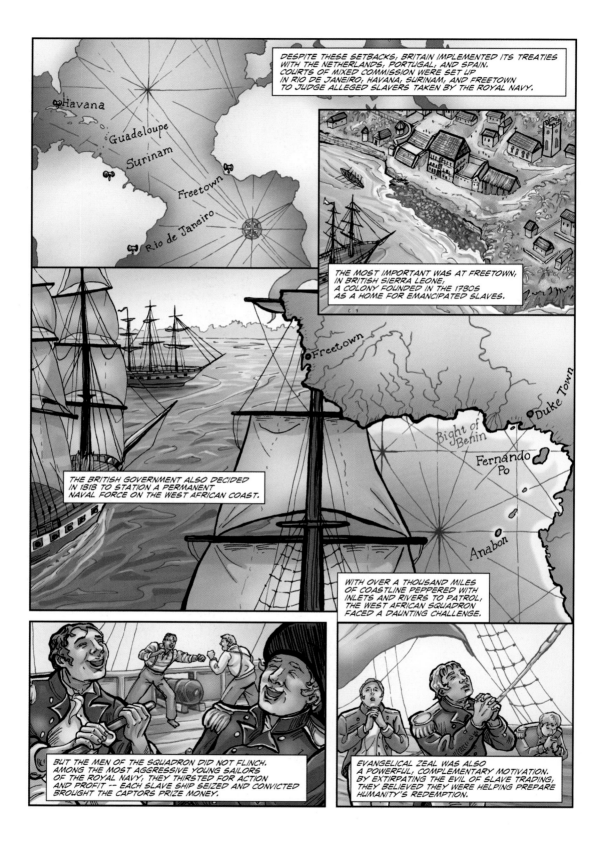

DESPITE THESE SETBACKS, BRITAIN IMPLEMENTED ITS TREATIES WITH THE NETHERLANDS, PORTUGAL, AND SPAIN. COURTS OF MIXED COMMISSION WERE SET UP IN RIO DE JANEIRO, HAVANA, SURINAM, AND FREETOWN TO JUDGE ALLEGED SLAVERS TAKEN BY THE ROYAL NAVY.

THE MOST IMPORTANT WAS AT FREETOWN, IN BRITISH SIERRA LEONE, A COLONY FOUNDED IN THE 1780S AS A HOME FOR EMANCIPATED SLAVES.

THE BRITISH GOVERNMENT ALSO DECIDED IN 1818 TO STATION A PERMANENT NAVAL FORCE ON THE WEST AFRICAN COAST.

WITH OVER A THOUSAND MILES OF COASTLINE PEPPERED WITH INLETS AND RIVERS TO PATROL, THE WEST AFRICAN SQUADRON FACED A DAUNTING CHALLENGE.

BUT THE MEN OF THE SQUADRON DID NOT FLINCH. AMONG THE MOST AGGRESSIVE YOUNG SAILORS OF THE ROYAL NAVY, THEY THIRSTED FOR ACTION AND PROFIT -- EACH SLAVE SHIP SEIZED AND CONVICTED BROUGHT THE CAPTORS PRIZE MONEY.

EVANGELICAL ZEAL WAS ALSO A POWERFUL, COMPLEMENTARY MOTIVATION. BY EXTIRPATING THE EVIL OF SLAVE TRADING, THEY BELIEVED THEY WERE HELPING PREPARE HUMANITY'S REDEMPTION.

Havana
Guadeloupe
Surinam
Freetown
Rio de Janeiro

Freetown
Duke Town
Bight of Benin
Fernando Po
Anabon

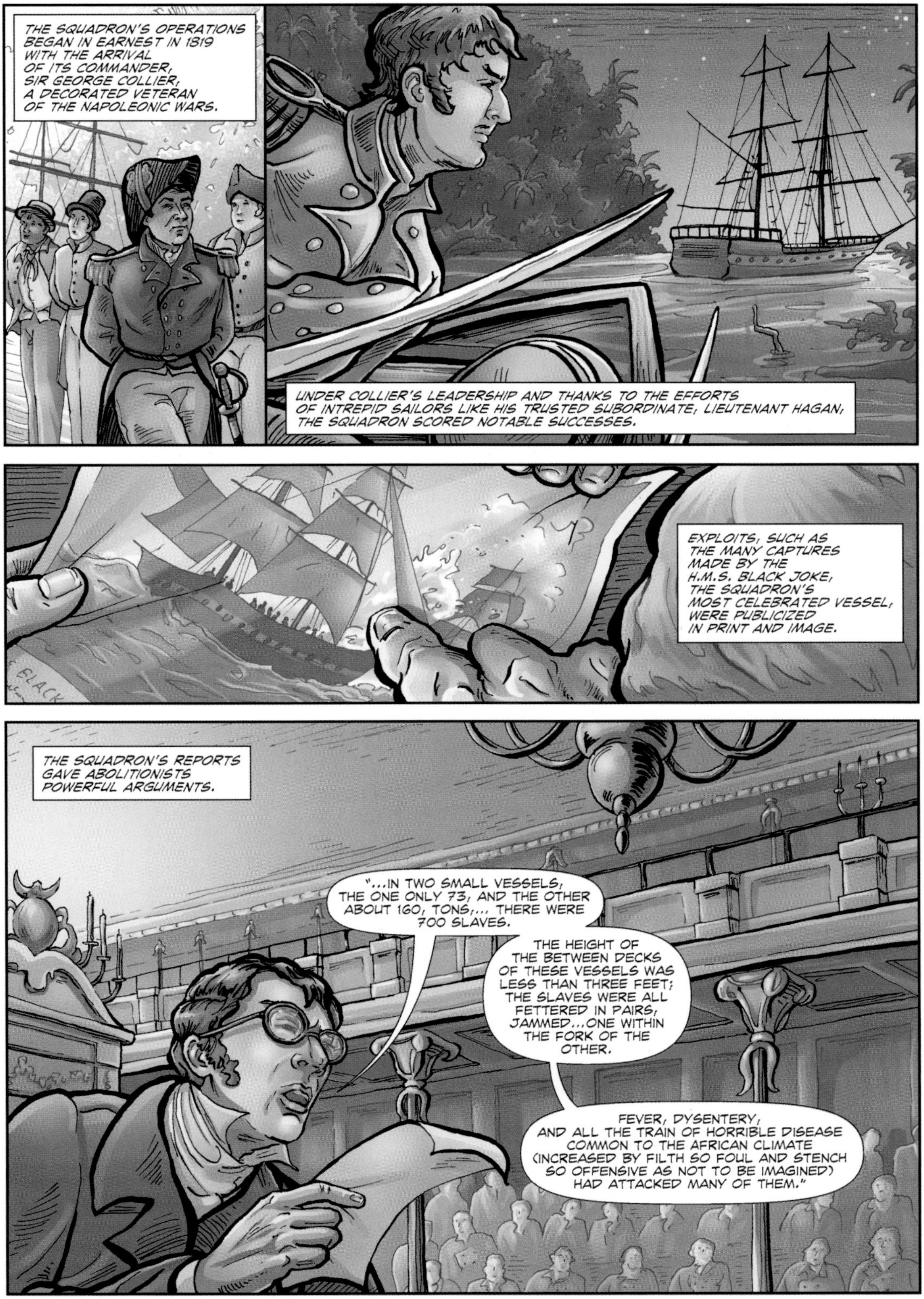
THE SQUADRON'S OPERATIONS BEGAN IN EARNEST IN 1819 WITH THE ARRIVAL OF ITS COMMANDER, SIR GEORGE COLLIER, A DECORATED VETERAN OF THE NAPOLEONIC WARS.
UNDER COLLIER'S LEADERSHIP AND THANKS TO THE EFFORTS OF INTREPID SAILORS LIKE HIS TRUSTED SUBORDINATE, LIEUTENANT HAGAN, THE SQUADRON SCORED NOTABLE SUCCESSES.
EXPLOITS, SUCH AS THE MANY CAPTURES MADE BY THE H.M.S. BLACK JOKE, THE SQUADRON'S MOST CELEBRATED VESSEL, WERE PUBLICIZED IN PRINT AND IMAGE.
THE SQUADRON'S REPORTS GAVE ABOLITIONISTS POWERFUL ARGUMENTS.
"...IN TWO SMALL VESSELS, THE ONE ONLY 73, AND THE OTHER ABOUT 160, TONS,... THERE WERE 700 SLAVES.
THE HEIGHT OF THE BETWEEN DECKS OF THESE VESSELS WAS LESS THAN THREE FEET; THE SLAVES WERE ALL FETTERED IN PAIRS, JAMMED...ONE WITHIN THE FORK OF THE OTHER.
FEVER, DYSENTERY, AND ALL THE TRAIN OF HORRIBLE DISEASE COMMON TO THE AFRICAN CLIMATE (INCREASED BY FILTH SO FOUL AND STENCH SO OFFENSIVE AS NOT TO BE IMAGINED) HAD ATTACKED MANY OF THEM."

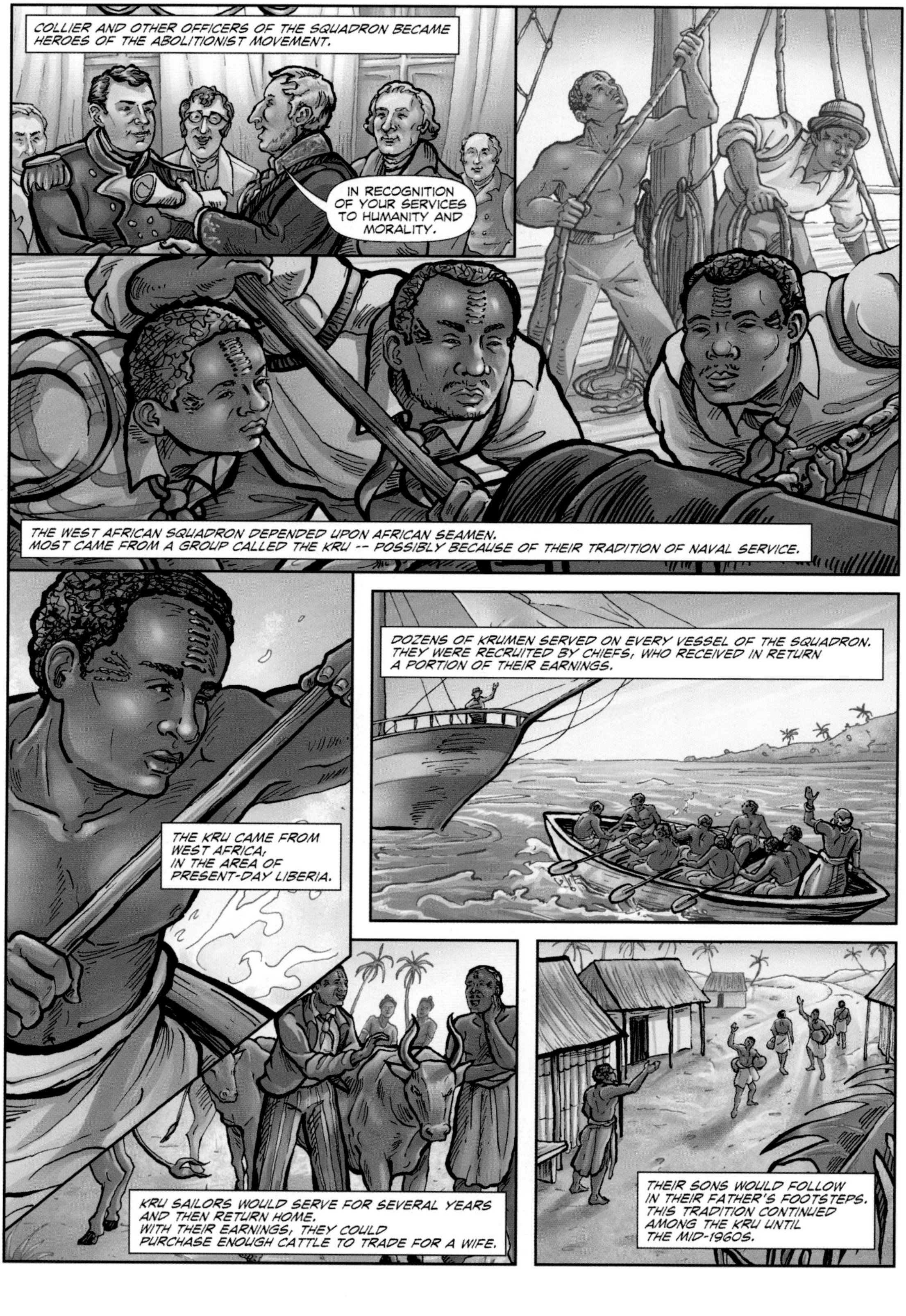
COLLIER AND OTHER OFFICERS OF THE SQUADRON BECAME HEROES OF THE ABOLITIONIST MOVEMENT.
IN RECOGNITION OF YOUR SERVICES TO HUMANITY AND MORALITY.
THE WEST AFRICAN SQUADRON DEPENDED UPON AFRICAN SEAMEN. MOST CAME FROM A GROUP CALLED THE KRU -- POSSIBLY BECAUSE OF THEIR TRADITION OF NAVAL SERVICE.
THE KRU CAME FROM WEST AFRICA, IN THE AREA OF PRESENT-DAY LIBERIA.
DOZENS OF KRUMEN SERVED ON EVERY VESSEL OF THE SQUADRON. THEY WERE RECRUITED BY CHIEFS, WHO RECEIVED IN RETURN A PORTION OF THEIR EARNINGS.
KRU SAILORS WOULD SERVE FOR SEVERAL YEARS AND THEN RETURN HOME. WITH THEIR EARNINGS, THEY COULD PURCHASE ENOUGH CATTLE TO TRADE FOR A WIFE.
THEIR SONS WOULD FOLLOW IN THEIR FATHER'S FOOTSTEPS. THIS TRADITION CONTINUED AMONG THE KRU UNTIL THE MID-1960S.

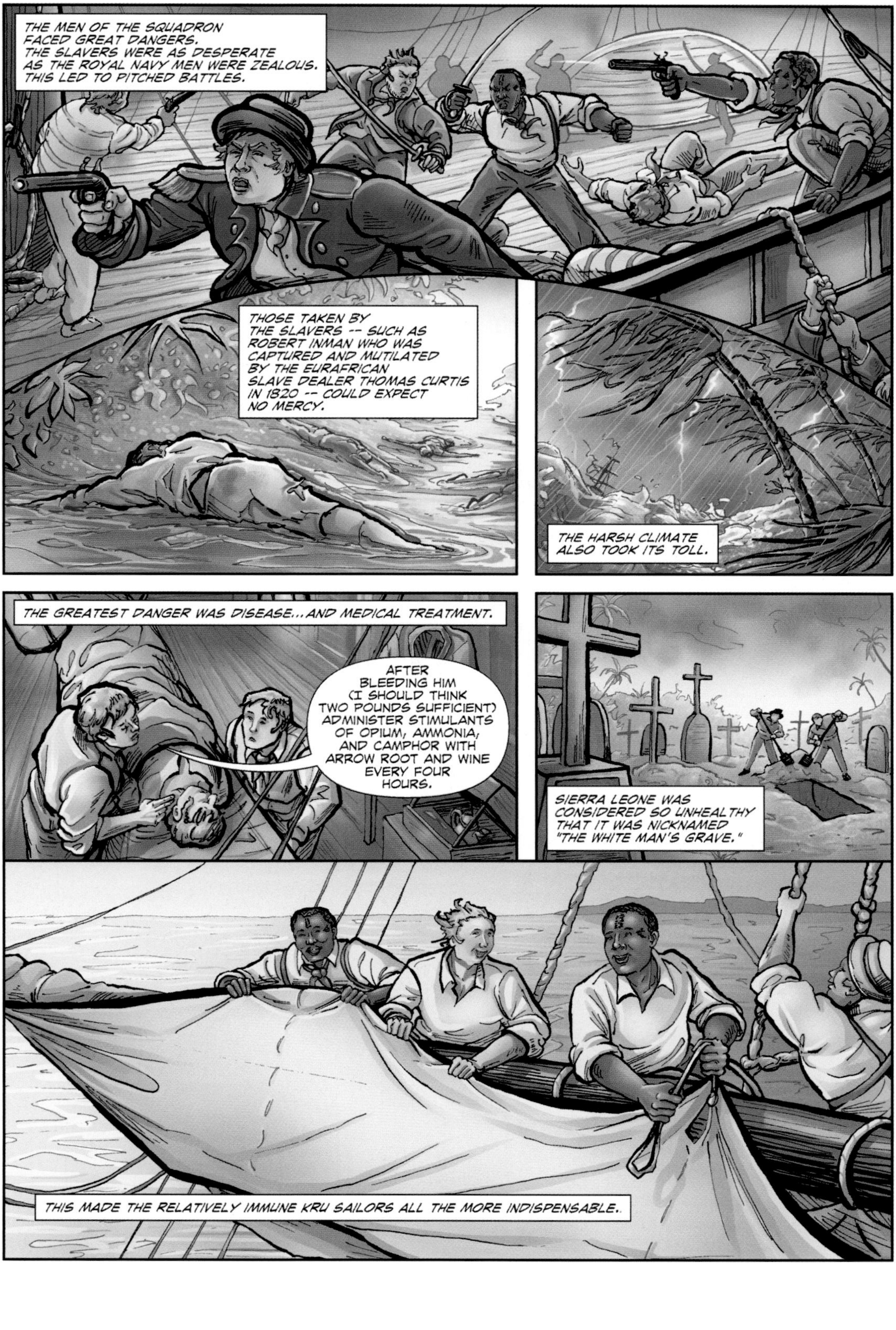
THE MEN OF THE SQUADRON FACED GREAT DANGERS. THE SLAVERS WERE AS DESPERATE AS THE ROYAL NAVY MEN WERE ZEALOUS. THIS LED TO PITCHED BATTLES.
THOSE TAKEN BY THE SLAVERS -- SUCH AS ROBERT INMAN WHO WAS CAPTURED AND MUTILATED BY THE EURAFRICAN SLAVE DEALER THOMAS CURTIS IN 1820 -- COULD EXPECT NO MERCY.
THE HARSH CLIMATE ALSO TOOK ITS TOLL.
THE GREATEST DANGER WAS DISEASE...AND MEDICAL TREATMENT.
AFTER BLEEDING HIM (I SHOULD THINK TWO POUNDS SUFFICIENT) ADMINISTER STIMULANTS OF OPIUM, AMMONIA, AND CAMPHOR WITH ARROW ROOT AND WINE EVERY FOUR HOURS.
SIERRA LEONE WAS CONSIDERED SO UNHEALTHY THAT IT WAS NICKNAMED "THE WHITE MAN'S GRAVE."
THIS MADE THE RELATIVELY IMMUNE KRU SAILORS ALL THE MORE INDISPENSABLE.

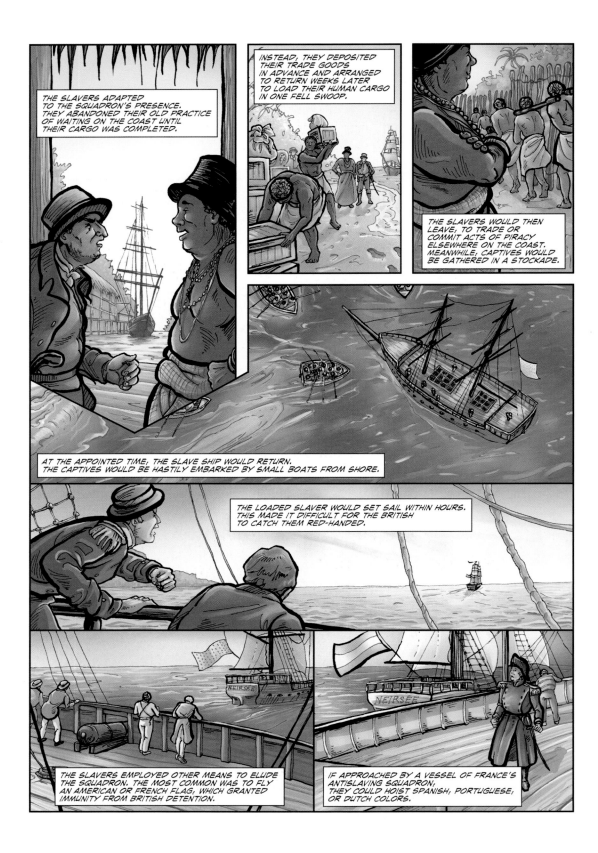

THE SLAVERS ADAPTED TO THE SQUADRON'S PRESENCE. THEY ABANDONED THEIR OLD PRACTICE OF WAITING ON THE COAST UNTIL THEIR CARGO WAS COMPLETED.

INSTEAD, THEY DEPOSITED THEIR TRADE GOODS IN ADVANCE AND ARRANGED TO RETURN WEEKS LATER TO LOAD THEIR HUMAN CARGO IN ONE FELL SWOOP.

THE SLAVERS WOULD THEN LEAVE, TO TRADE OR COMMIT ACTS OF PIRACY ELSEWHERE ON THE COAST. MEANWHILE, CAPTIVES WOULD BE GATHERED IN A STOCKADE.

AT THE APPOINTED TIME, THE SLAVE SHIP WOULD RETURN. THE CAPTIVES WOULD BE HASTILY EMBARKED BY SMALL BOATS FROM SHORE.

THE LOADED SLAVER WOULD SET SAIL WITHIN HOURS. THIS MADE IT DIFFICULT FOR THE BRITISH TO CATCH THEM RED-HANDED.

THE SLAVERS EMPLOYED OTHER MEANS TO ELUDE THE SQUADRON. THE MOST COMMON WAS TO FLY AN AMERICAN OR FRENCH FLAG, WHICH GRANTED IMMUNITY FROM BRITISH DETENTION.

IF APPROACHED BY A VESSEL OF FRANCE'S ANTISLAVING SQUADRON, THEY COULD HOIST SPANISH, PORTUGUESE, OR DUTCH COLORS.

62

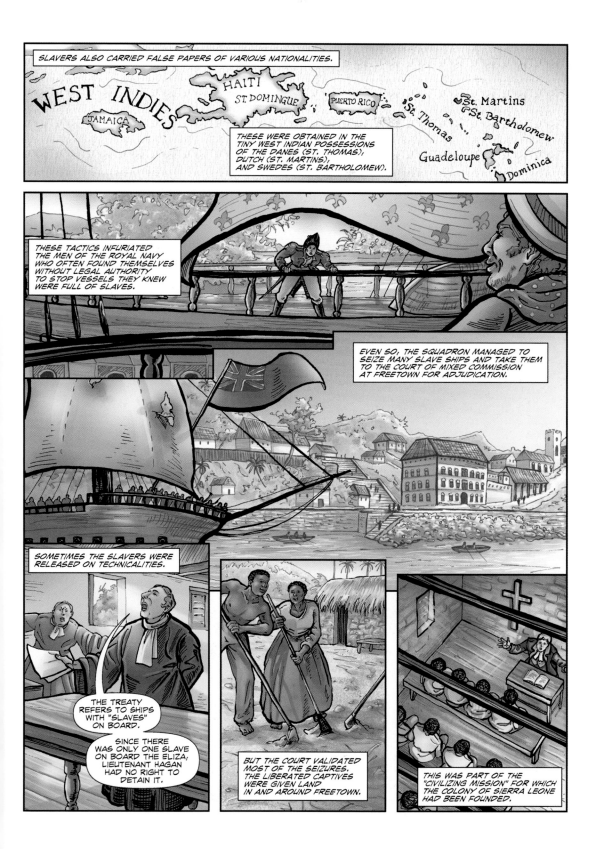

SLAVERS ALSO CARRIED FALSE PAPERS OF VARIOUS NATIONALITIES.

WEST INDIES

JAMAICA

HAITI
ST. DOMINGUE

PUERTO RICO

St. Thomas

St. Martins
St. Bartholomew

Guadeloupe

Dominica

THESE WERE OBTAINED IN THE TINY WEST INDIAN POSSESSIONS OF THE DANES (ST. THOMAS), DUTCH (ST. MARTINS), AND SWEDES (ST. BARTHOLOMEW).

THESE TACTICS INFURIATED THE MEN OF THE ROYAL NAVY WHO OFTEN FOUND THEMSELVES WITHOUT LEGAL AUTHORITY TO STOP VESSELS THEY KNEW WERE FULL OF SLAVES.

EVEN SO, THE SQUADRON MANAGED TO SEIZE MANY SLAVE SHIPS AND TAKE THEM TO THE COURT OF MIXED COMMISSION AT FREETOWN FOR ADJUDICATION.

SOMETIMES THE SLAVERS WERE RELEASED ON TECHNICALITIES.

THE TREATY REFERS TO SHIPS WITH "SLAVES" ON BOARD.

SINCE THERE WAS ONLY ONE SLAVE ON BOARD THE ELIZA, LIEUTENANT HAGAN HAD NO RIGHT TO DETAIN IT.

BUT THE COURT VALIDATED MOST OF THE SEIZURES. THE LIBERATED CAPTIVES WERE GIVEN LAND IN AND AROUND FREETOWN.

THIS WAS PART OF THE "CIVILIZING MISSION" FOR WHICH THE COLONY OF SIERRA LEONE HAD BEEN FOUNDED.

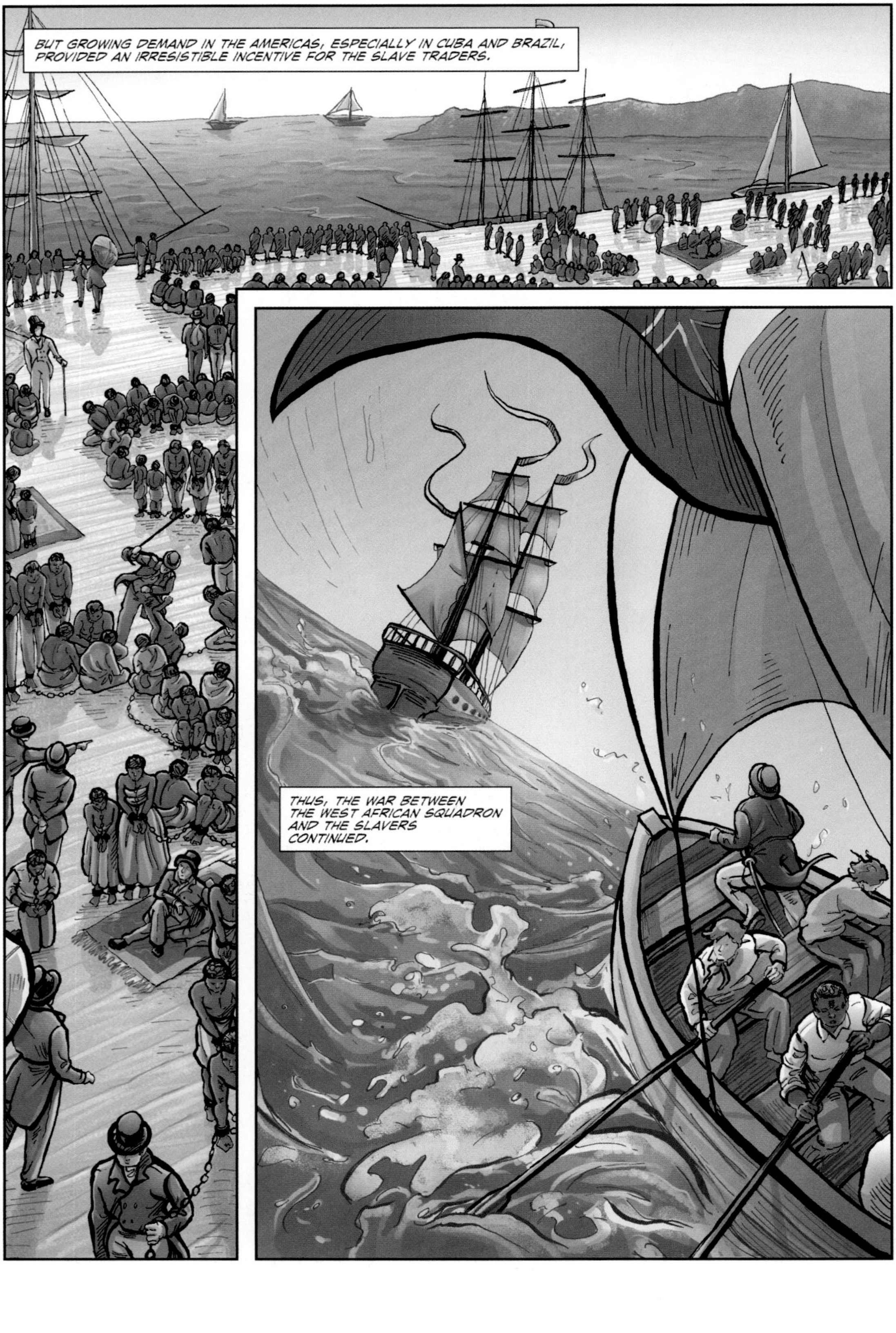
BUT GROWING DEMAND IN THE AMERICAS, ESPECIALLY IN CUBA AND BRAZIL, PROVIDED AN IRRESISTIBLE INCENTIVE FOR THE SLAVE TRADERS.
THUS, THE WAR BETWEEN THE WEST AFRICAN SQUADRON AND THE SLAVERS CONTINUED.

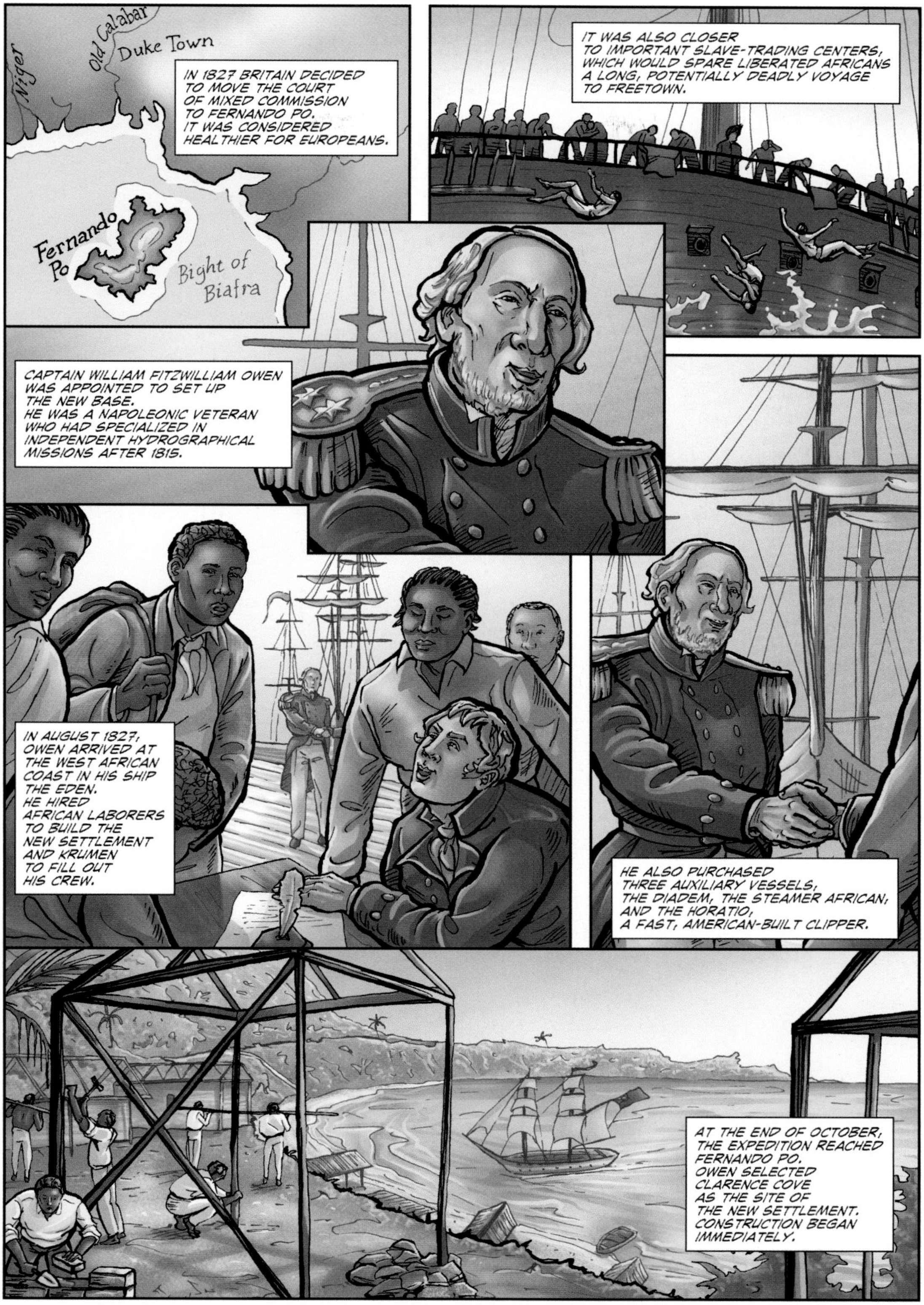
Old Calabar
Duke Town
Niger
Fernando Po
Bight of Biafra
IN 1827 BRITAIN DECIDED TO MOVE THE COURT OF MIXED COMMISSION TO FERNANDO PO. IT WAS CONSIDERED HEALTHIER FOR EUROPEANS.
IT WAS ALSO CLOSER TO IMPORTANT SLAVE-TRADING CENTERS, WHICH WOULD SPARE LIBERATED AFRICANS A LONG, POTENTIALLY DEADLY VOYAGE TO FREETOWN.
CAPTAIN WILLIAM FITZWILLIAM OWEN WAS APPOINTED TO SET UP THE NEW BASE. HE WAS A NAPOLEONIC VETERAN WHO HAD SPECIALIZED IN INDEPENDENT HYDROGRAPHICAL MISSIONS AFTER 1815.
IN AUGUST 1827, OWEN ARRIVED AT THE WEST AFRICAN COAST IN HIS SHIP THE EDEN. HE HIRED AFRICAN LABORERS TO BUILD THE NEW SETTLEMENT AND KRUMEN TO FILL OUT HIS CREW.
HE ALSO PURCHASED THREE AUXILIARY VESSELS, THE DIADEM, THE STEAMER AFRICAN, AND THE HORATIO, A FAST, AMERICAN-BUILT CLIPPER.
AT THE END OF OCTOBER, THE EXPEDITION REACHED FERNANDO PO. OWEN SELECTED CLARENCE COVE AS THE SITE OF THE NEW SETTLEMENT. CONSTRUCTION BEGAN IMMEDIATELY.

CHAPTER 2
THE *NEIRSÉE* INCIDENT

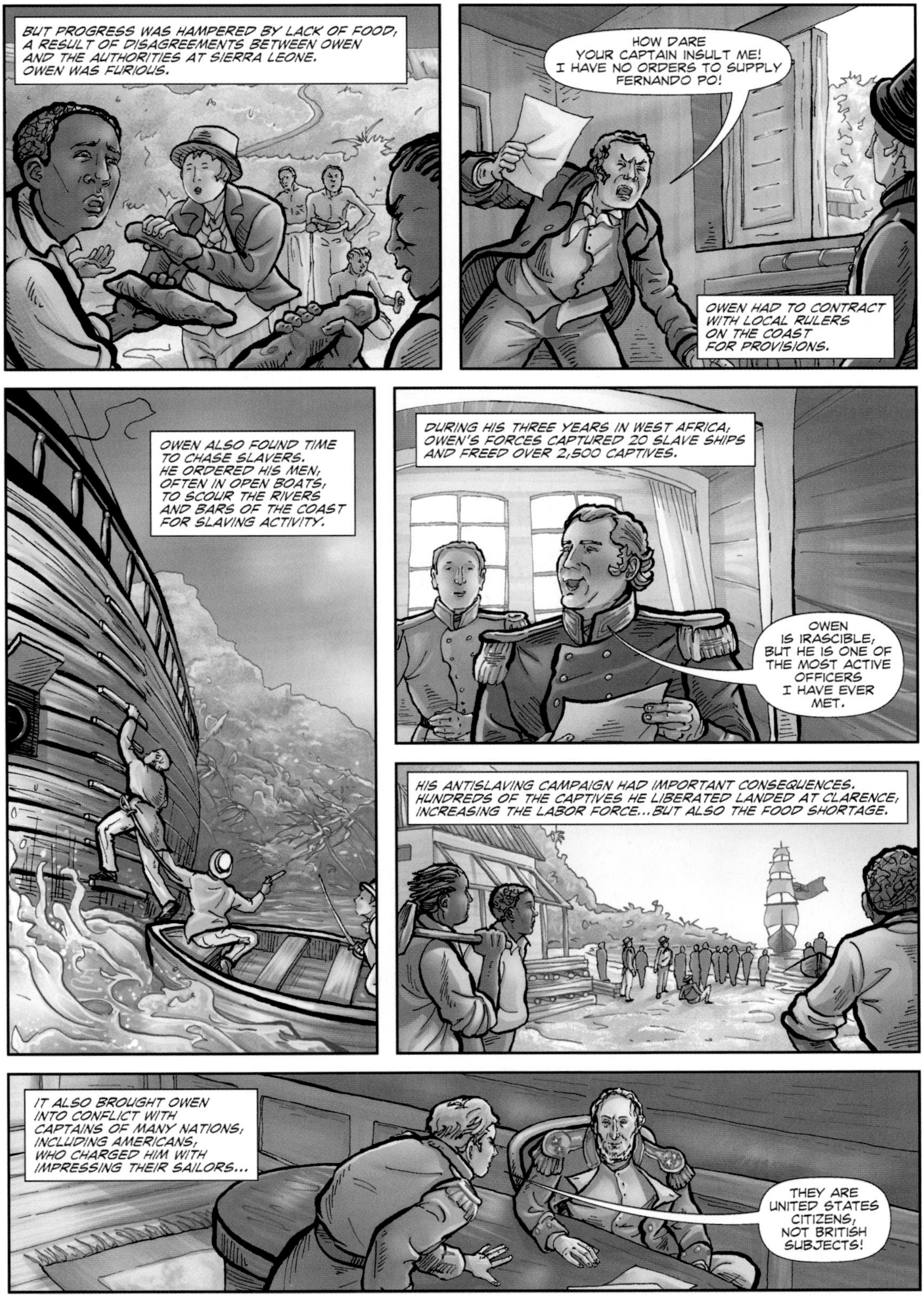
BUT PROGRESS WAS HAMPERED BY LACK OF FOOD, A RESULT OF DISAGREEMENTS BETWEEN OWEN AND THE AUTHORITIES AT SIERRA LEONE. OWEN WAS FURIOUS.
HOW DARE YOUR CAPTAIN INSULT ME! I HAVE NO ORDERS TO SUPPLY FERNANDO PO!
OWEN HAD TO CONTRACT WITH LOCAL RULERS ON THE COAST FOR PROVISIONS.
OWEN ALSO FOUND TIME TO CHASE SLAVERS. HE ORDERED HIS MEN, OFTEN IN OPEN BOATS, TO SCOUR THE RIVERS AND BARS OF THE COAST FOR SLAVING ACTIVITY.
DURING HIS THREE YEARS IN WEST AFRICA, OWEN'S FORCES CAPTURED 20 SLAVE SHIPS AND FREED OVER 2,500 CAPTIVES.
OWEN IS IRASCIBLE, BUT HE IS ONE OF THE MOST ACTIVE OFFICERS I HAVE EVER MET.
HIS ANTISLAVING CAMPAIGN HAD IMPORTANT CONSEQUENCES. HUNDREDS OF THE CAPTIVES HE LIBERATED LANDED AT CLARENCE, INCREASING THE LABOR FORCE...BUT ALSO THE FOOD SHORTAGE.
IT ALSO BROUGHT OWEN INTO CONFLICT WITH CAPTAINS OF MANY NATIONS, INCLUDING AMERICANS, WHO CHARGED HIM WITH IMPRESSING THEIR SAILORS...
THEY ARE UNITED STATES CITIZENS, NOT BRITISH SUBJECTS!

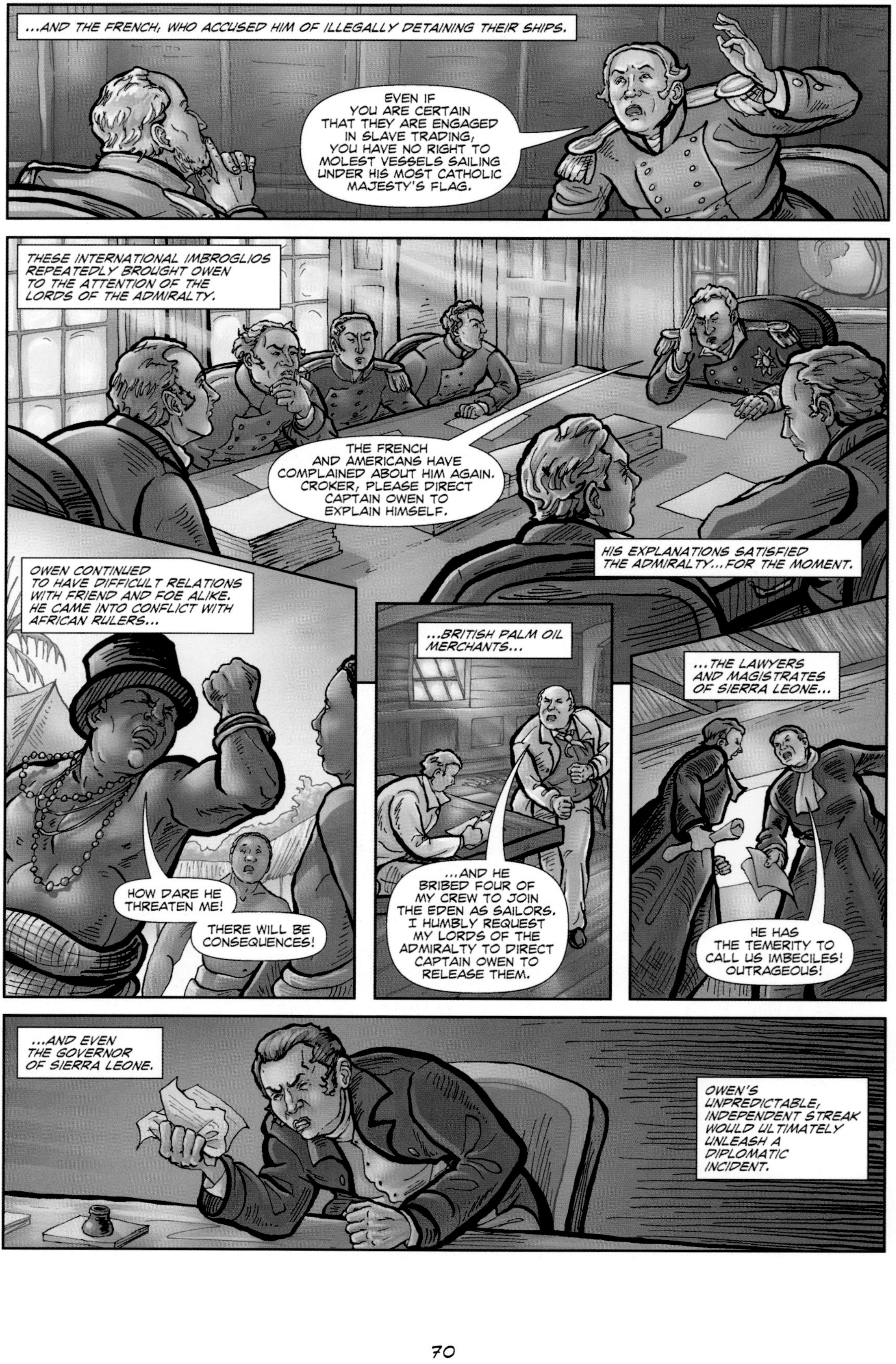
...AND THE FRENCH, WHO ACCUSED HIM OF ILLEGALLY DETAINING THEIR SHIPS.
EVEN IF YOU ARE CERTAIN THAT THEY ARE ENGAGED IN SLAVE TRADING, YOU HAVE NO RIGHT TO MOLEST VESSELS SAILING UNDER HIS MOST CATHOLIC MAJESTY'S FLAG.
THESE INTERNATIONAL IMBROGLIOS REPEATEDLY BROUGHT OWEN TO THE ATTENTION OF THE LORDS OF THE ADMIRALTY.
THE FRENCH AND AMERICANS HAVE COMPLAINED ABOUT HIM AGAIN. CROKER, PLEASE DIRECT CAPTAIN OWEN TO EXPLAIN HIMSELF.
HIS EXPLANATIONS SATISFIED THE ADMIRALTY...FOR THE MOMENT.
OWEN CONTINUED TO HAVE DIFFICULT RELATIONS WITH FRIEND AND FOE ALIKE. HE CAME INTO CONFLICT WITH AFRICAN RULERS...
HOW DARE HE THREATEN ME!
THERE WILL BE CONSEQUENCES!
...BRITISH PALM OIL MERCHANTS...
...AND HE BRIBED FOUR OF MY CREW TO JOIN THE EDEN AS SAILORS. I HUMBLY REQUEST MY LORDS OF THE ADMIRALTY TO DIRECT CAPTAIN OWEN TO RELEASE THEM.
...THE LAWYERS AND MAGISTRATES OF SIERRA LEONE...
HE HAS THE TEMERITY TO CALL US IMBECILES! OUTRAGEOUS!
...AND EVEN THE GOVERNOR OF SIERRA LEONE.
OWEN'S UNPREDICTABLE, INDEPENDENT STREAK WOULD ULTIMATELY UNLEASH A DIPLOMATIC INCIDENT.

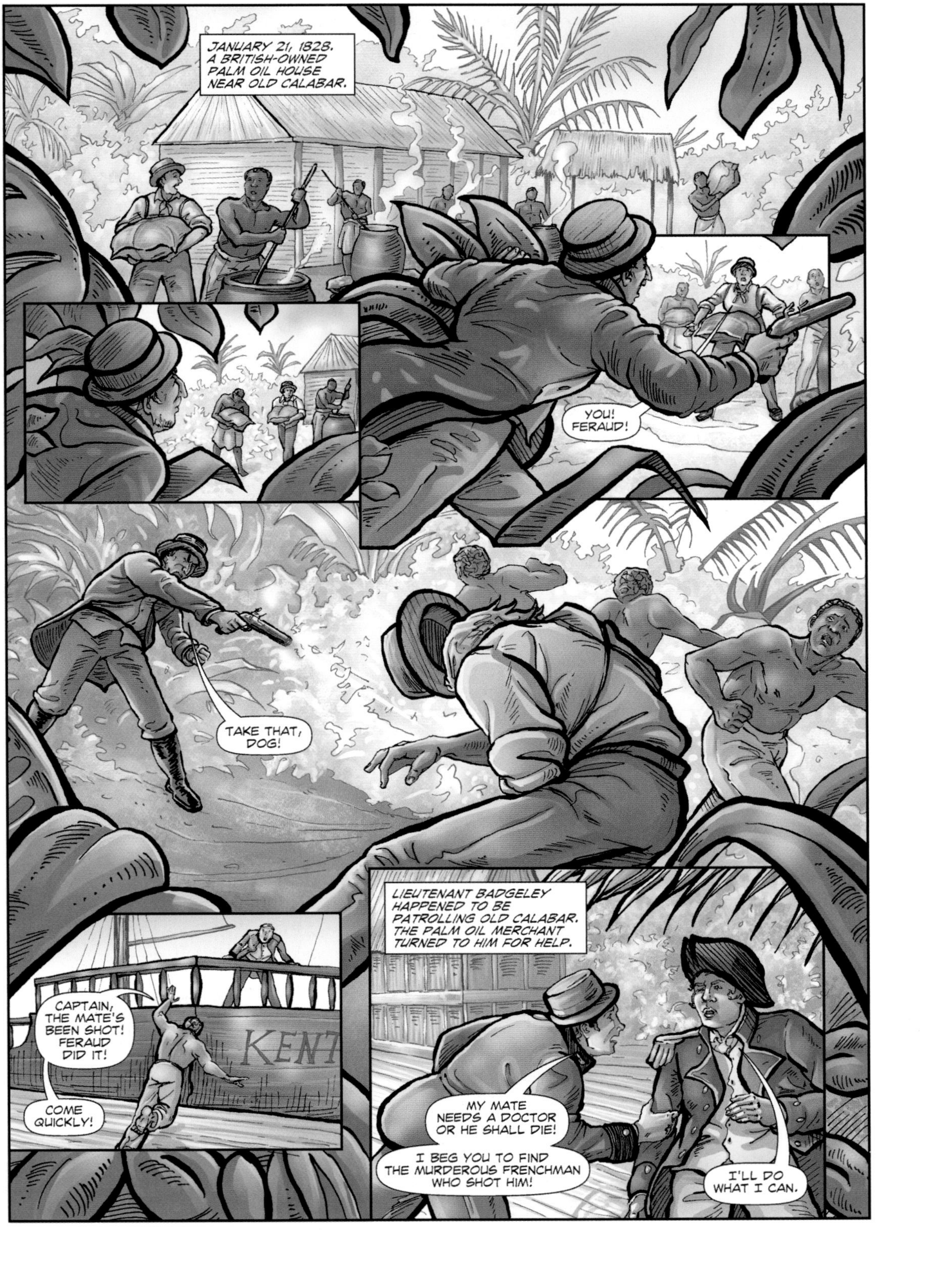
JANUARY 21, 1828. A BRITISH-OWNED PALM OIL HOUSE NEAR OLD CALABAR.
YOU! FERAUD!
TAKE THAT, DOG!
CAPTAIN, THE MATE'S BEEN SHOT! FERAUD DID IT!
COME QUICKLY!
KENT
LIEUTENANT BADGELEY HAPPENED TO BE PATROLLING OLD CALABAR. THE PALM OIL MERCHANT TURNED TO HIM FOR HELP.
MY MATE NEEDS A DOCTOR OR HE SHALL DIE!
I BEG YOU TO FIND THE MURDEROUS FRENCHMAN WHO SHOT HIM!
I'LL DO WHAT I CAN.

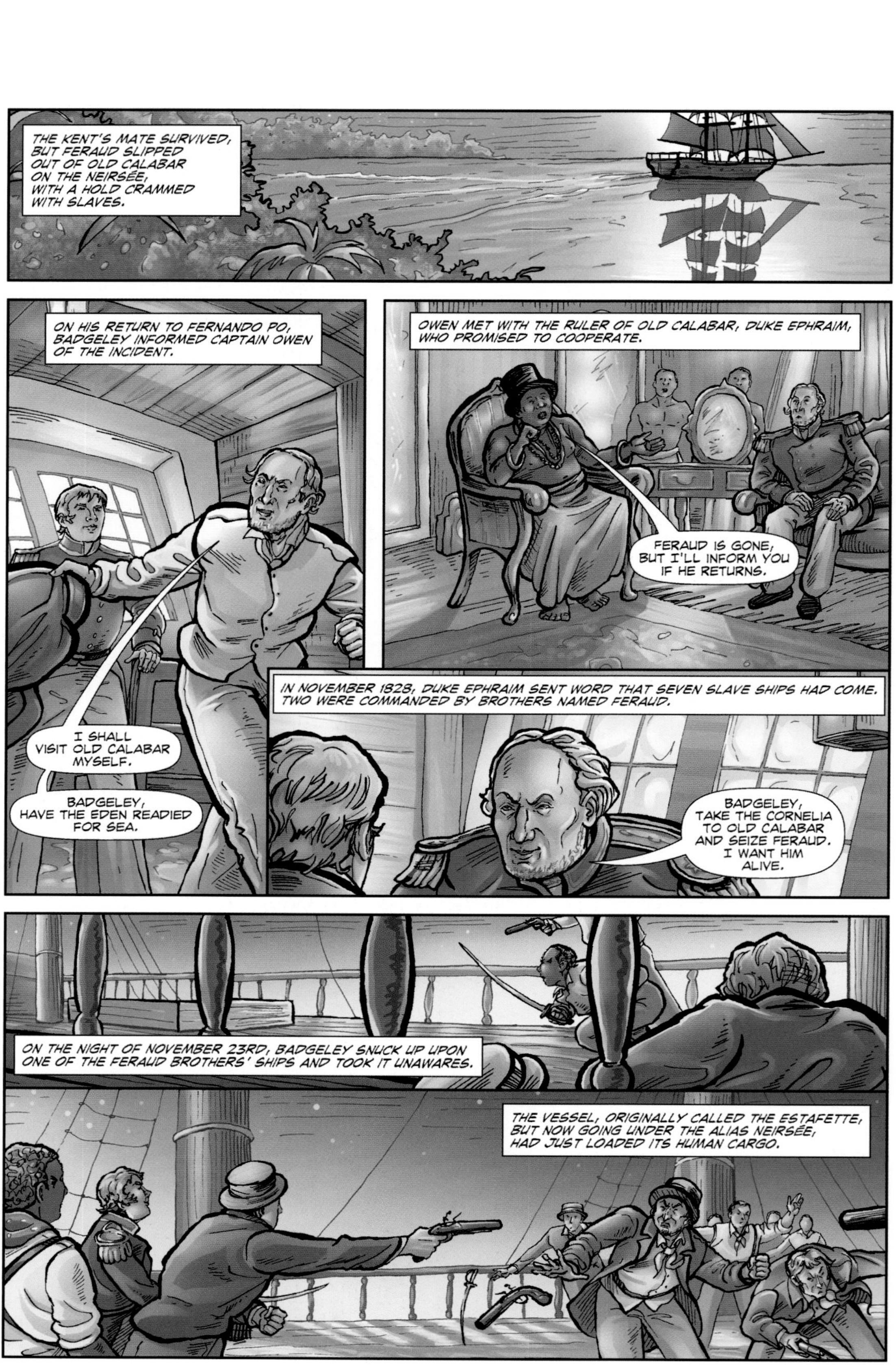
THE KENT'S MATE SURVIVED, BUT FERAUD SLIPPED OUT OF OLD CALABAR ON THE NEIRSÉE, WITH A HOLD CRAMMED WITH SLAVES.
ON HIS RETURN TO FERNANDO PO, BADGELEY INFORMED CAPTAIN OWEN OF THE INCIDENT.
I SHALL VISIT OLD CALABAR MYSELF.
BADGELEY, HAVE THE EDEN READIED FOR SEA.
OWEN MET WITH THE RULER OF OLD CALABAR, DUKE EPHRAIM, WHO PROMISED TO COOPERATE.
FERAUD IS GONE, BUT I'LL INFORM YOU IF HE RETURNS.
IN NOVEMBER 1828, DUKE EPHRAIM SENT WORD THAT SEVEN SLAVE SHIPS HAD COME. TWO WERE COMMANDED BY BROTHERS NAMED FERAUD.
BADGELEY, TAKE THE CORNELIA TO OLD CALABAR AND SEIZE FERAUD. I WANT HIM ALIVE.
ON THE NIGHT OF NOVEMBER 23RD, BADGELEY SNUCK UP UPON ONE OF THE FERAUD BROTHERS' SHIPS AND TOOK IT UNAWARES.
THE VESSEL, ORIGINALLY CALLED THE ESTAFETTE, BUT NOW GOING UNDER THE ALIAS NEIRSÉE, HAD JUST LOADED ITS HUMAN CARGO.

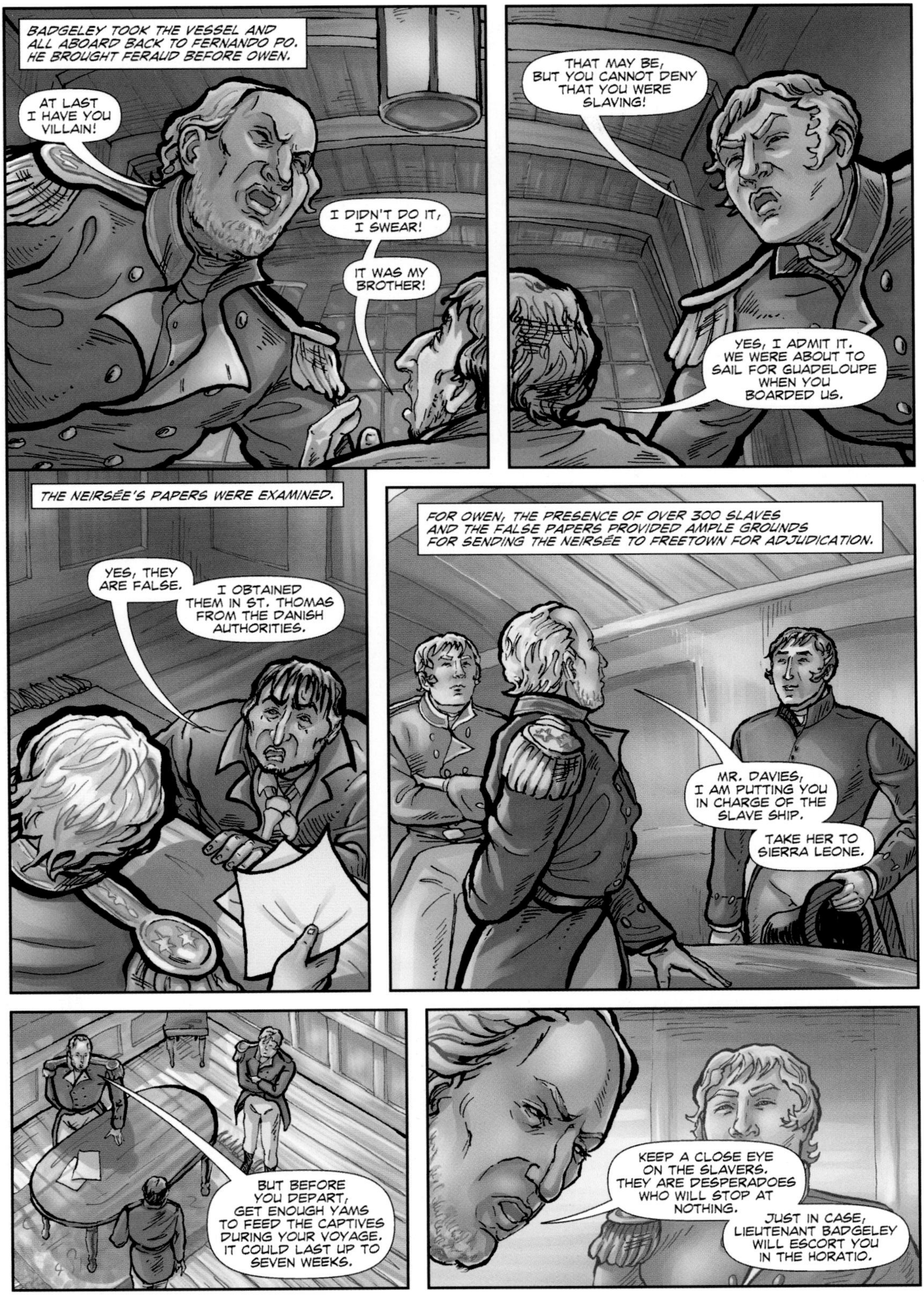
BADGELEY TOOK THE VESSEL AND ALL ABOARD BACK TO FERNANDO PO. HE BROUGHT FERAUD BEFORE OWEN.
AT LAST I HAVE YOU VILLAIN!
I DIDN'T DO IT, I SWEAR!
IT WAS MY BROTHER!
THAT MAY BE, BUT YOU CANNOT DENY THAT YOU WERE SLAVING!
YES, I ADMIT IT. WE WERE ABOUT TO SAIL FOR GUADELOUPE WHEN YOU BOARDED US.
THE NEIRSÉE'S PAPERS WERE EXAMINED.
YES, THEY ARE FALSE.
I OBTAINED THEM IN ST. THOMAS FROM THE DANISH AUTHORITIES.
FOR OWEN, THE PRESENCE OF OVER 300 SLAVES AND THE FALSE PAPERS PROVIDED AMPLE GROUNDS FOR SENDING THE NEIRSÉE TO FREETOWN FOR ADJUDICATION.
MR. DAVIES, I AM PUTTING YOU IN CHARGE OF THE SLAVE SHIP.
TAKE HER TO SIERRA LEONE.
BUT BEFORE YOU DEPART, GET ENOUGH YAMS TO FEED THE CAPTIVES DURING YOUR VOYAGE. IT COULD LAST UP TO SEVEN WEEKS.
KEEP A CLOSE EYE ON THE SLAVERS. THEY ARE DESPERADOES WHO WILL STOP AT NOTHING.
JUST IN CASE, LIEUTENANT BADGELEY WILL ESCORT YOU IN THE HORATIO.

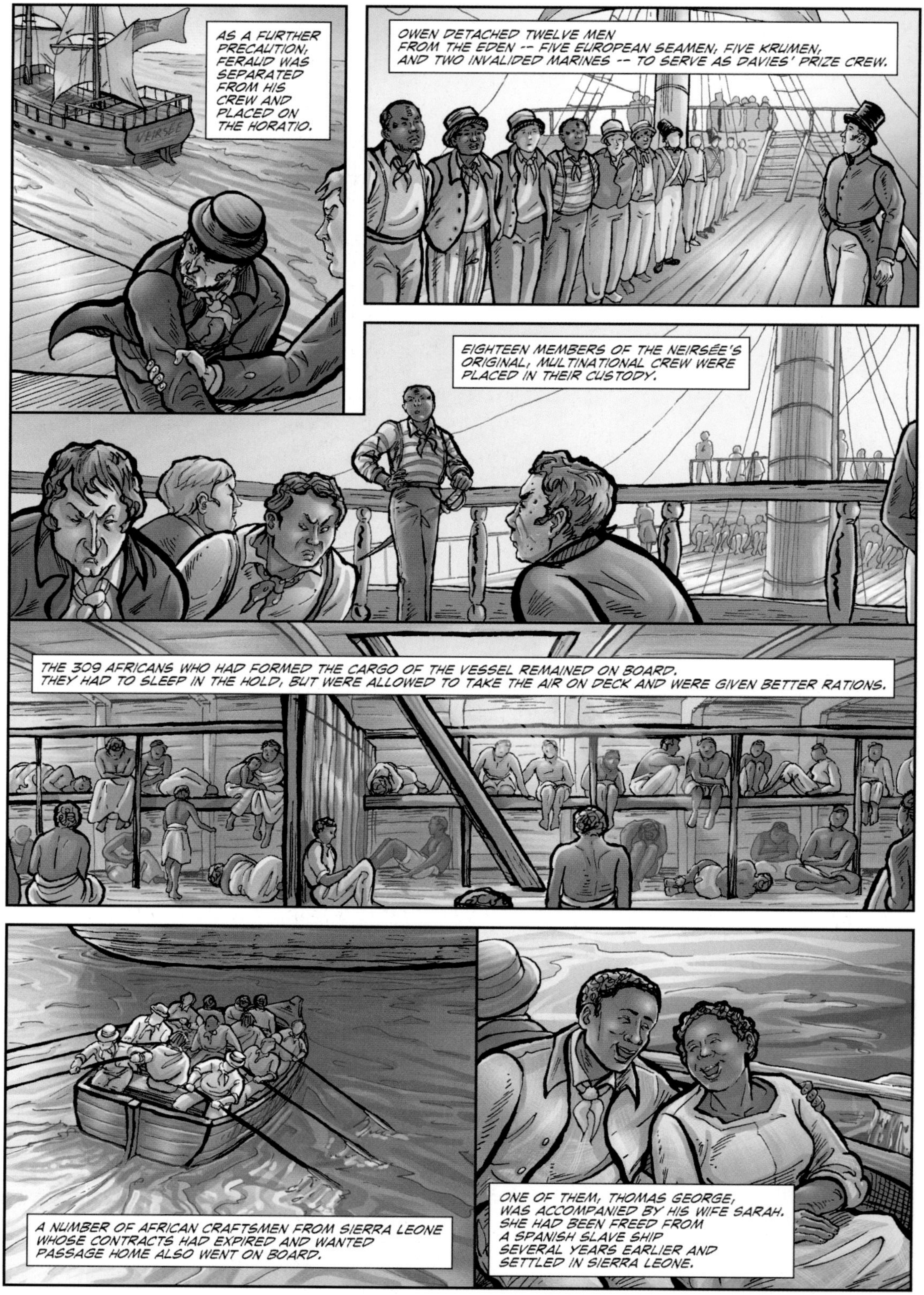
AS A FURTHER PRECAUTION, FERAUD WAS SEPARATED FROM HIS CREW AND PLACED ON THE HORATIO.
NEIRSÉE
OWEN DETACHED TWELVE MEN FROM THE EDEN -- FIVE EUROPEAN SEAMEN, FIVE KRUMEN, AND TWO INVALIDED MARINES -- TO SERVE AS DAVIES' PRIZE CREW.
EIGHTEEN MEMBERS OF THE NEIRSÉE'S ORIGINAL, MULTINATIONAL CREW WERE PLACED IN THEIR CUSTODY.
THE 309 AFRICANS WHO HAD FORMED THE CARGO OF THE VESSEL REMAINED ON BOARD. THEY HAD TO SLEEP IN THE HOLD, BUT WERE ALLOWED TO TAKE THE AIR ON DECK AND WERE GIVEN BETTER RATIONS.
A NUMBER OF AFRICAN CRAFTSMEN FROM SIERRA LEONE WHOSE CONTRACTS HAD EXPIRED AND WANTED PASSAGE HOME ALSO WENT ON BOARD.
ONE OF THEM, THOMAS GEORGE, WAS ACCOMPANIED BY HIS WIFE SARAH. SHE HAD BEEN FREED FROM A SPANISH SLAVE SHIP SEVERAL YEARS EARLIER AND SETTLED IN SIERRA LEONE.

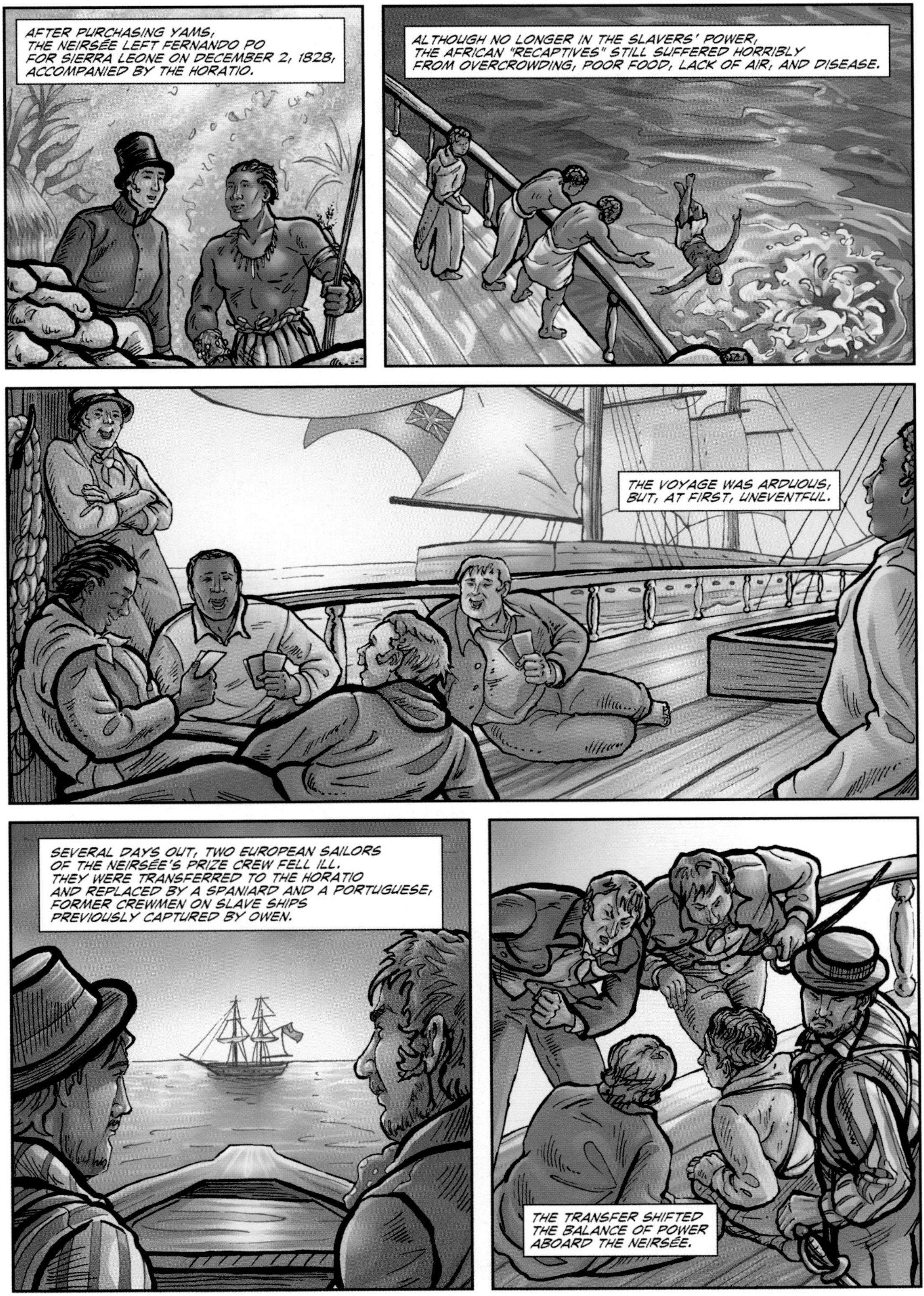
AFTER PURCHASING YAMS, THE NEIRSÉE LEFT FERNANDO PO FOR SIERRA LEONE ON DECEMBER 2, 1828, ACCOMPANIED BY THE HORATIO.
ALTHOUGH NO LONGER IN THE SLAVERS' POWER, THE AFRICAN "RECAPTIVES" STILL SUFFERED HORRIBLY FROM OVERCROWDING, POOR FOOD, LACK OF AIR, AND DISEASE.
THE VOYAGE WAS ARDUOUS, BUT, AT FIRST, UNEVENTFUL.
SEVERAL DAYS OUT, TWO EUROPEAN SAILORS OF THE NEIRSÉE'S PRIZE CREW FELL ILL. THEY WERE TRANSFERRED TO THE HORATIO AND REPLACED BY A SPANIARD AND A PORTUGUESE, FORMER CREWMEN ON SLAVE SHIPS PREVIOUSLY CAPTURED BY OWEN.
THE TRANSFER SHIFTED THE BALANCE OF POWER ABOARD THE NEIRSÉE.

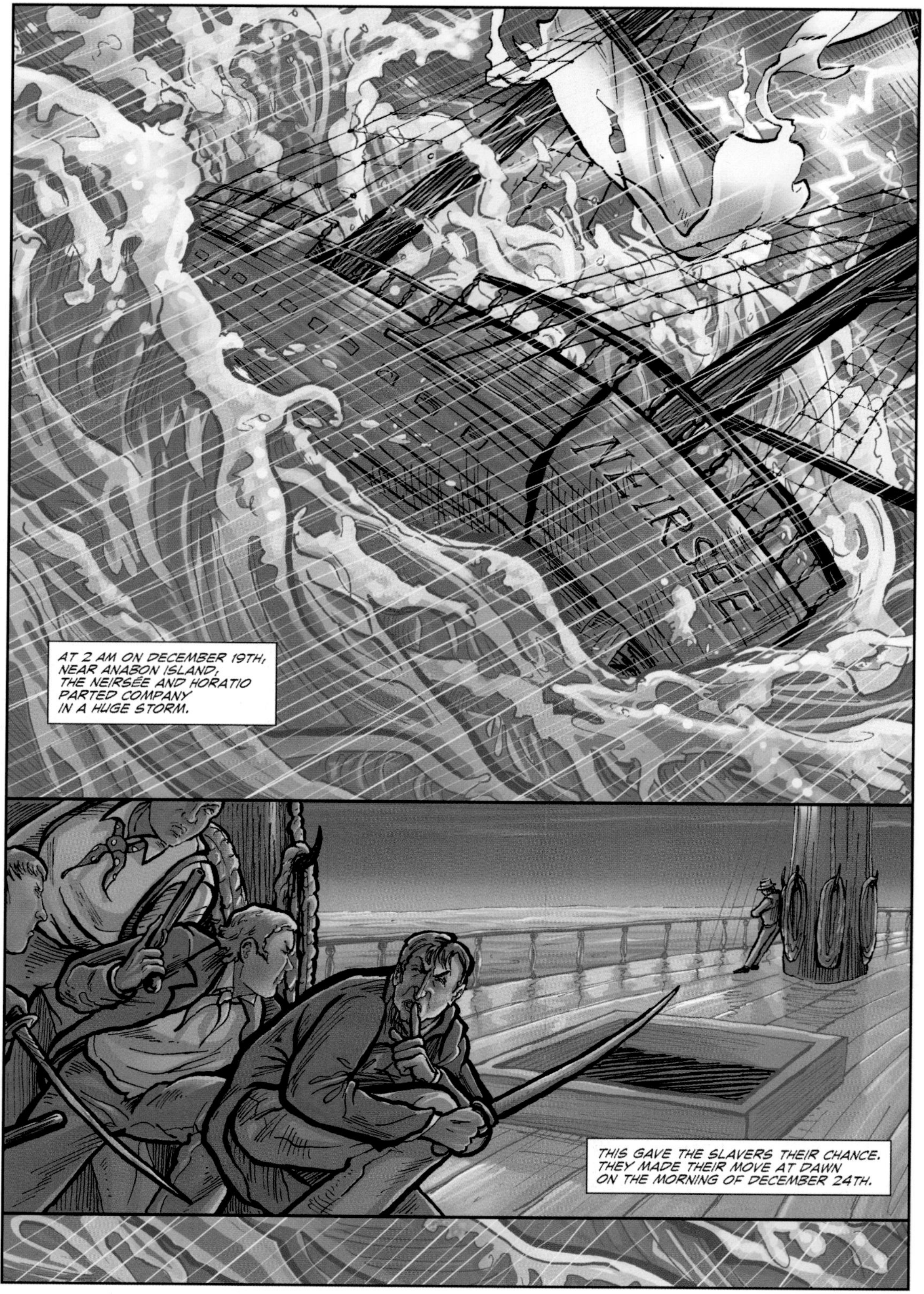
AT 2 AM ON DECEMBER 19TH, NEAR ANABON ISLAND, THE NEIRSÉE AND HORATIO PARTED COMPANY IN A HUGE STORM.
THIS GAVE THE SLAVERS THEIR CHANCE. THEY MADE THEIR MOVE AT DAWN ON THE MORNING OF DECEMBER 24TH.

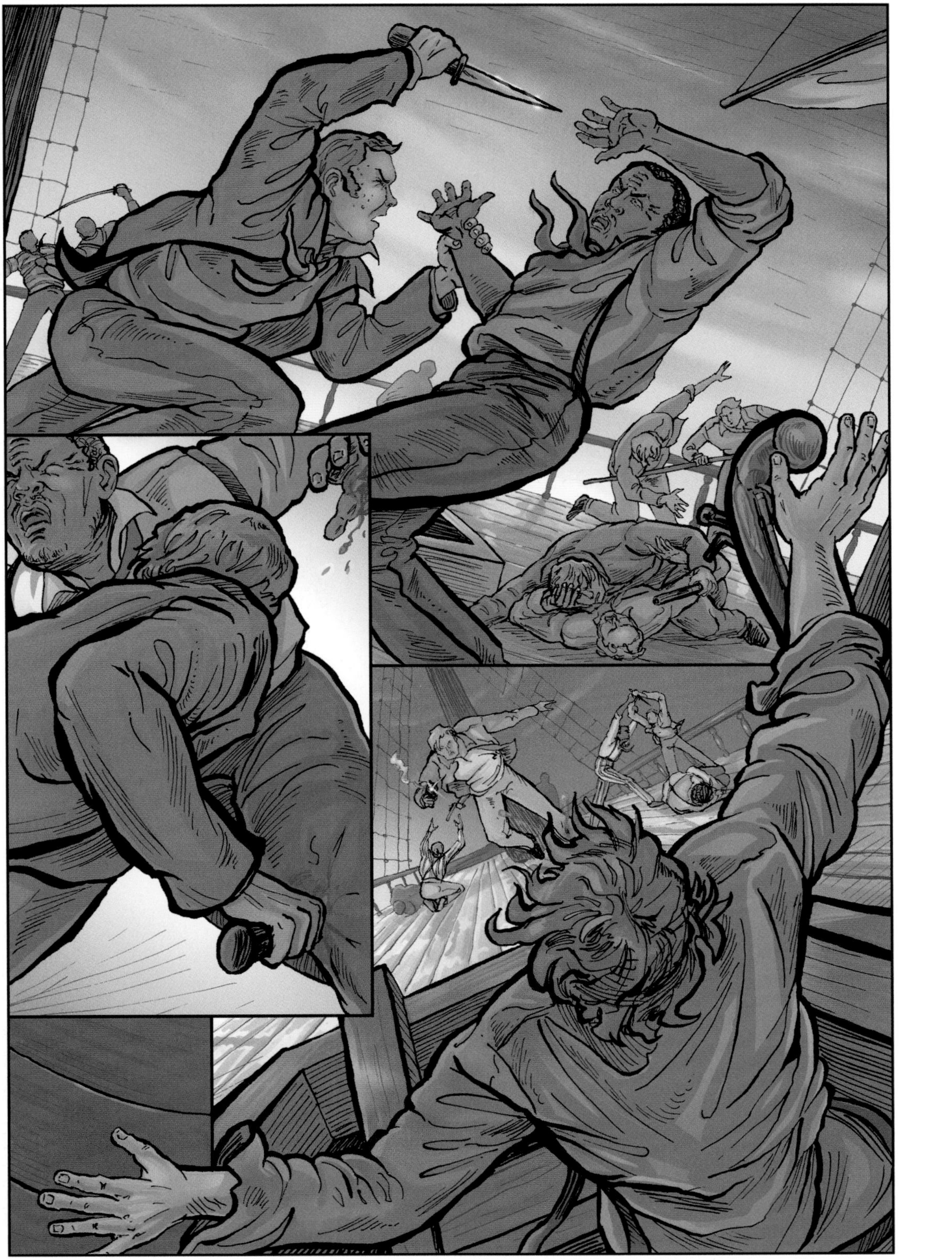

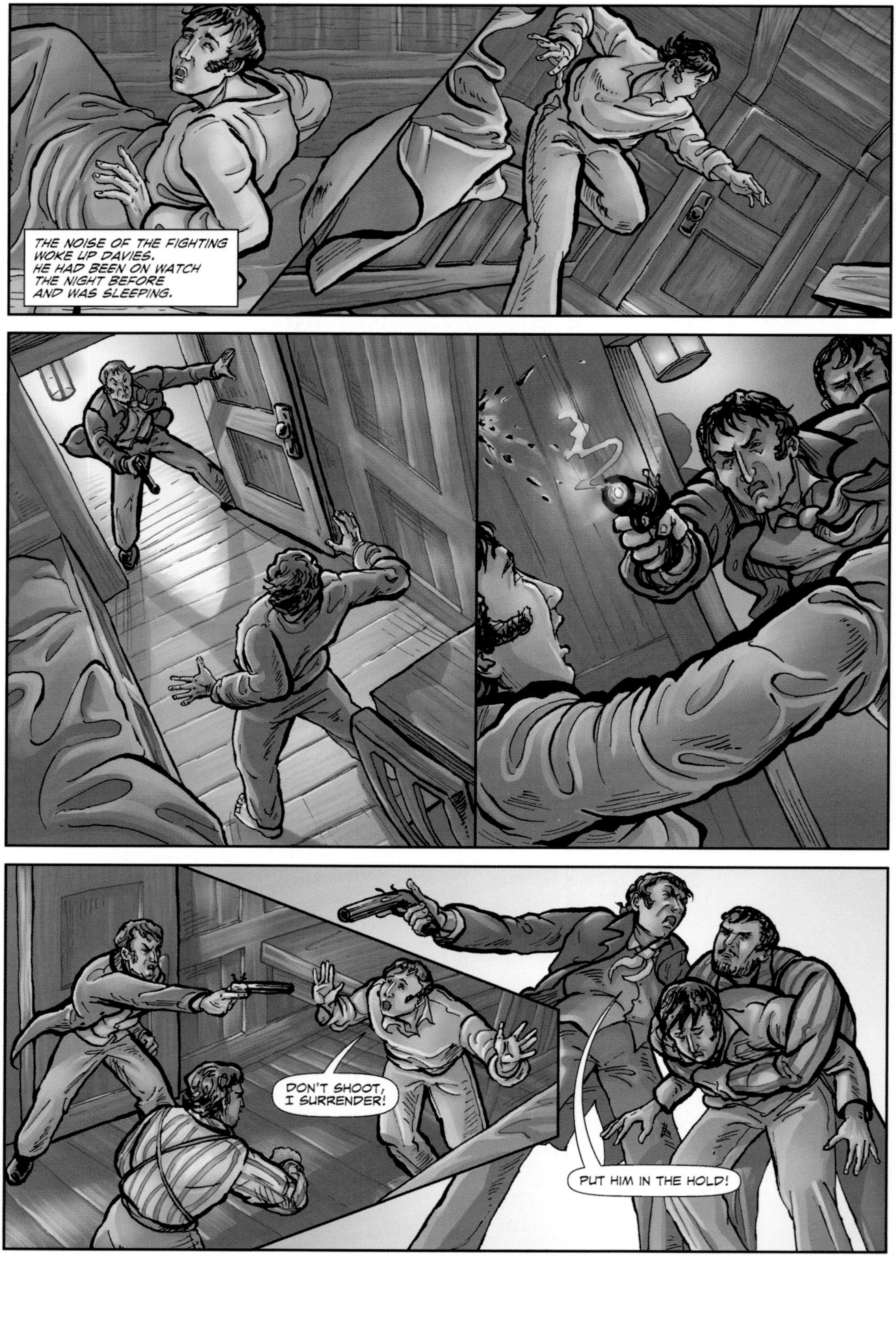
THE NOISE OF THE FIGHTING WOKE UP DAVIES. HE HAD BEEN ON WATCH THE NIGHT BEFORE AND WAS SLEEPING.
DON'T SHOOT, I SURRENDER!
PUT HIM IN THE HOLD!

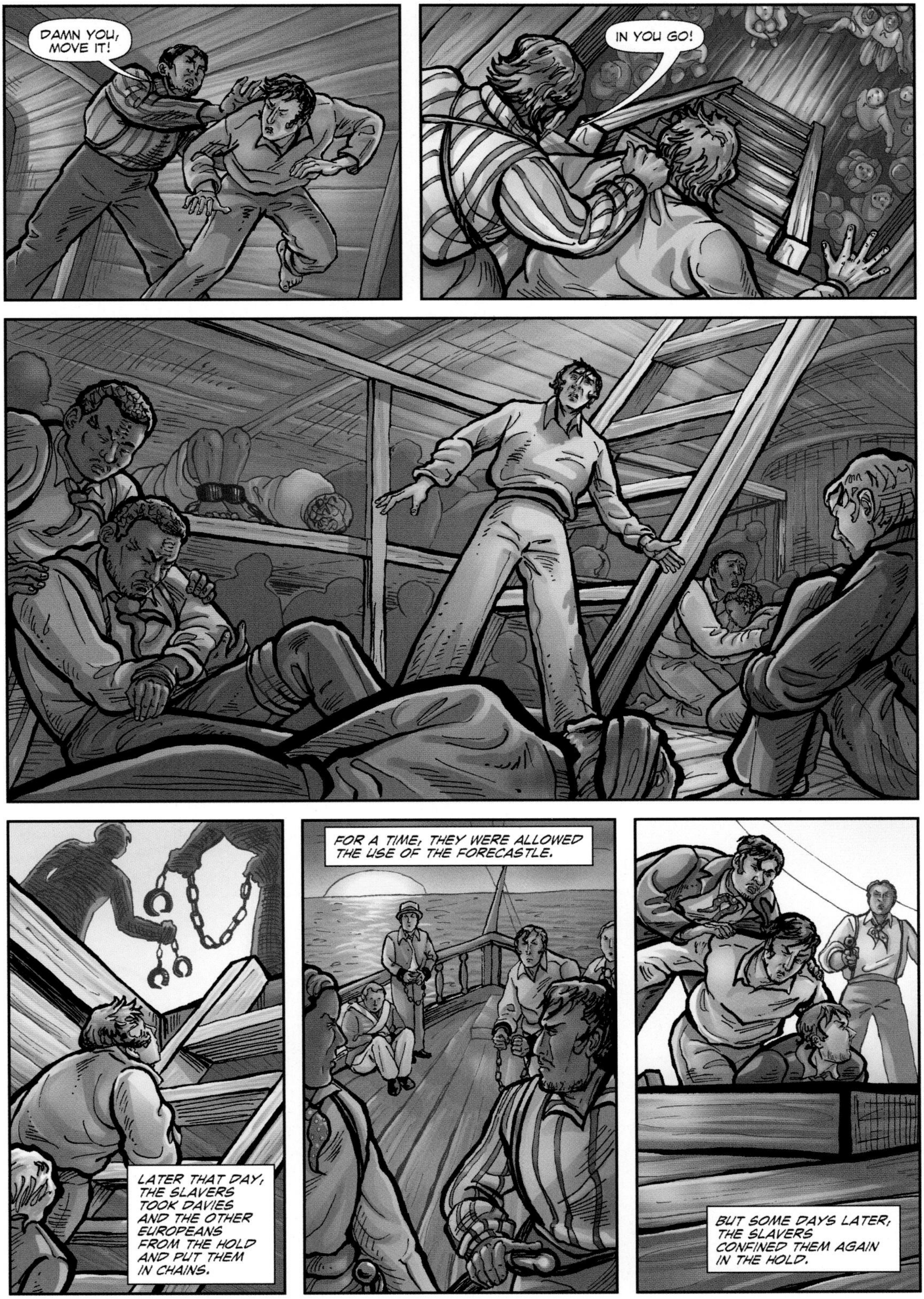
DAMN YOU, MOVE IT!
IN YOU GO!
LATER THAT DAY, THE SLAVERS TOOK DAVIES AND THE OTHER EUROPEANS FROM THE HOLD AND PUT THEM IN CHAINS.
FOR A TIME, THEY WERE ALLOWED THE USE OF THE FORECASTLE.
BUT SOME DAYS LATER, THE SLAVERS CONFINED THEM AGAIN IN THE HOLD.

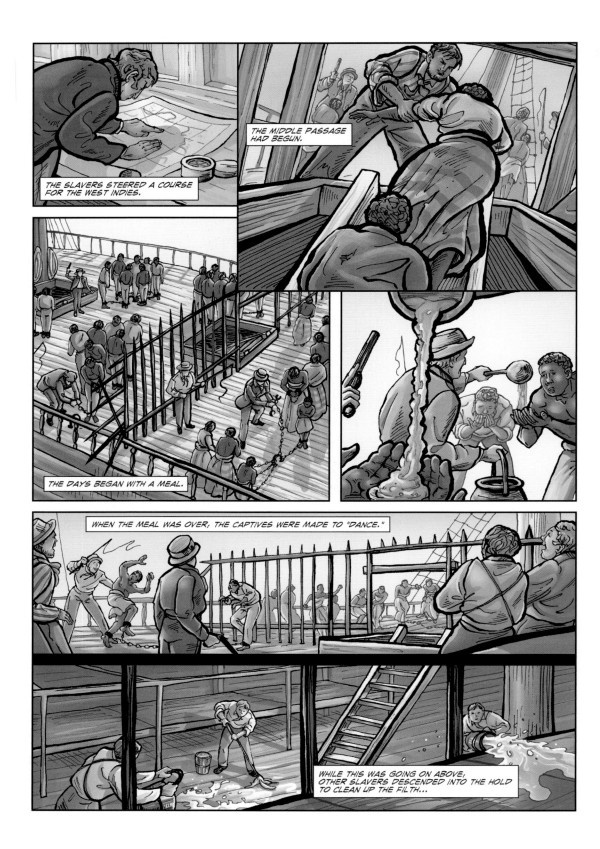

THE SLAVERS STEERED A COURSE FOR THE WEST INDIES.

THE MIDDLE PASSAGE HAD BEGUN.

THE DAYS BEGAN WITH A MEAL.

WHEN THE MEAL WAS OVER, THE CAPTIVES WERE MADE TO "DANCE."

WHILE THIS WAS GOING ON ABOVE, OTHER SLAVERS DESCENDED INTO THE HOLD TO CLEAN UP THE FILTH...

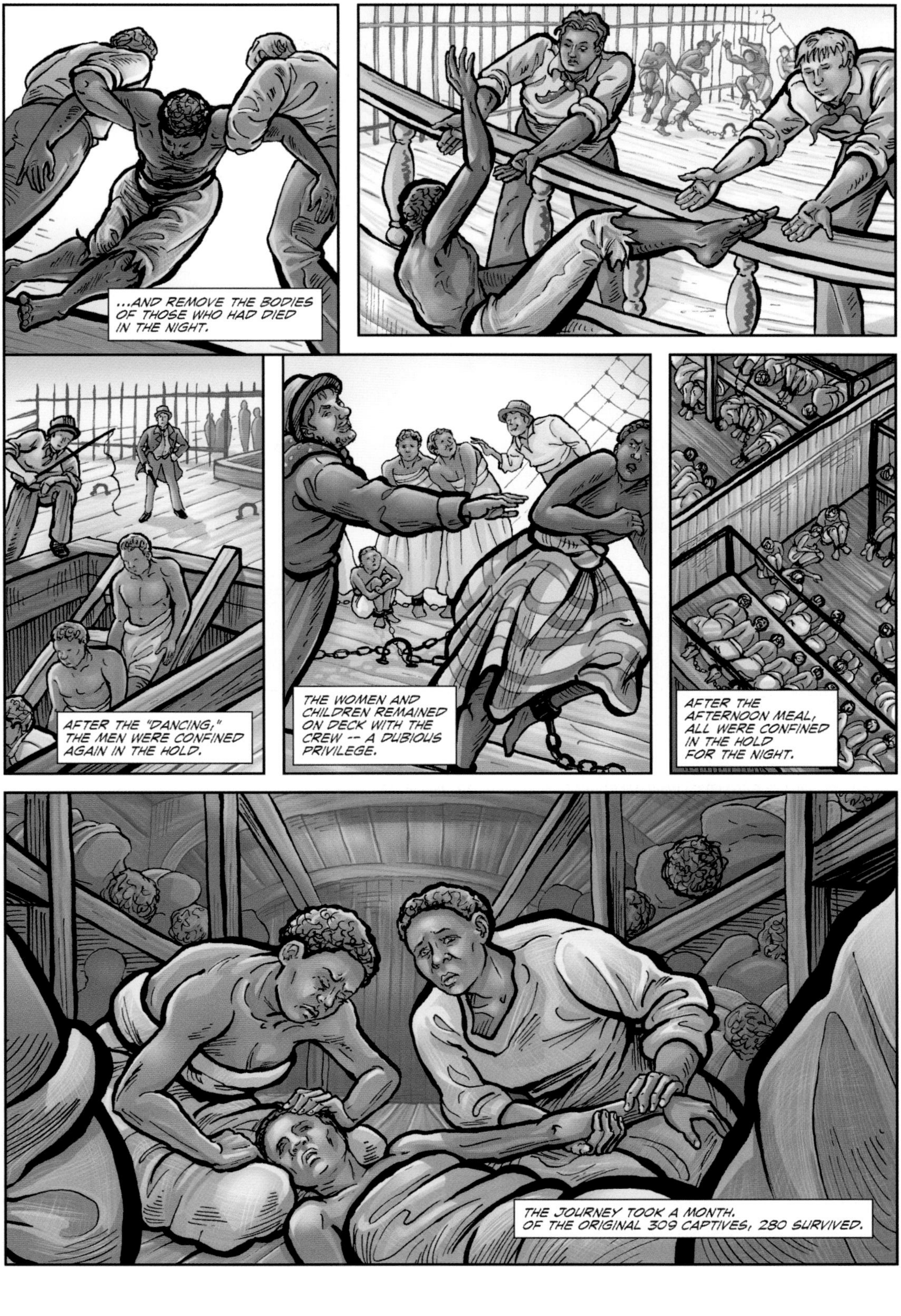
...AND REMOVE THE BODIES OF THOSE WHO HAD DIED IN THE NIGHT.
AFTER THE "DANCING," THE MEN WERE CONFINED AGAIN IN THE HOLD.
THE WOMEN AND CHILDREN REMAINED ON DECK WITH THE CREW -- A DUBIOUS PRIVILEGE.
AFTER THE AFTERNOON MEAL, ALL WERE CONFINED IN THE HOLD FOR THE NIGHT.
THE JOURNEY TOOK A MONTH. OF THE ORIGINAL 309 CAPTIVES, 280 SURVIVED.

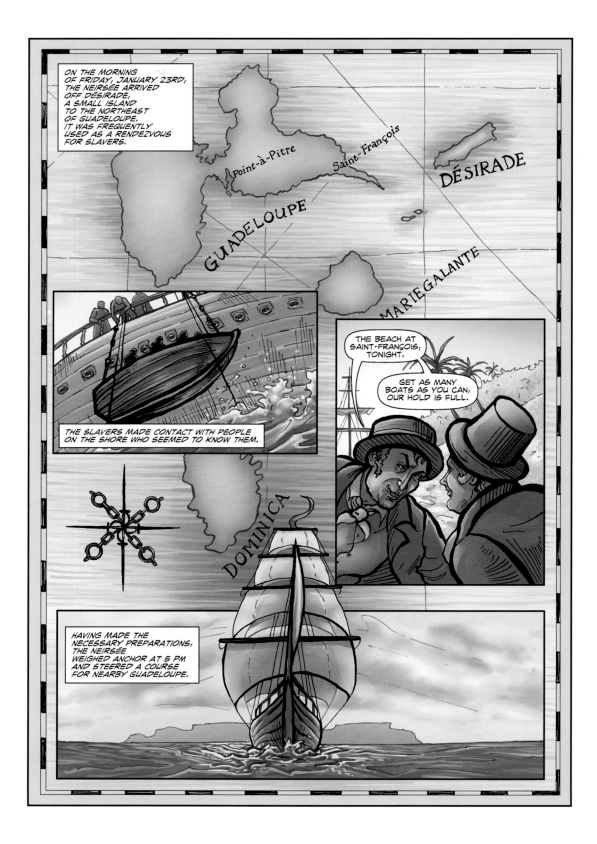

ON THE MORNING OF FRIDAY, JANUARY 23RD, THE NEIRSÉE ARRIVED OFF DÉSIRADE, A SMALL ISLAND TO THE NORTHEAST OF GUADELOUPE. IT WAS FREQUENTLY USED AS A RENDEZVOUS FOR SLAVERS.

Point-à-Pitre

Saint-François

DÉSIRADE

GUADELOUPE

MARIEGALANTE

THE SLAVERS MADE CONTACT WITH PEOPLE ON THE SHORE WHO SEEMED TO KNOW THEM.

THE BEACH AT SAINT-FRANÇOIS, TONIGHT.

GET AS MANY BOATS AS YOU CAN, OUR HOLD IS FULL.

DOMINICA

HAVING MADE THE NECESSARY PREPARATIONS, THE NEIRSÉE WEIGHED ANCHOR AT 5 PM AND STEERED A COURSE FOR NEARBY GUADELOUPE.

CHAPTER 3
SOLD INTO SLAVERY

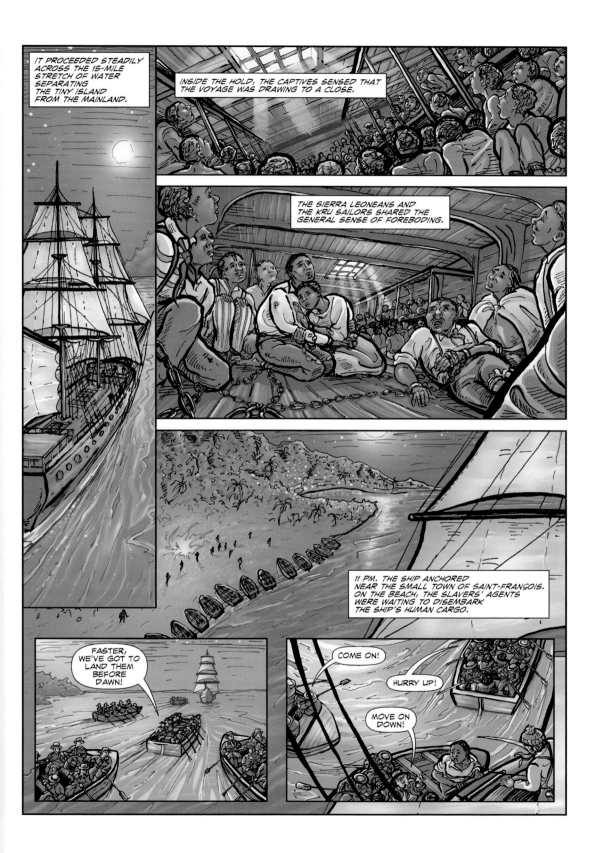

IT PROCEEDED STEADILY ACROSS THE 15-MILE STRETCH OF WATER SEPARATING THE TINY ISLAND FROM THE MAINLAND.

INSIDE THE HOLD, THE CAPTIVES SENSED THAT THE VOYAGE WAS DRAWING TO A CLOSE.

THE SIERRA LEONEANS AND THE KRU SAILORS SHARED THE GENERAL SENSE OF FOREBODING.

11 PM. THE SHIP ANCHORED NEAR THE SMALL TOWN OF SAINT-FRANÇOIS. ON THE BEACH, THE SLAVERS' AGENTS WERE WAITING TO DISEMBARK THE SHIP'S HUMAN CARGO.

FASTER, WE'VE GOT TO LAND THEM BEFORE DAWN!

COME ON!

HURRY UP!

MOVE ON DOWN!

BY 7 AM THE DISEMBARKATION WAS COMPLETED, AND THE CAPTIVES WERE MARCHED INLAND.

SEVERAL HOURS LATER, THEY ARRIVED AT THEIR DESTINATION -- A SUGAR PLANTATION THREE MILES FROM THE COAST.

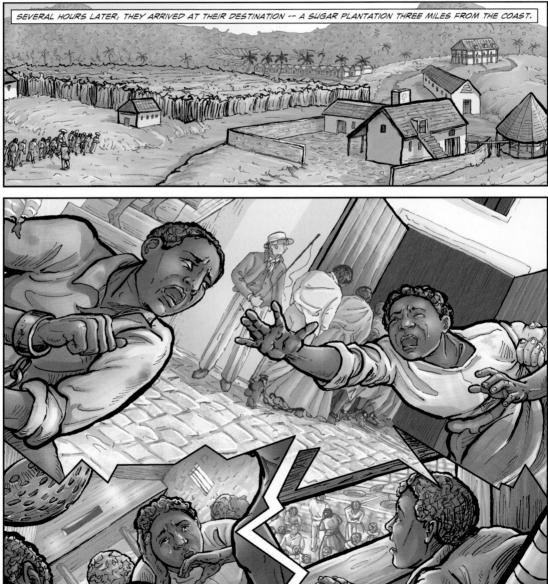

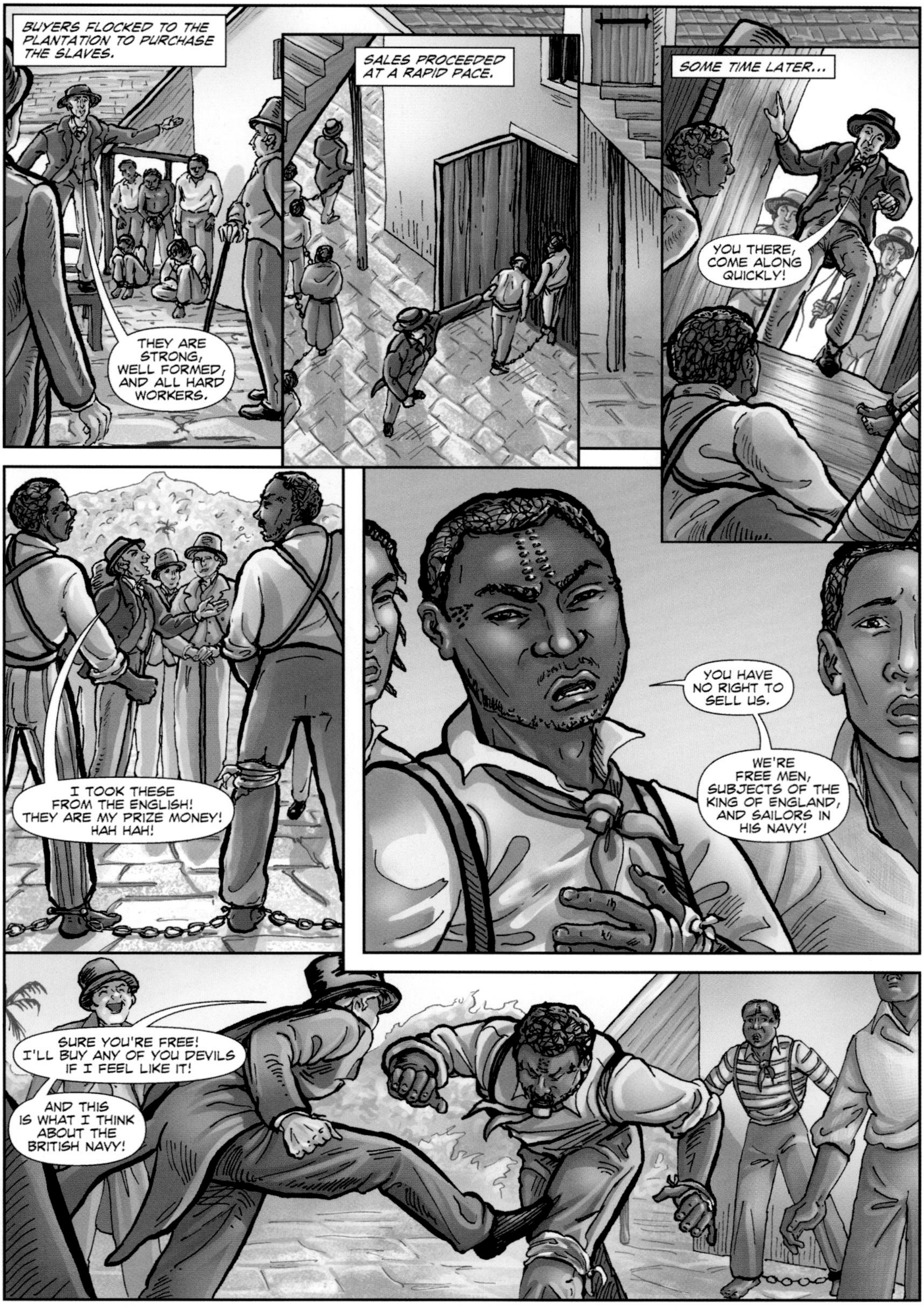
BUYERS FLOCKED TO THE PLANTATION TO PURCHASE THE SLAVES.
THEY ARE STRONG, WELL FORMED, AND ALL HARD WORKERS.
SALES PROCEEDED AT A RAPID PACE.
SOME TIME LATER...
YOU THERE, COME ALONG QUICKLY!
I TOOK THESE FROM THE ENGLISH! THEY ARE MY PRIZE MONEY! HAH HAH!
YOU HAVE NO RIGHT TO SELL US.
WE'RE FREE MEN, SUBJECTS OF THE KING OF ENGLAND, AND SAILORS IN HIS NAVY!
SURE YOU'RE FREE! I'LL BUY ANY OF YOU DEVILS IF I FEEL LIKE IT!
AND THIS IS WHAT I THINK ABOUT THE BRITISH NAVY!

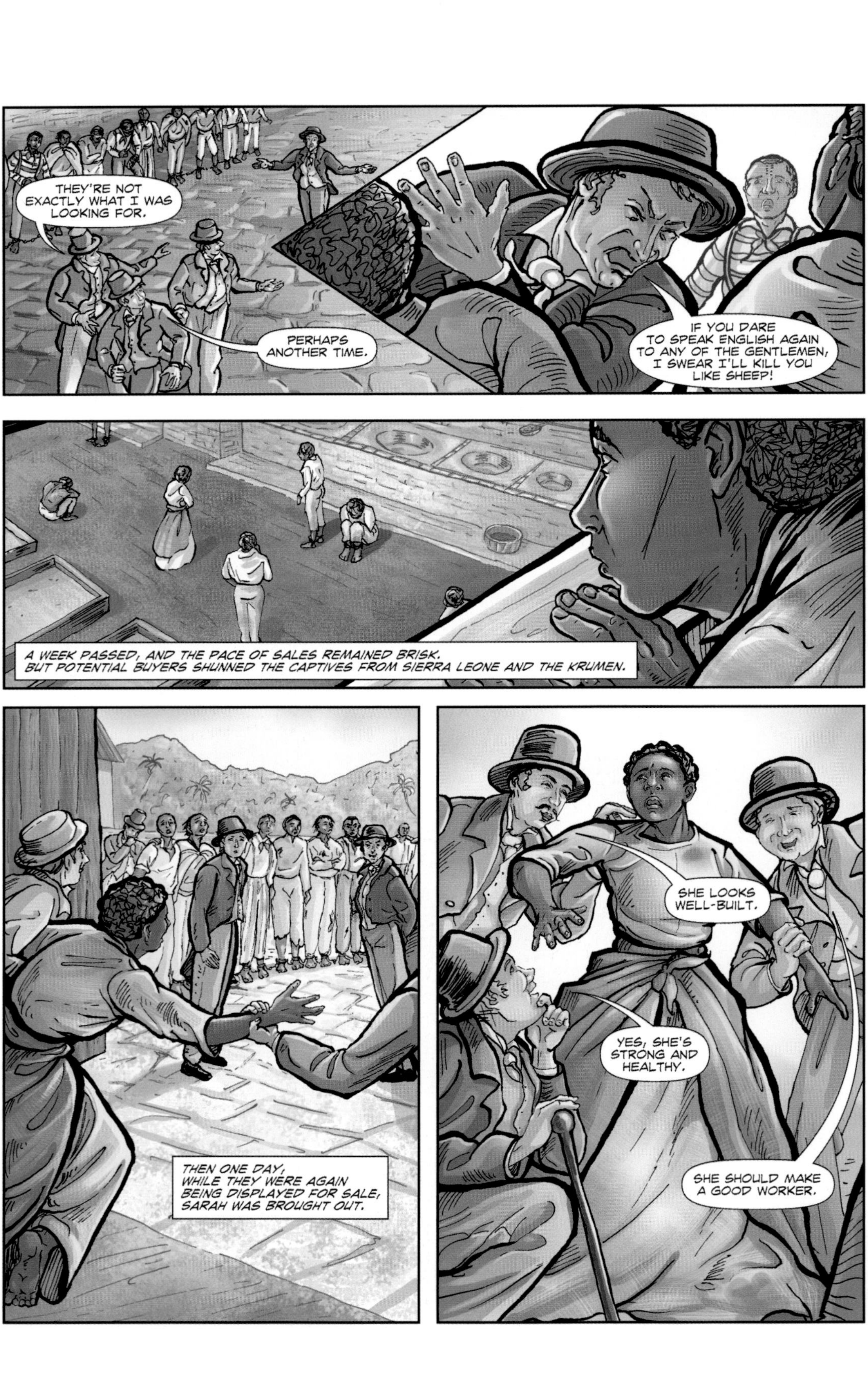

THEY'RE NOT EXACTLY WHAT I WAS LOOKING FOR.
PERHAPS ANOTHER TIME.
IF YOU DARE TO SPEAK ENGLISH AGAIN TO ANY OF THE GENTLEMEN, I SWEAR I'LL KILL YOU LIKE SHEEP!
A WEEK PASSED, AND THE PACE OF SALES REMAINED BRISK. BUT POTENTIAL BUYERS SHUNNED THE CAPTIVES FROM SIERRA LEONE AND THE KRUMEN.
THEN ONE DAY, WHILE THEY WERE AGAIN BEING DISPLAYED FOR SALE, SARAH WAS BROUGHT OUT.
SHE LOOKS WELL-BUILT.
YES, SHE'S STRONG AND HEALTHY.
SHE SHOULD MAKE A GOOD WORKER.

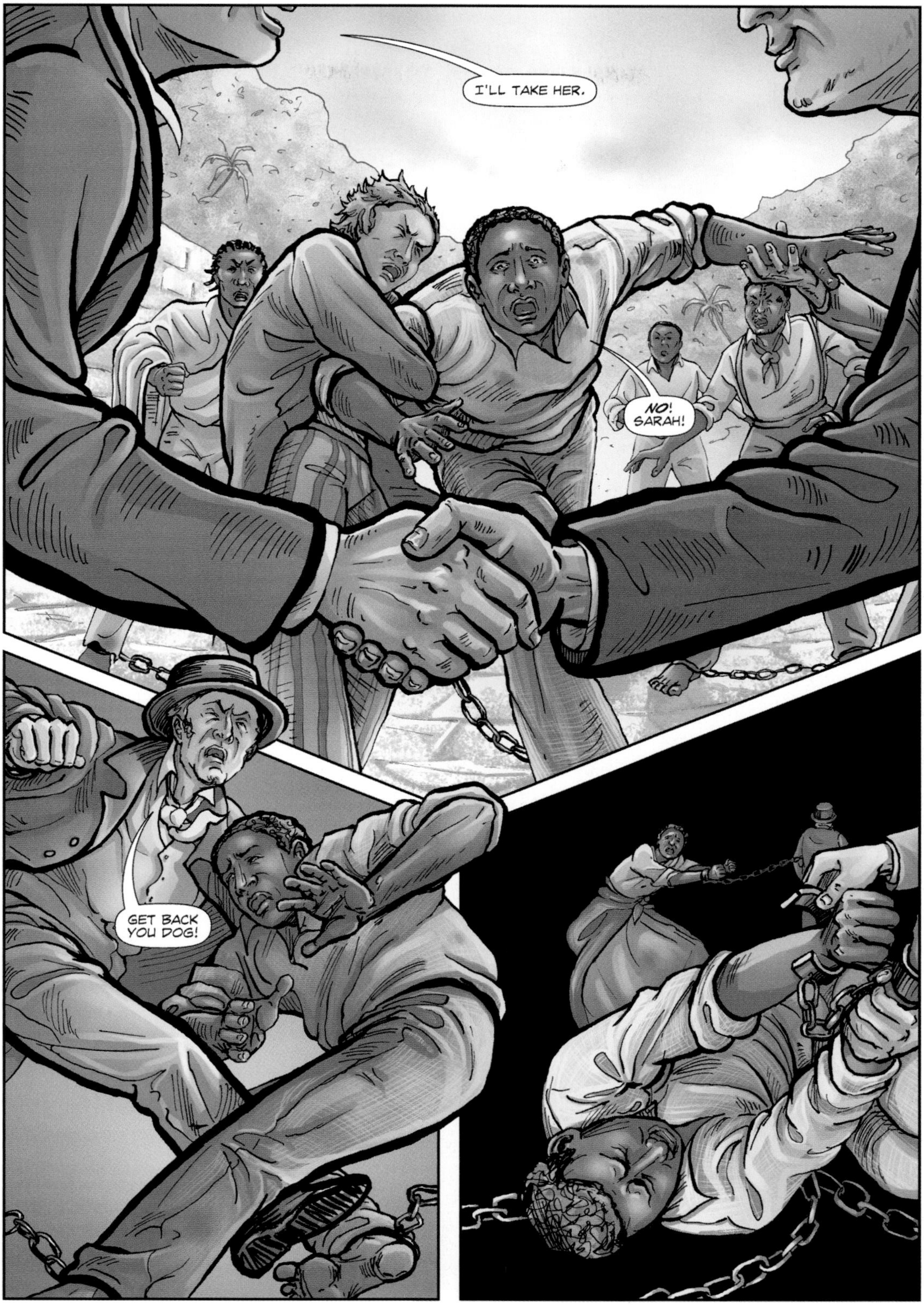
I'LL TAKE HER.
NO! SARAH!
GET BACK YOU DOG!

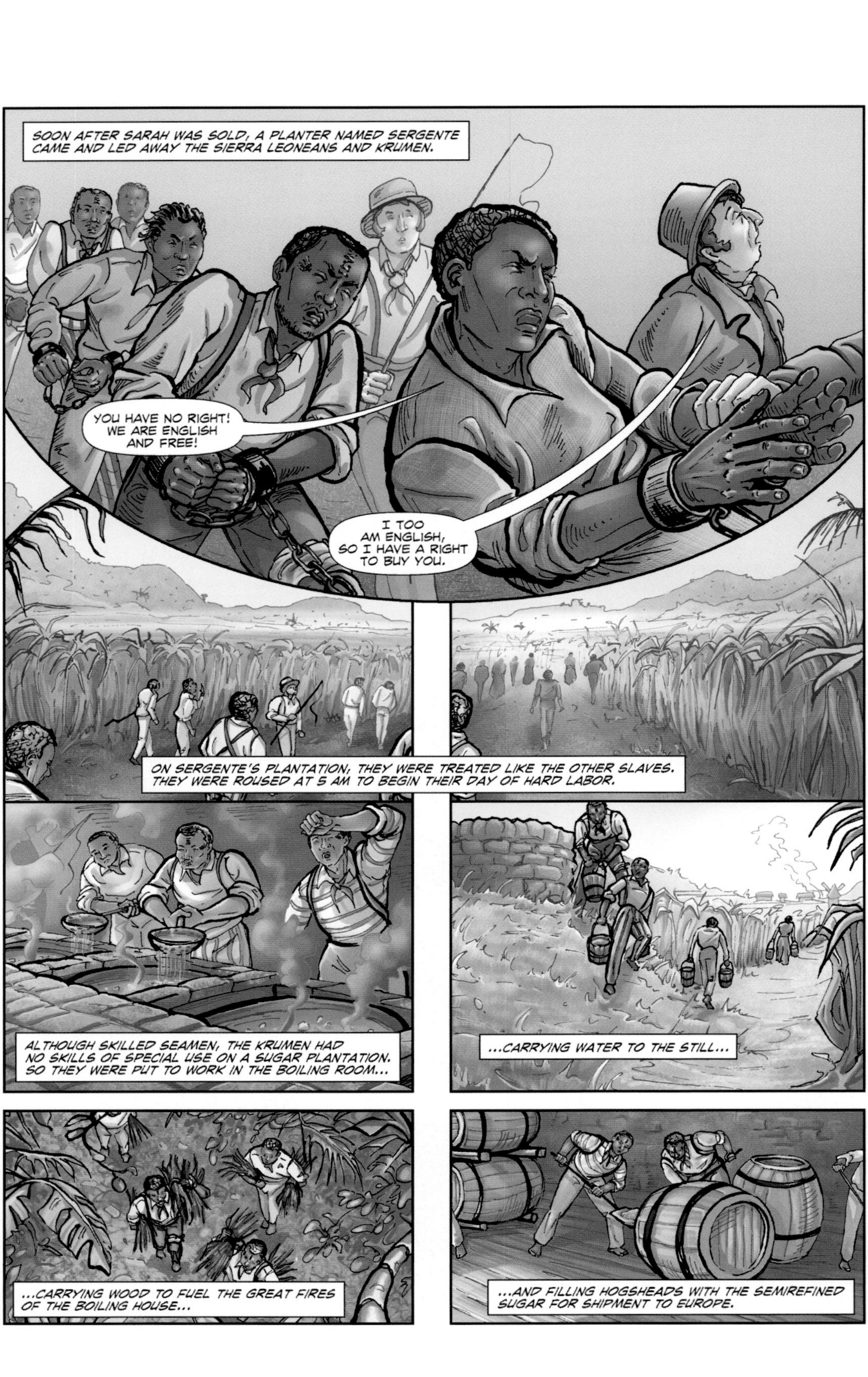
SOON AFTER SARAH WAS SOLD, A PLANTER NAMED SERGENTE CAME AND LED AWAY THE SIERRA LEONEANS AND KRUMEN.
YOU HAVE NO RIGHT! WE ARE ENGLISH AND FREE!
I TOO AM ENGLISH, SO I HAVE A RIGHT TO BUY YOU.
ON SERGENTE'S PLANTATION, THEY WERE TREATED LIKE THE OTHER SLAVES. THEY WERE ROUSED AT 5 AM TO BEGIN THEIR DAY OF HARD LABOR.
ALTHOUGH SKILLED SEAMEN, THE KRUMEN HAD NO SKILLS OF SPECIAL USE ON A SUGAR PLANTATION. SO THEY WERE PUT TO WORK IN THE BOILING ROOM...
...CARRYING WATER TO THE STILL...
...CARRYING WOOD TO FUEL THE GREAT FIRES OF THE BOILING HOUSE...
...AND FILLING HOGSHEADS WITH THE SEMIREFINED SUGAR FOR SHIPMENT TO EUROPE.

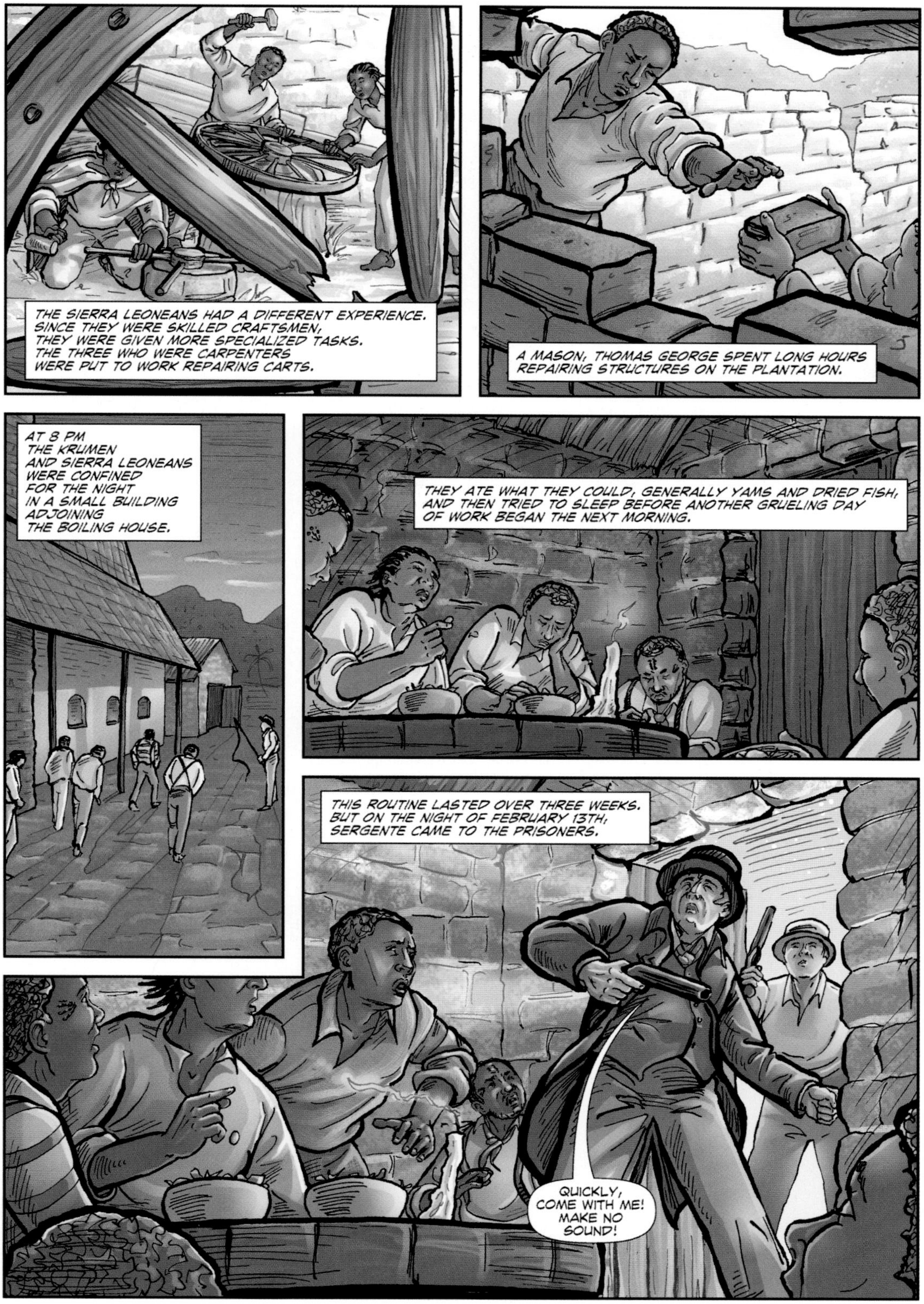
THE SIERRA LEONEANS HAD A DIFFERENT EXPERIENCE. SINCE THEY WERE SKILLED CRAFTSMEN, THEY WERE GIVEN MORE SPECIALIZED TASKS. THE THREE WHO WERE CARPENTERS WERE PUT TO WORK REPAIRING CARTS.
A MASON, THOMAS GEORGE SPENT LONG HOURS REPAIRING STRUCTURES ON THE PLANTATION.
AT 8 PM THE KRUMEN AND SIERRA LEONEANS WERE CONFINED FOR THE NIGHT IN A SMALL BUILDING ADJOINING THE BOILING HOUSE.
THEY ATE WHAT THEY COULD, GENERALLY YAMS AND DRIED FISH, AND THEN TRIED TO SLEEP BEFORE ANOTHER GRUELING DAY OF WORK BEGAN THE NEXT MORNING.
THIS ROUTINE LASTED OVER THREE WEEKS. BUT ON THE NIGHT OF FEBRUARY 13TH, SERGENTE CAME TO THE PRISONERS.
QUICKLY, COME WITH ME! MAKE NO SOUND!

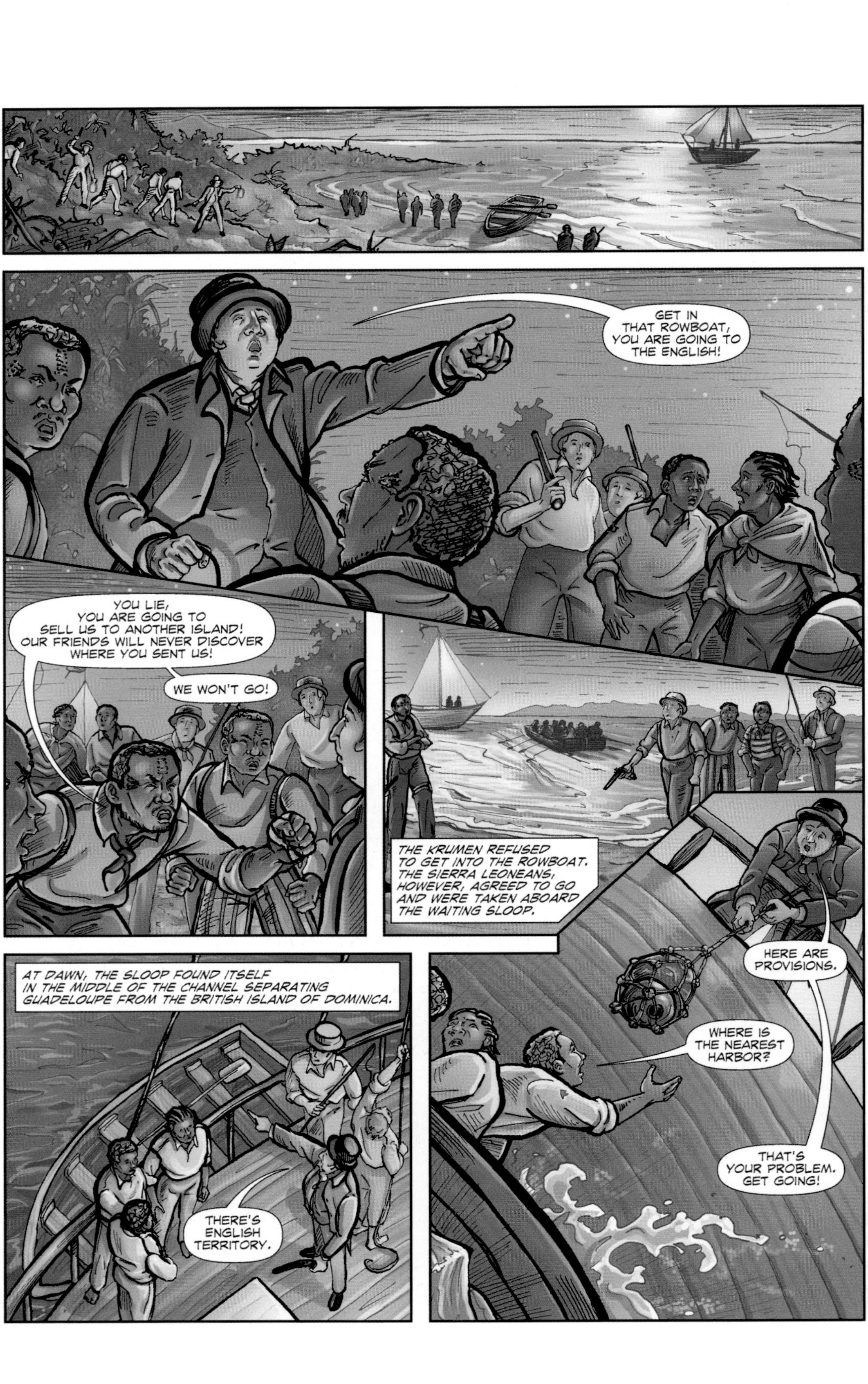
GET IN THAT ROWBOAT, YOU ARE GOING TO THE ENGLISH!
YOU LIE, YOU ARE GOING TO SELL US TO ANOTHER ISLAND! OUR FRIENDS WILL NEVER DISCOVER WHERE YOU SENT US!
WE WON'T GO!
THE KRUMEN REFUSED TO GET INTO THE ROWBOAT. THE SIERRA LEONEANS, HOWEVER, AGREED TO GO AND WERE TAKEN ABOARD THE WAITING SLOOP.
AT DAWN, THE SLOOP FOUND ITSELF IN THE MIDDLE OF THE CHANNEL SEPARATING GUADELOUPE FROM THE BRITISH ISLAND OF DOMINICA.
THERE'S ENGLISH TERRITORY.
HERE ARE PROVISIONS.
WHERE IS THE NEAREST HARBOR?
THAT'S YOUR PROBLEM. GET GOING!

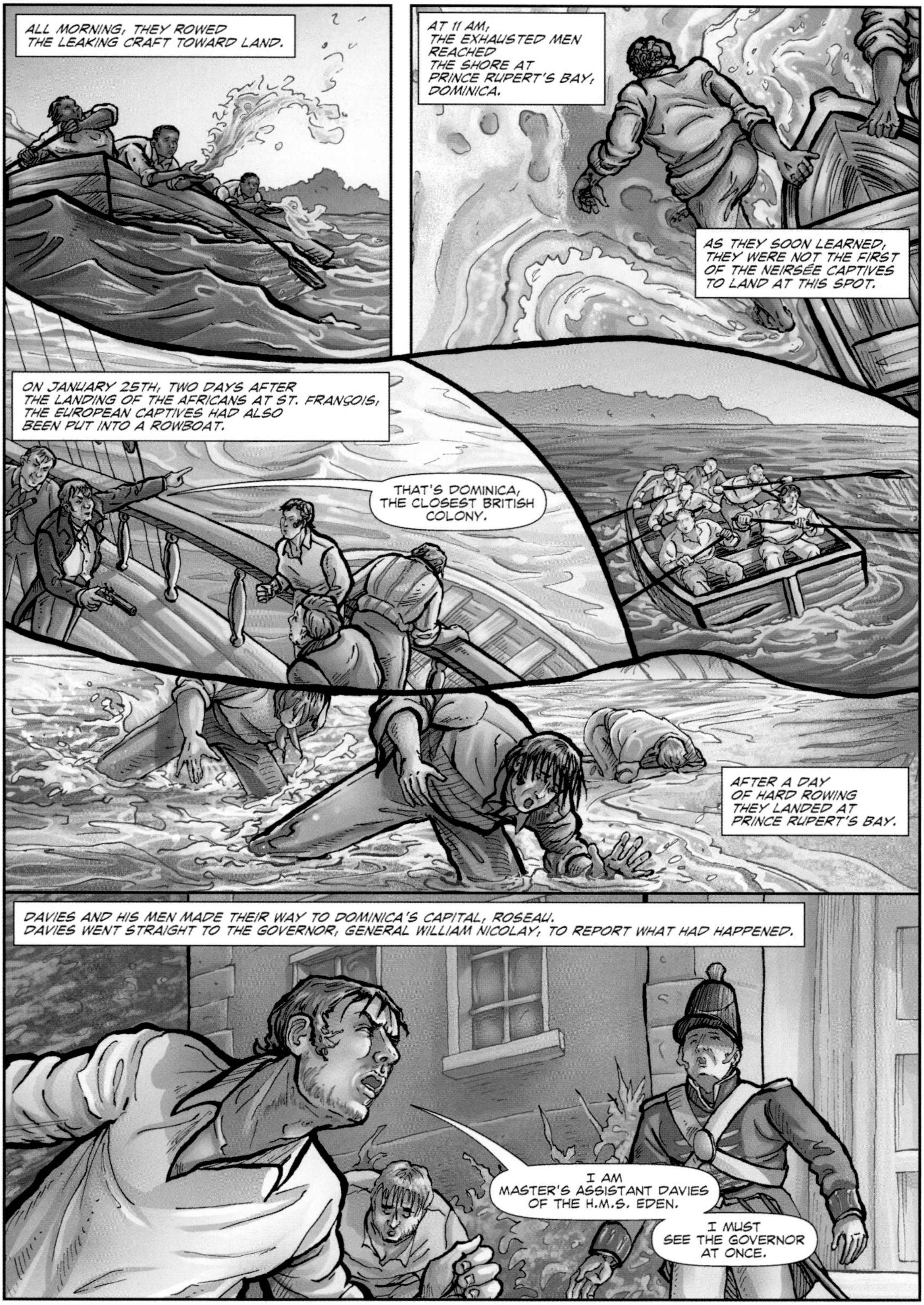
ALL MORNING, THEY ROWED THE LEAKING CRAFT TOWARD LAND.
AT 11 AM, THE EXHAUSTED MEN REACHED THE SHORE AT PRINCE RUPERT'S BAY, DOMINICA.
AS THEY SOON LEARNED, THEY WERE NOT THE FIRST OF THE NEIRSÉE CAPTIVES TO LAND AT THIS SPOT.
ON JANUARY 25TH, TWO DAYS AFTER THE LANDING OF THE AFRICANS AT ST. FRANÇOIS, THE EUROPEAN CAPTIVES HAD ALSO BEEN PUT INTO A ROWBOAT.
THAT'S DOMINICA, THE CLOSEST BRITISH COLONY.
AFTER A DAY OF HARD ROWING THEY LANDED AT PRINCE RUPERT'S BAY.
DAVIES AND HIS MEN MADE THEIR WAY TO DOMINICA'S CAPITAL, ROSEAU. DAVIES WENT STRAIGHT TO THE GOVERNOR, GENERAL WILLIAM NICOLAY, TO REPORT WHAT HAD HAPPENED.
I AM MASTER'S ASSISTANT DAVIES OF THE H.M.S. EDEN.
I MUST SEE THE GOVERNOR AT ONCE.

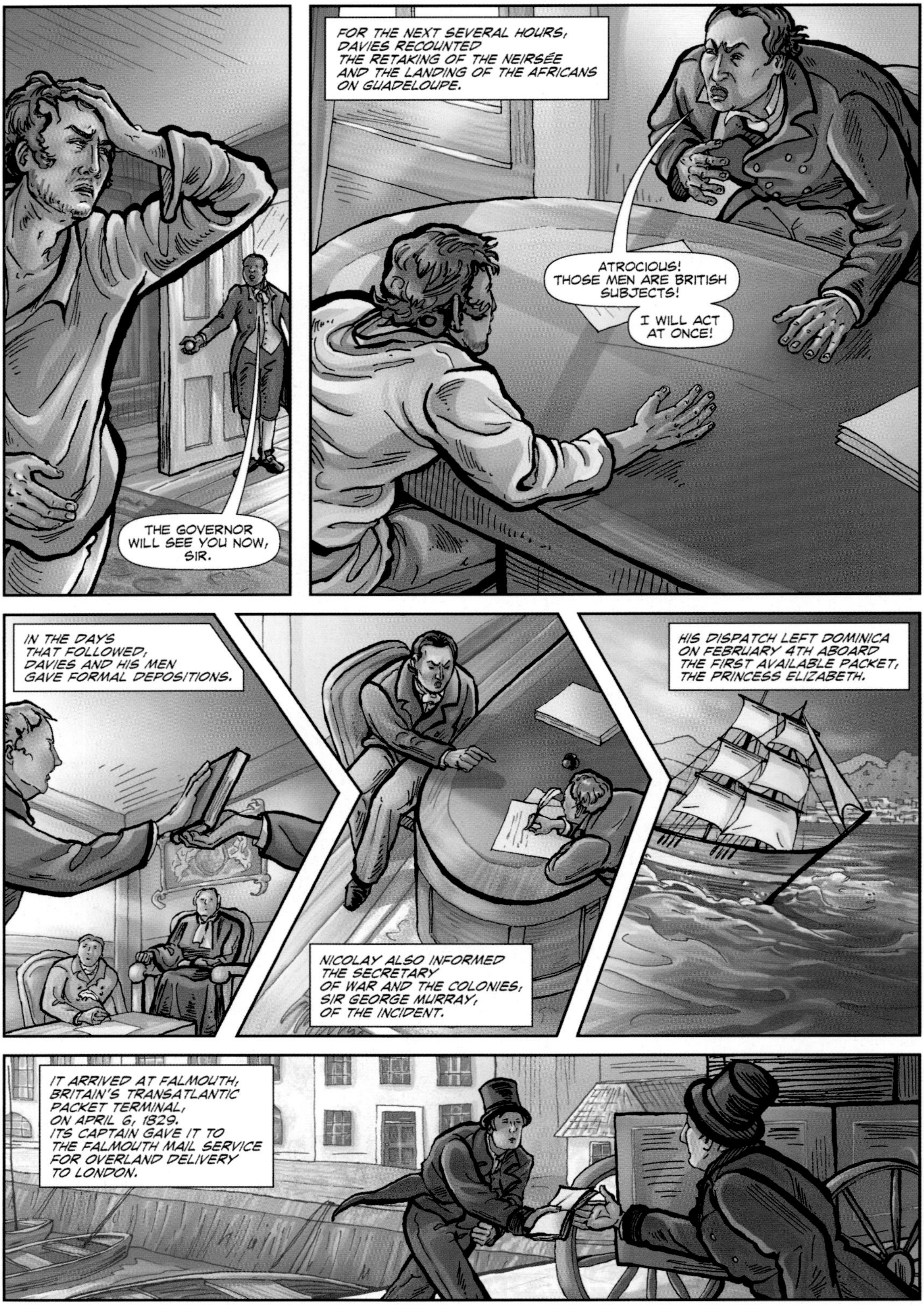
THE GOVERNOR WILL SEE YOU NOW, SIR.
FOR THE NEXT SEVERAL HOURS, DAVIES RECOUNTED THE RETAKING OF THE NEIRSÉE AND THE LANDING OF THE AFRICANS ON GUADELOUPE.
ATROCIOUS! THOSE MEN ARE BRITISH SUBJECTS!
I WILL ACT AT ONCE!
IN THE DAYS THAT FOLLOWED, DAVIES AND HIS MEN GAVE FORMAL DEPOSITIONS.
NICOLAY ALSO INFORMED THE SECRETARY OF WAR AND THE COLONIES, SIR GEORGE MURRAY, OF THE INCIDENT.
HIS DISPATCH LEFT DOMINICA ON FEBRUARY 4TH ABOARD THE FIRST AVAILABLE PACKET, THE PRINCESS ELIZABETH.
IT ARRIVED AT FALMOUTH, BRITAIN'S TRANSATLANTIC PACKET TERMINAL, ON APRIL 6, 1829. ITS CAPTAIN GAVE IT TO THE FALMOUTH MAIL SERVICE FOR OVERLAND DELIVERY TO LONDON.

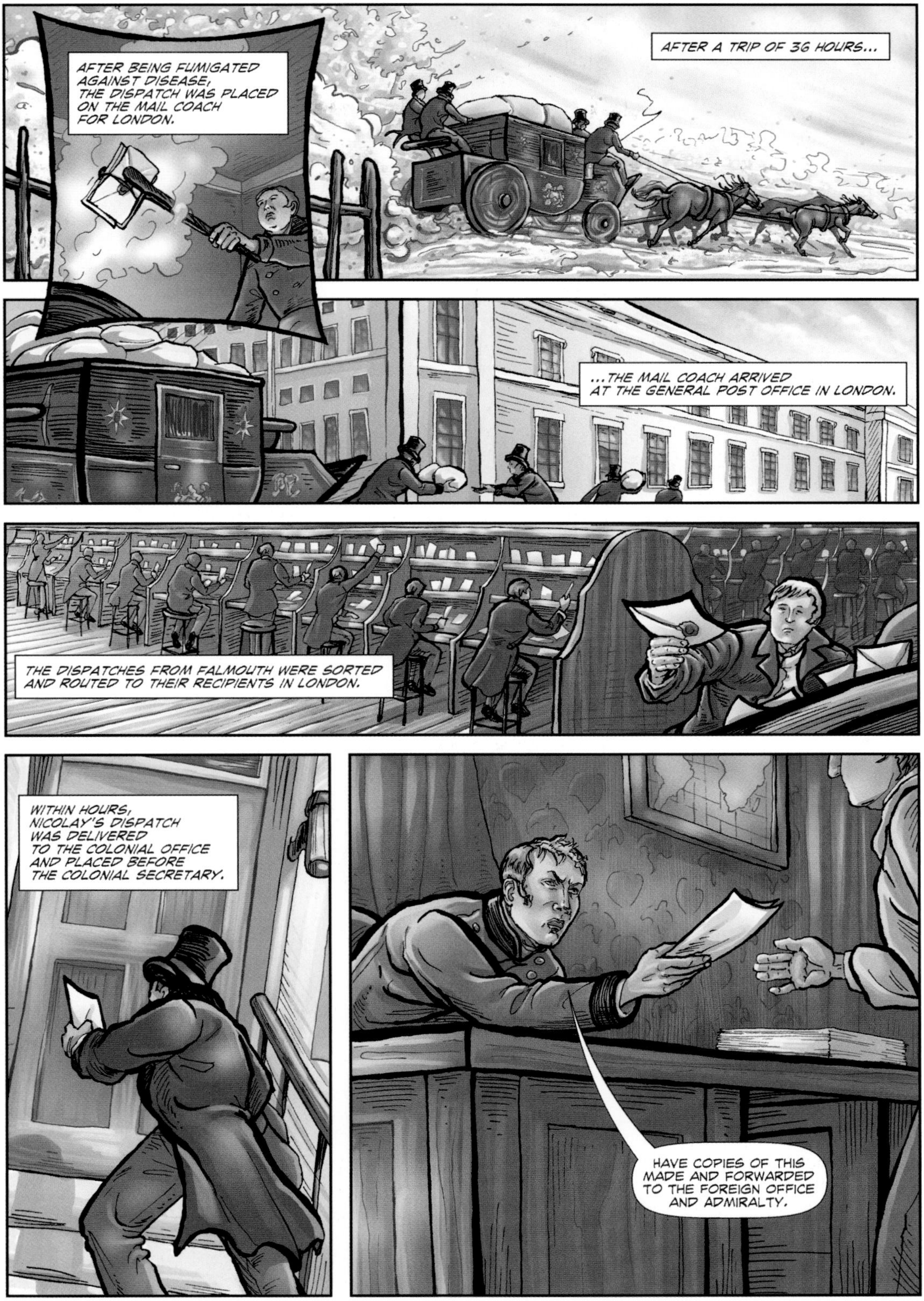
AFTER BEING FUMIGATED AGAINST DISEASE, THE DISPATCH WAS PLACED ON THE MAIL COACH FOR LONDON.
AFTER A TRIP OF 36 HOURS...
...THE MAIL COACH ARRIVED AT THE GENERAL POST OFFICE IN LONDON.
THE DISPATCHES FROM FALMOUTH WERE SORTED AND ROUTED TO THEIR RECIPIENTS IN LONDON.
WITHIN HOURS, NICOLAY'S DISPATCH WAS DELIVERED TO THE COLONIAL OFFICE AND PLACED BEFORE THE COLONIAL SECRETARY.
HAVE COPIES OF THIS MADE AND FORWARDED TO THE FOREIGN OFFICE AND ADMIRALTY.

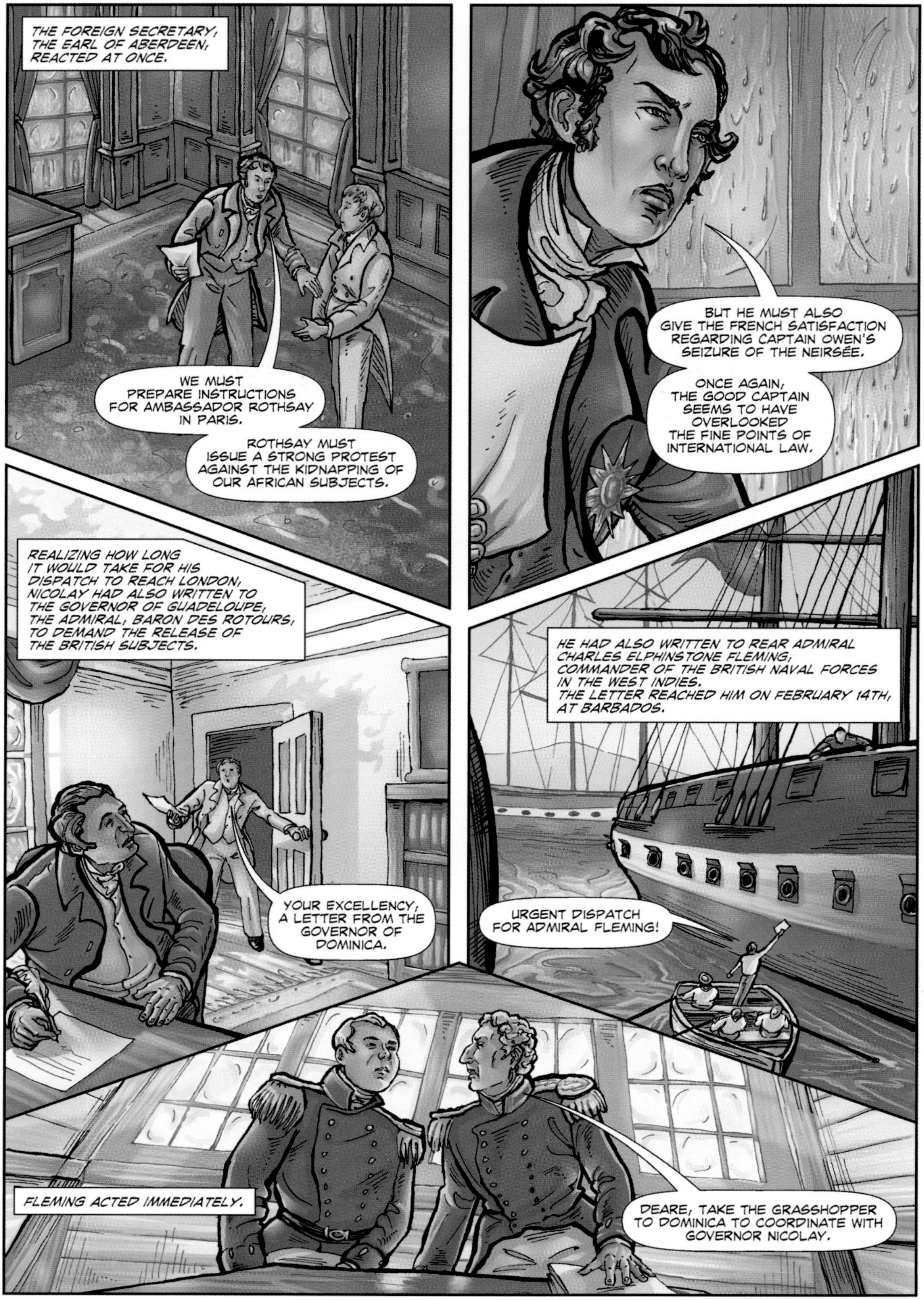

THE FOREIGN SECRETARY, THE EARL OF ABERDEEN, REACTED AT ONCE.
WE MUST PREPARE INSTRUCTIONS FOR AMBASSADOR ROTHSAY IN PARIS.
ROTHSAY MUST ISSUE A STRONG PROTEST AGAINST THE KIDNAPPING OF OUR AFRICAN SUBJECTS.
BUT HE MUST ALSO GIVE THE FRENCH SATISFACTION REGARDING CAPTAIN OWEN'S SEIZURE OF THE NEIRSÉE.
ONCE AGAIN, THE GOOD CAPTAIN SEEMS TO HAVE OVERLOOKED THE FINE POINTS OF INTERNATIONAL LAW.
REALIZING HOW LONG IT WOULD TAKE FOR HIS DISPATCH TO REACH LONDON, NICOLAY HAD ALSO WRITTEN TO THE GOVERNOR OF GUADELOUPE, THE ADMIRAL, BARON DES ROTOURS, TO DEMAND THE RELEASE OF THE BRITISH SUBJECTS.
YOUR EXCELLENCY, A LETTER FROM THE GOVERNOR OF DOMINICA.
HE HAD ALSO WRITTEN TO REAR ADMIRAL CHARLES ELPHINSTONE FLEMING, COMMANDER OF THE BRITISH NAVAL FORCES IN THE WEST INDIES. THE LETTER REACHED HIM ON FEBRUARY 14TH, AT BARBADOS.
URGENT DISPATCH FOR ADMIRAL FLEMING!
FLEMING ACTED IMMEDIATELY.
DEARE, TAKE THE GRASSHOPPER TO DOMINICA TO COORDINATE WITH GOVERNOR NICOLAY.

CHAPTER 4
AN INTERNATIONAL INCIDENT

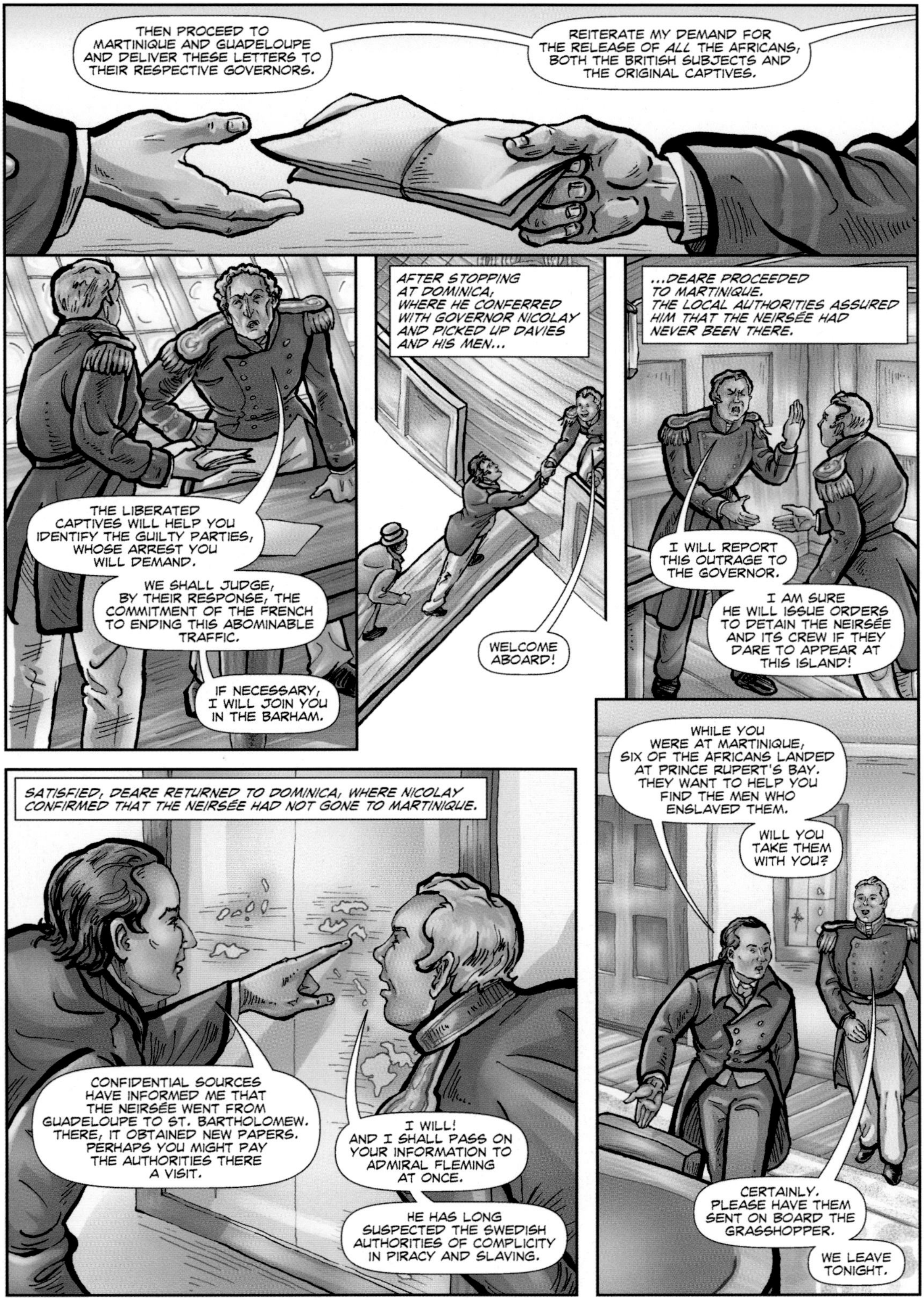

THEN PROCEED TO MARTINIQUE AND GUADELOUPE AND DELIVER THESE LETTERS TO THEIR RESPECTIVE GOVERNORS.
REITERATE MY DEMAND FOR THE RELEASE OF *ALL* THE AFRICANS, BOTH THE BRITISH SUBJECTS AND THE ORIGINAL CAPTIVES.
THE LIBERATED CAPTIVES WILL HELP YOU IDENTIFY THE GUILTY PARTIES, WHOSE ARREST YOU WILL DEMAND.
WE SHALL JUDGE, BY THEIR RESPONSE, THE COMMITMENT OF THE FRENCH TO ENDING THIS ABOMINABLE TRAFFIC.
IF NECESSARY, I WILL JOIN YOU IN THE BARHAM.
AFTER STOPPING AT DOMINICA, WHERE HE CONFERRED WITH GOVERNOR NICOLAY AND PICKED UP DAVIES AND HIS MEN...
WELCOME ABOARD!
...DEARE PROCEEDED TO MARTINIQUE. THE LOCAL AUTHORITIES ASSURED HIM THAT THE NEIRSÉE HAD NEVER BEEN THERE.
I WILL REPORT THIS OUTRAGE TO THE GOVERNOR.
I AM SURE HE WILL ISSUE ORDERS TO DETAIN THE NEIRSÉE AND ITS CREW IF THEY DARE TO APPEAR AT THIS ISLAND!
SATISFIED, DEARE RETURNED TO DOMINICA, WHERE NICOLAY CONFIRMED THAT THE NEIRSÉE HAD NOT GONE TO MARTINIQUE.
CONFIDENTIAL SOURCES HAVE INFORMED ME THAT THE NEIRSÉE WENT FROM GUADELOUPE TO ST. BARTHOLOMEW. THERE, IT OBTAINED NEW PAPERS. PERHAPS YOU MIGHT PAY THE AUTHORITIES THERE A VISIT.
I WILL! AND I SHALL PASS ON YOUR INFORMATION TO ADMIRAL FLEMING AT ONCE.
HE HAS LONG SUSPECTED THE SWEDISH AUTHORITIES OF COMPLICITY IN PIRACY AND SLAVING.
WHILE YOU WERE AT MARTINIQUE, SIX OF THE AFRICANS LANDED AT PRINCE RUPERT'S BAY. THEY WANT TO HELP YOU FIND THE MEN WHO ENSLAVED THEM.
WILL YOU TAKE THEM WITH YOU?
CERTAINLY. PLEASE HAVE THEM SENT ON BOARD THE GRASSHOPPER.
WE LEAVE TONIGHT.

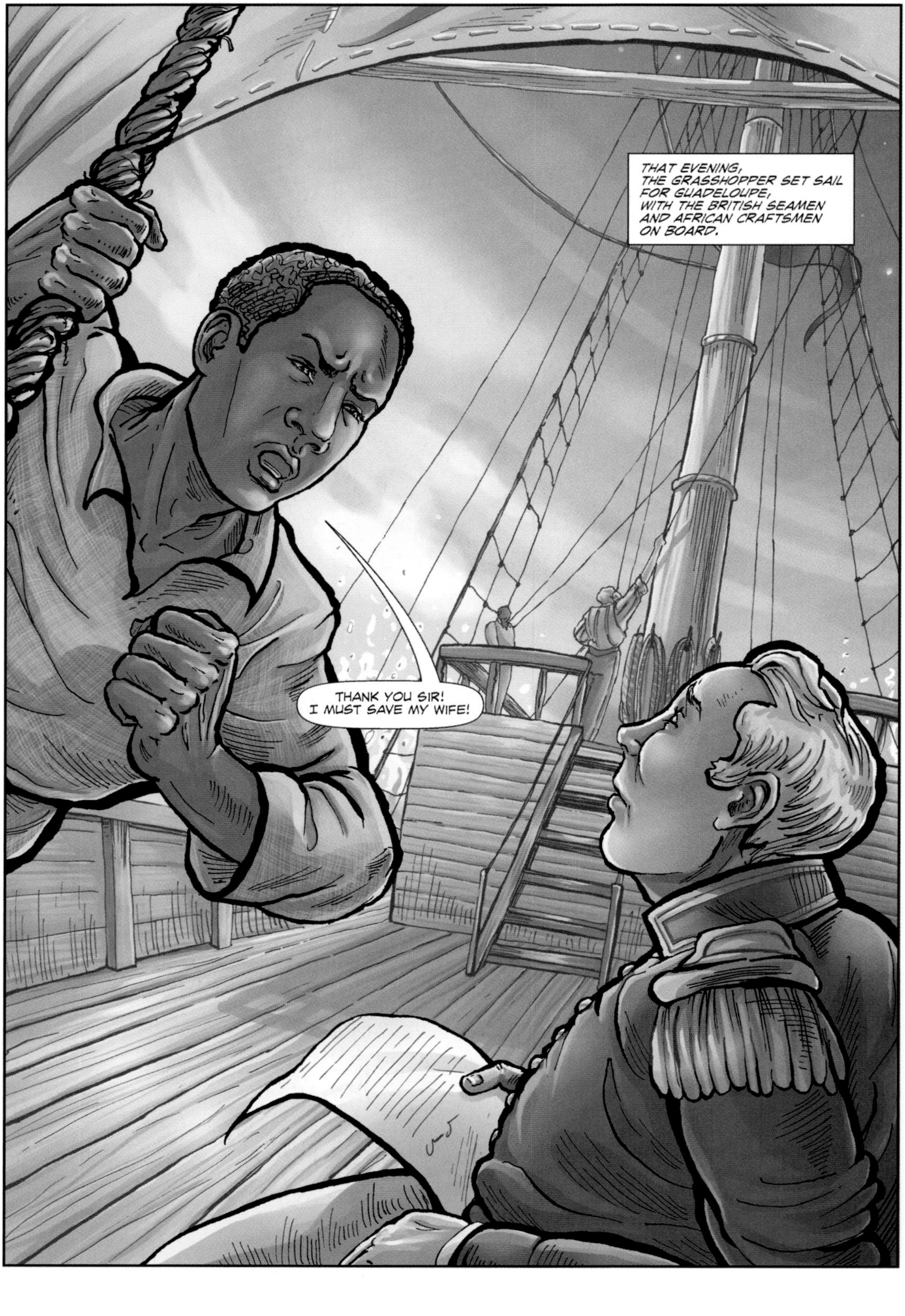
THAT EVENING, THE GRASSHOPPER SET SAIL FOR GUADELOUPE, WITH THE BRITISH SEAMEN AND AFRICAN CRAFTSMEN ON BOARD.
THANK YOU SIR! I MUST SAVE MY WIFE!

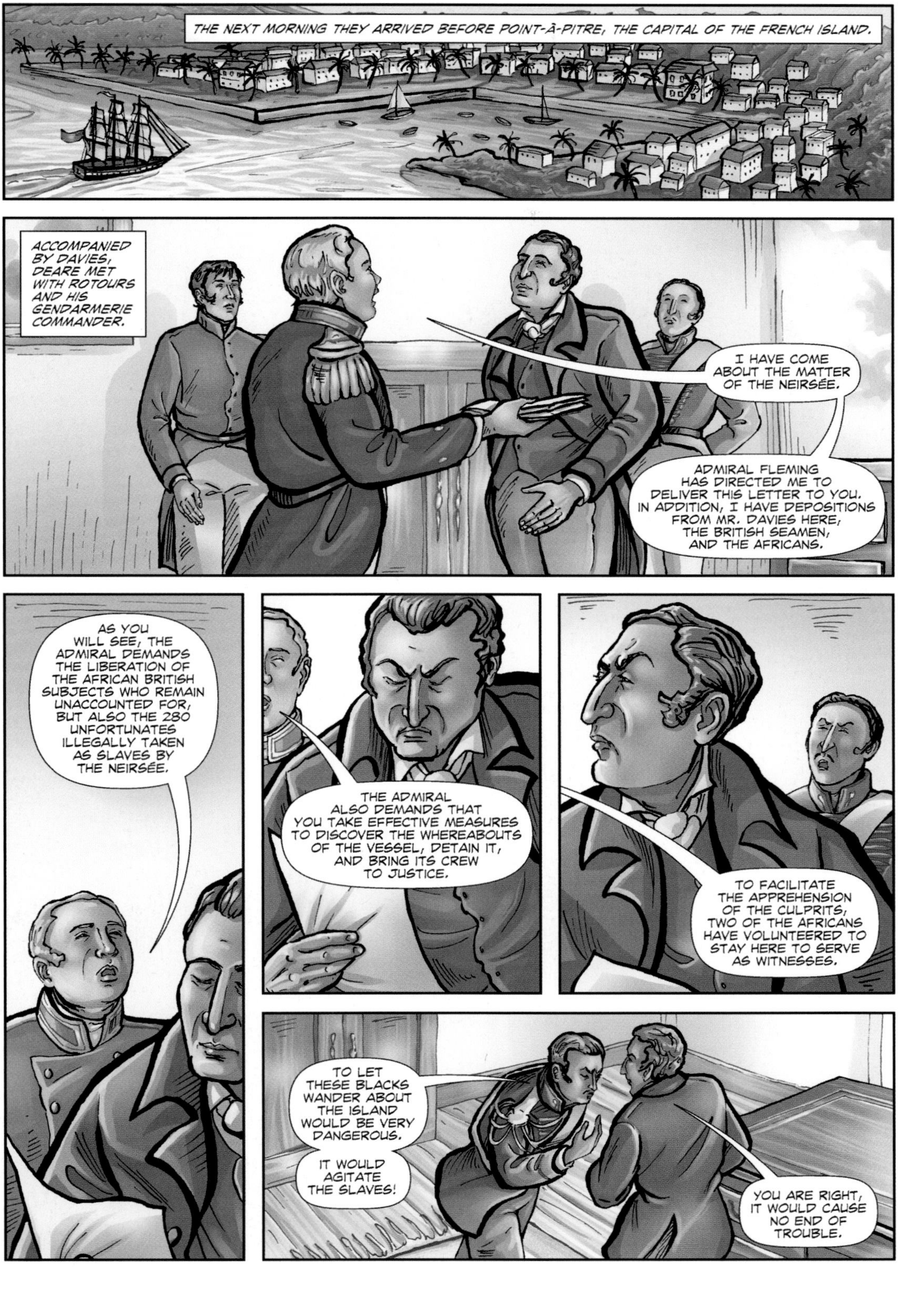
THE NEXT MORNING THEY ARRIVED BEFORE POINT-À-PITRE, THE CAPITAL OF THE FRENCH ISLAND.
ACCOMPANIED BY DAVIES, DEARE MET WITH ROTOURS AND HIS GENDARMERIE COMMANDER.
I HAVE COME ABOUT THE MATTER OF THE NEIRSÉE.
ADMIRAL FLEMING HAS DIRECTED ME TO DELIVER THIS LETTER TO YOU. IN ADDITION, I HAVE DEPOSITIONS FROM MR. DAVIES HERE, THE BRITISH SEAMEN, AND THE AFRICANS.
AS YOU WILL SEE, THE ADMIRAL DEMANDS THE LIBERATION OF THE AFRICAN BRITISH SUBJECTS WHO REMAIN UNACCOUNTED FOR, BUT ALSO THE 280 UNFORTUNATES ILLEGALLY TAKEN AS SLAVES BY THE NEIRSÉE.
THE ADMIRAL ALSO DEMANDS THAT YOU TAKE EFFECTIVE MEASURES TO DISCOVER THE WHEREABOUTS OF THE VESSEL, DETAIN IT, AND BRING ITS CREW TO JUSTICE.
TO FACILITATE THE APPREHENSION OF THE CULPRITS, TWO OF THE AFRICANS HAVE VOLUNTEERED TO STAY HERE TO SERVE AS WITNESSES.
TO LET THESE BLACKS WANDER ABOUT THE ISLAND WOULD BE VERY DANGEROUS.
IT WOULD AGITATE THE SLAVES!
YOU ARE RIGHT, IT WOULD CAUSE NO END OF TROUBLE.

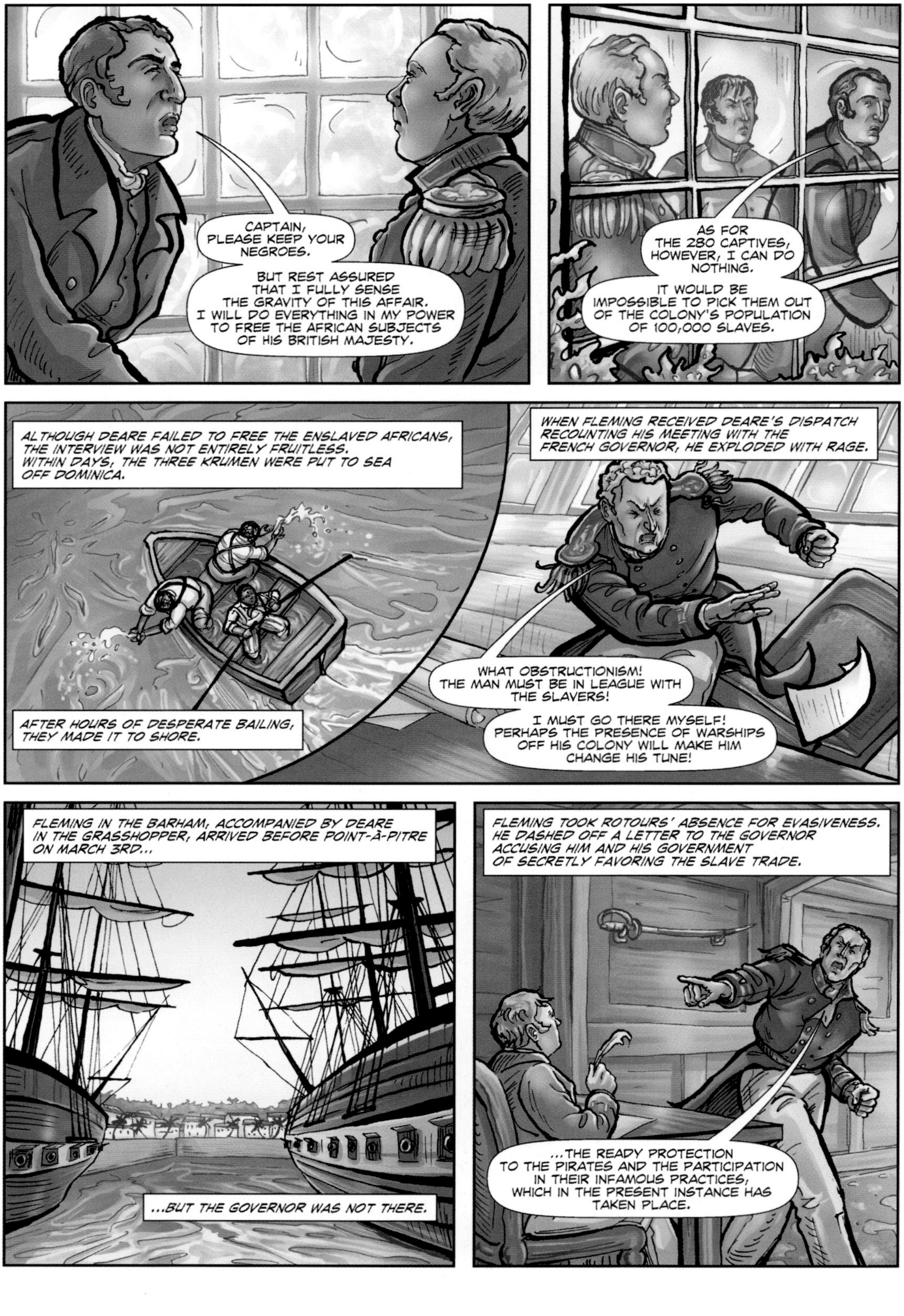

CAPTAIN, PLEASE KEEP YOUR NEGROES.
BUT REST ASSURED THAT I FULLY SENSE THE GRAVITY OF THIS AFFAIR. I WILL DO EVERYTHING IN MY POWER TO FREE THE AFRICAN SUBJECTS OF HIS BRITISH MAJESTY.
AS FOR THE 280 CAPTIVES, HOWEVER, I CAN DO NOTHING.
IT WOULD BE IMPOSSIBLE TO PICK THEM OUT OF THE COLONY'S POPULATION OF 100,000 SLAVES.
ALTHOUGH DEARE FAILED TO FREE THE ENSLAVED AFRICANS, THE INTERVIEW WAS NOT ENTIRELY FRUITLESS. WITHIN DAYS, THE THREE KRUMEN WERE PUT TO SEA OFF DOMINICA.
AFTER HOURS OF DESPERATE BAILING, THEY MADE IT TO SHORE.
WHEN FLEMING RECEIVED DEARE'S DISPATCH RECOUNTING HIS MEETING WITH THE FRENCH GOVERNOR, HE EXPLODED WITH RAGE.
WHAT OBSTRUCTIONISM! THE MAN MUST BE IN LEAGUE WITH THE SLAVERS!
I MUST GO THERE MYSELF! PERHAPS THE PRESENCE OF WARSHIPS OFF HIS COLONY WILL MAKE HIM CHANGE HIS TUNE!
FLEMING IN THE BARHAM, ACCOMPANIED BY DEARE IN THE GRASSHOPPER, ARRIVED BEFORE POINT-À-PITRE ON MARCH 3RD...
...BUT THE GOVERNOR WAS NOT THERE.
FLEMING TOOK ROTOURS' ABSENCE FOR EVASIVENESS. HE DASHED OFF A LETTER TO THE GOVERNOR ACCUSING HIM AND HIS GOVERNMENT OF SECRETLY FAVORING THE SLAVE TRADE.
...THE READY PROTECTION TO THE PIRATES AND THE PARTICIPATION IN THEIR INFAMOUS PRACTICES, WHICH IN THE PRESENT INSTANCE HAS TAKEN PLACE.

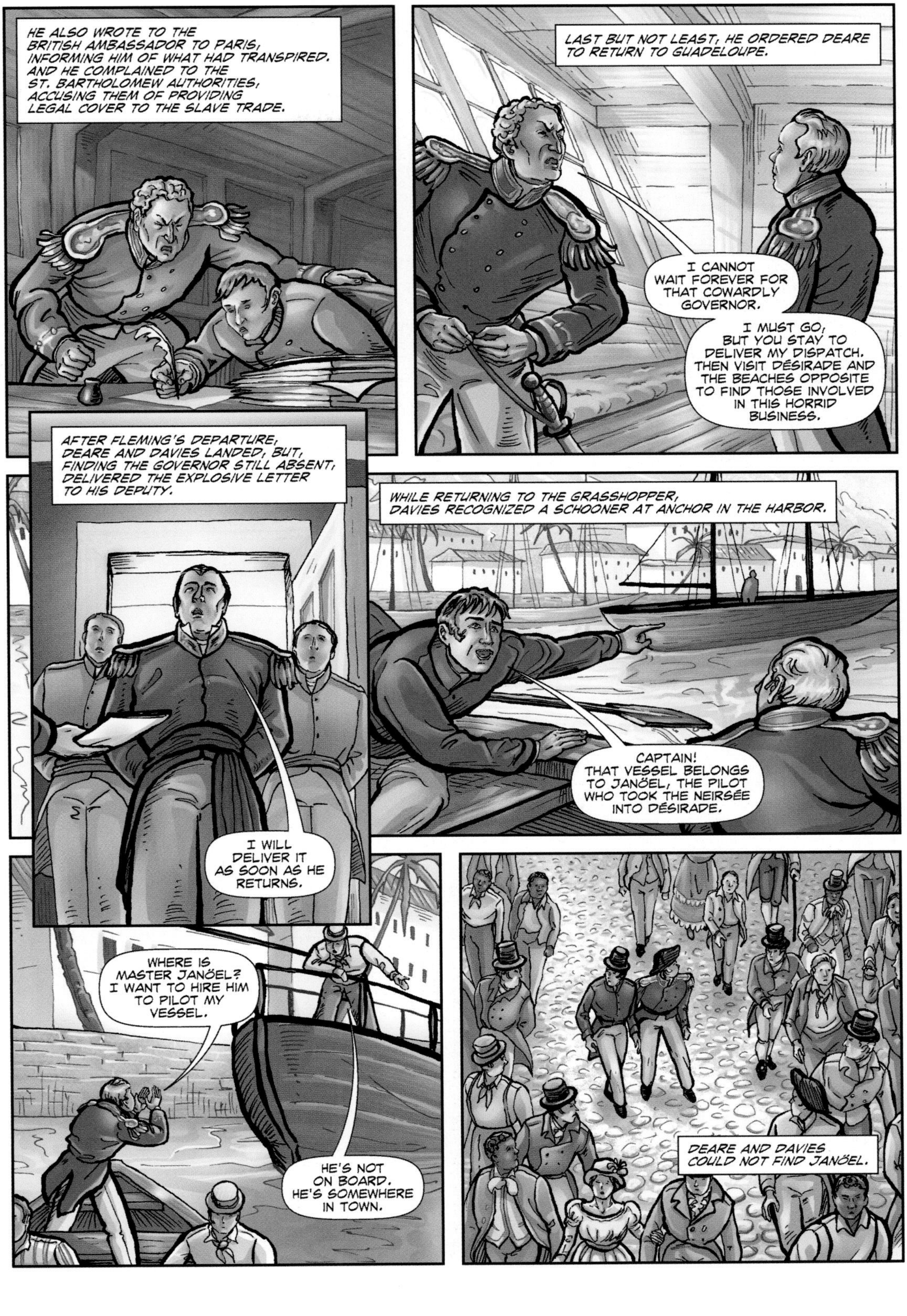
HE ALSO WROTE TO THE BRITISH AMBASSADOR TO PARIS, INFORMING HIM OF WHAT HAD TRANSPIRED. AND HE COMPLAINED TO THE ST. BARTHOLOMEW AUTHORITIES, ACCUSING THEM OF PROVIDING LEGAL COVER TO THE SLAVE TRADE.
LAST BUT NOT LEAST, HE ORDERED DEARE TO RETURN TO GUADELOUPE.
I CANNOT WAIT FOREVER FOR THAT COWARDLY GOVERNOR.
I MUST GO, BUT YOU STAY TO DELIVER MY DISPATCH. THEN VISIT DÉSIRADE AND THE BEACHES OPPOSITE TO FIND THOSE INVOLVED IN THIS HORRID BUSINESS.
AFTER FLEMING'S DEPARTURE, DEARE AND DAVIES LANDED, BUT, FINDING THE GOVERNOR STILL ABSENT, DELIVERED THE EXPLOSIVE LETTER TO HIS DEPUTY.
I WILL DELIVER IT AS SOON AS HE RETURNS.
WHILE RETURNING TO THE GRASSHOPPER, DAVIES RECOGNIZED A SCHOONER AT ANCHOR IN THE HARBOR.
CAPTAIN! THAT VESSEL BELONGS TO JANÖEL, THE PILOT WHO TOOK THE NEIRSÉE INTO DÉSIRADE.
WHERE IS MASTER JANÖEL? I WANT TO HIRE HIM TO PILOT MY VESSEL.
HE'S NOT ON BOARD. HE'S SOMEWHERE IN TOWN.
DEARE AND DAVIES COULD NOT FIND JANÖEL.

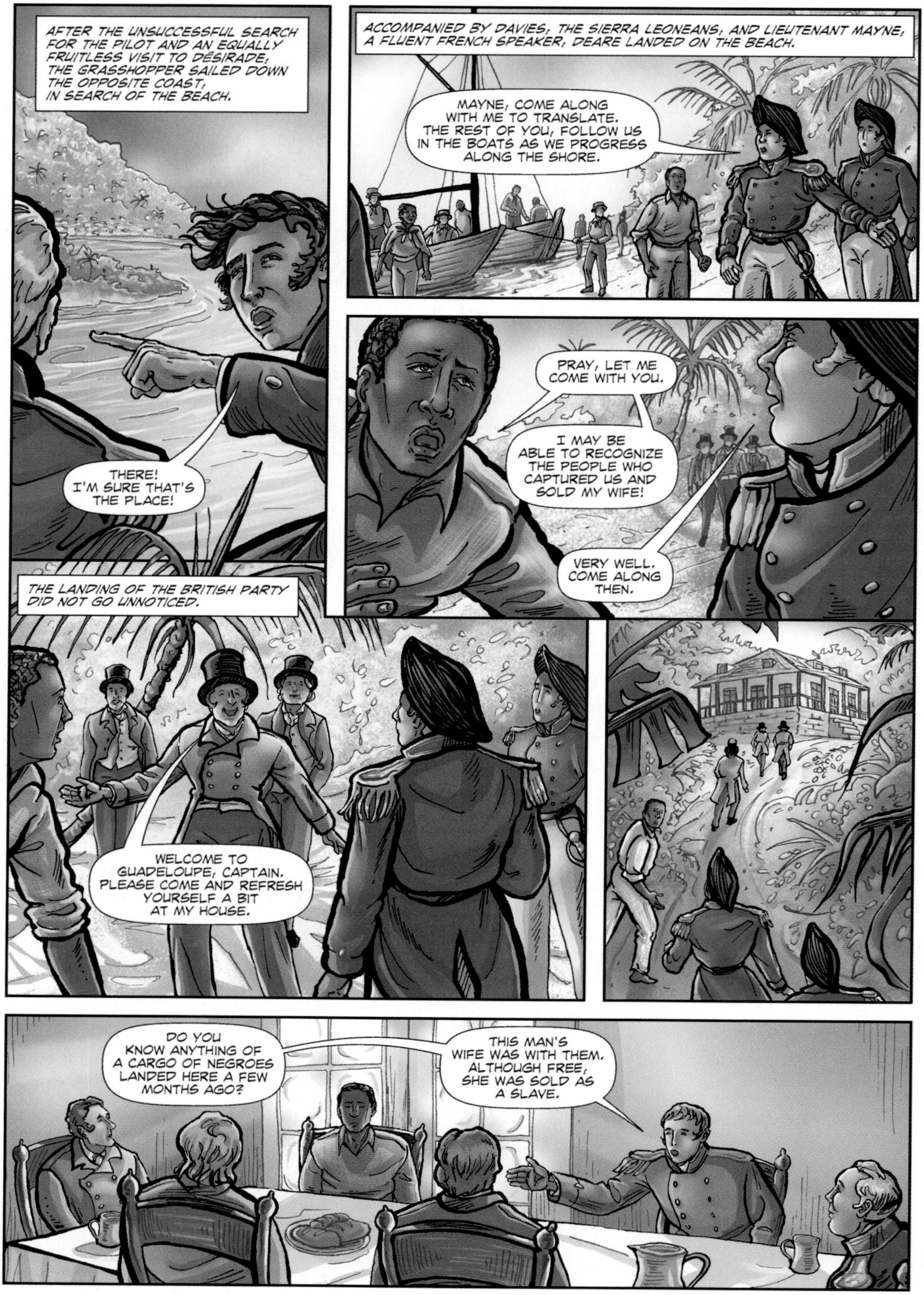
AFTER THE UNSUCCESSFUL SEARCH FOR THE PILOT AND AN EQUALLY FRUITLESS VISIT TO DÉSIRADE, THE GRASSHOPPER SAILED DOWN THE OPPOSITE COAST, IN SEARCH OF THE BEACH.
THERE! I'M SURE THAT'S THE PLACE!
ACCOMPANIED BY DAVIES, THE SIERRA LEONEANS, AND LIEUTENANT MAYNE, A FLUENT FRENCH SPEAKER, DEARE LANDED ON THE BEACH.
MAYNE, COME ALONG WITH ME TO TRANSLATE. THE REST OF YOU, FOLLOW US IN THE BOATS AS WE PROGRESS ALONG THE SHORE.
PRAY, LET ME COME WITH YOU.
I MAY BE ABLE TO RECOGNIZE THE PEOPLE WHO CAPTURED US AND SOLD MY WIFE!
VERY WELL. COME ALONG THEN.
THE LANDING OF THE BRITISH PARTY DID NOT GO UNNOTICED.
WELCOME TO GUADELOUPE, CAPTAIN. PLEASE COME AND REFRESH YOURSELF A BIT AT MY HOUSE.
DO YOU KNOW ANYTHING OF A CARGO OF NEGROES LANDED HERE A FEW MONTHS AGO?
THIS MAN'S WIFE WAS WITH THEM. ALTHOUGH FREE, SHE WAS SOLD AS A SLAVE.

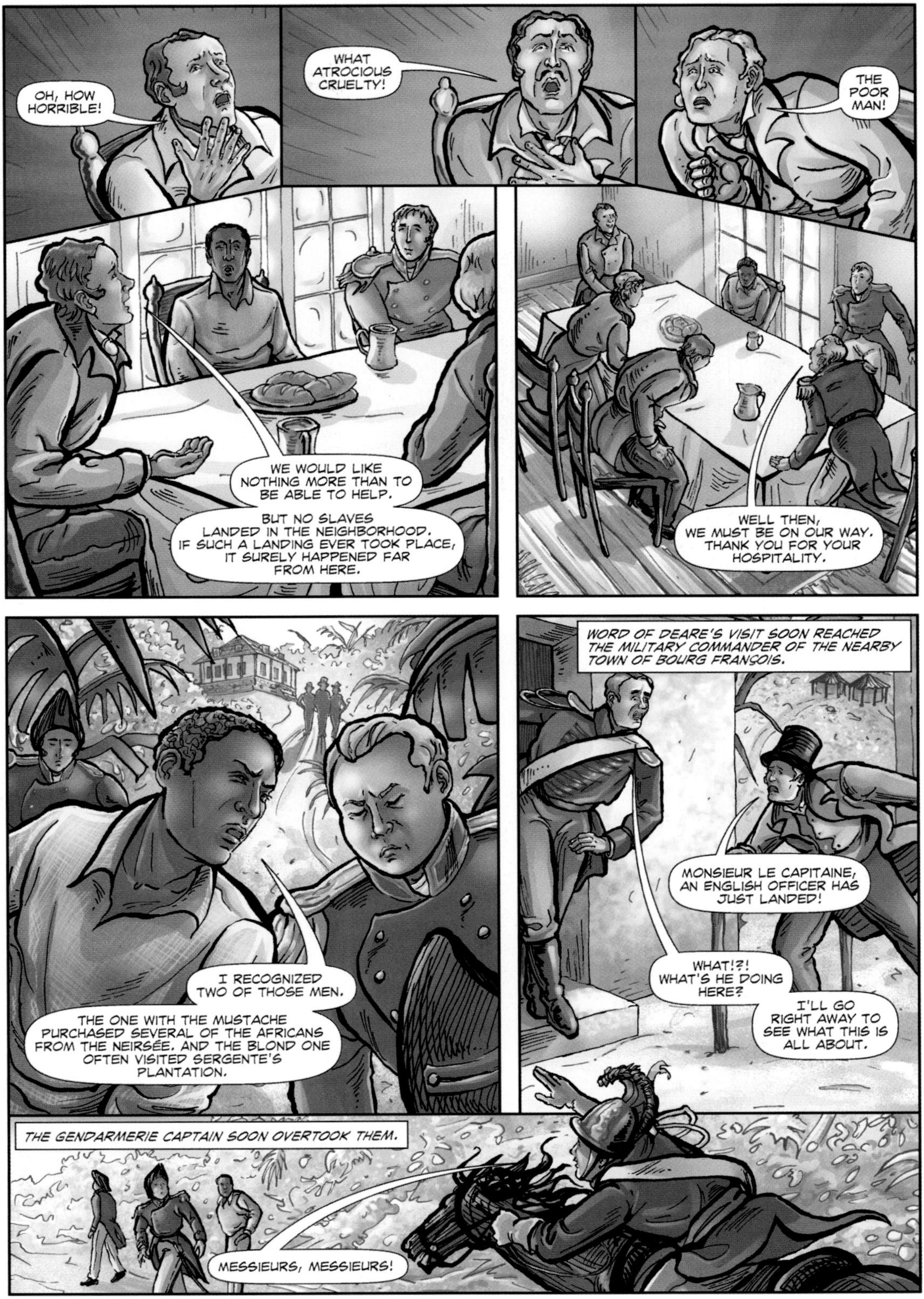

OH, HOW HORRIBLE!
WHAT ATROCIOUS CRUELTY!
THE POOR MAN!
WE WOULD LIKE NOTHING MORE THAN TO BE ABLE TO HELP.
BUT NO SLAVES LANDED IN THE NEIGHBORHOOD. IF SUCH A LANDING EVER TOOK PLACE, IT SURELY HAPPENED FAR FROM HERE.
WELL THEN, WE MUST BE ON OUR WAY. THANK YOU FOR YOUR HOSPITALITY.
I RECOGNIZED TWO OF THOSE MEN.
THE ONE WITH THE MUSTACHE PURCHASED SEVERAL OF THE AFRICANS FROM THE NEIRSÉE. AND THE BLOND ONE OFTEN VISITED SERGENTE'S PLANTATION.
WORD OF DEARE'S VISIT SOON REACHED THE MILITARY COMMANDER OF THE NEARBY TOWN OF BOURG FRANÇOIS.
MONSIEUR LE CAPITAINE, AN ENGLISH OFFICER HAS JUST LANDED!
WHAT!?! WHAT'S HE DOING HERE?
I'LL GO RIGHT AWAY TO SEE WHAT THIS IS ALL ABOUT.
THE GENDARMERIE CAPTAIN SOON OVERTOOK THEM.
MESSIEURS, MESSIEURS!

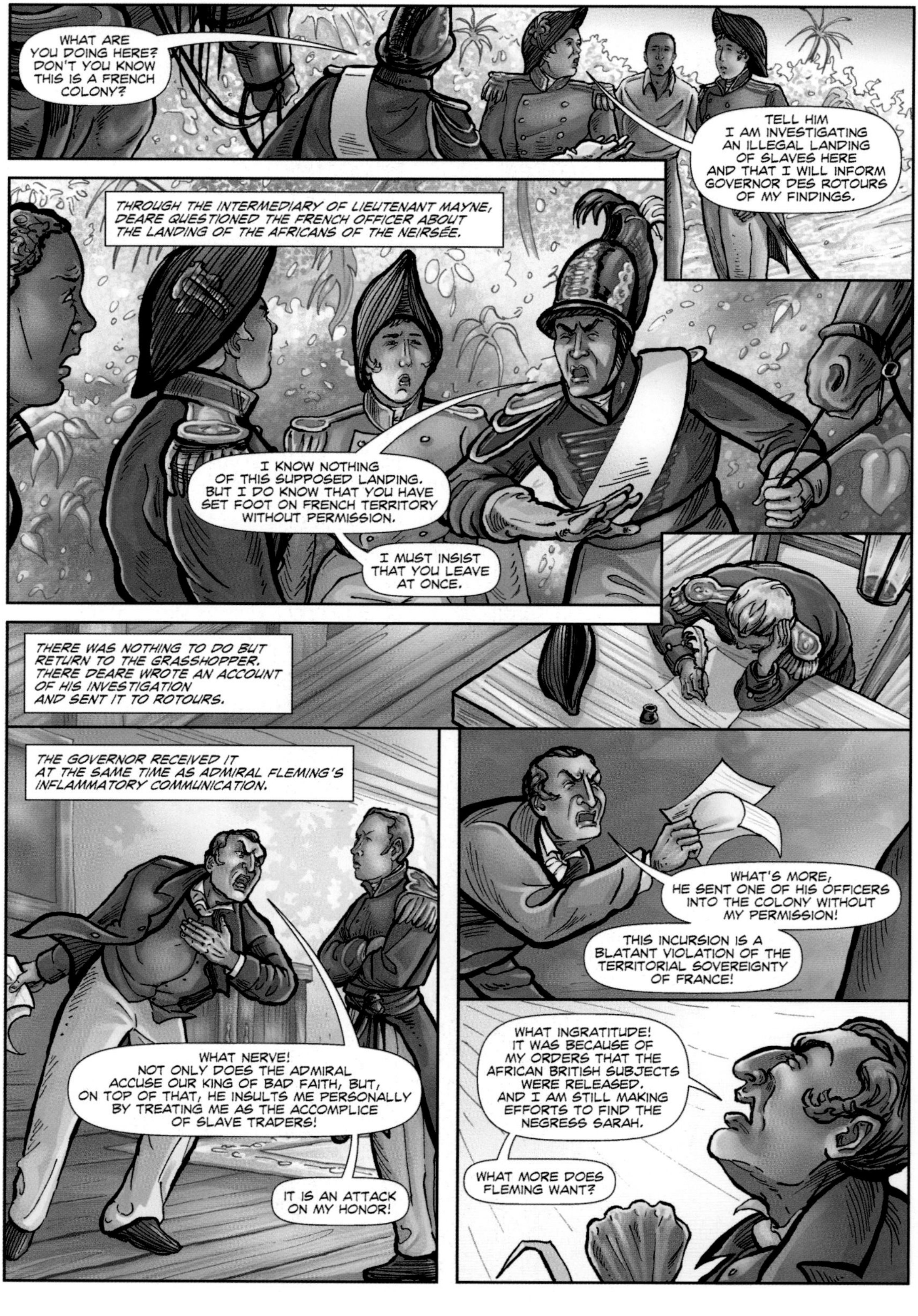
WHAT ARE YOU DOING HERE? DON'T YOU KNOW THIS IS A FRENCH COLONY?
TELL HIM I AM INVESTIGATING AN ILLEGAL LANDING OF SLAVES HERE AND THAT I WILL INFORM GOVERNOR DES ROTOURS OF MY FINDINGS.
THROUGH THE INTERMEDIARY OF LIEUTENANT MAYNE, DEARE QUESTIONED THE FRENCH OFFICER ABOUT THE LANDING OF THE AFRICANS OF THE NEIRSÉE.
I KNOW NOTHING OF THIS SUPPOSED LANDING. BUT I DO KNOW THAT YOU HAVE SET FOOT ON FRENCH TERRITORY WITHOUT PERMISSION.
I MUST INSIST THAT YOU LEAVE AT ONCE.
THERE WAS NOTHING TO DO BUT RETURN TO THE GRASSHOPPER. THERE DEARE WROTE AN ACCOUNT OF HIS INVESTIGATION AND SENT IT TO ROTOURS.
THE GOVERNOR RECEIVED IT AT THE SAME TIME AS ADMIRAL FLEMING'S INFLAMMATORY COMMUNICATION.
WHAT NERVE! NOT ONLY DOES THE ADMIRAL ACCUSE OUR KING OF BAD FAITH, BUT, ON TOP OF THAT, HE INSULTS ME PERSONALLY BY TREATING ME AS THE ACCOMPLICE OF SLAVE TRADERS!
IT IS AN ATTACK ON MY HONOR!
WHAT'S MORE, HE SENT ONE OF HIS OFFICERS INTO THE COLONY WITHOUT MY PERMISSION!
THIS INCURSION IS A BLATANT VIOLATION OF THE TERRITORIAL SOVEREIGNTY OF FRANCE!
WHAT INGRATITUDE! IT WAS BECAUSE OF MY ORDERS THAT THE AFRICAN BRITISH SUBJECTS WERE RELEASED. AND I AM STILL MAKING EFFORTS TO FIND THE NEGRESS SARAH.
WHAT MORE DOES FLEMING WANT?

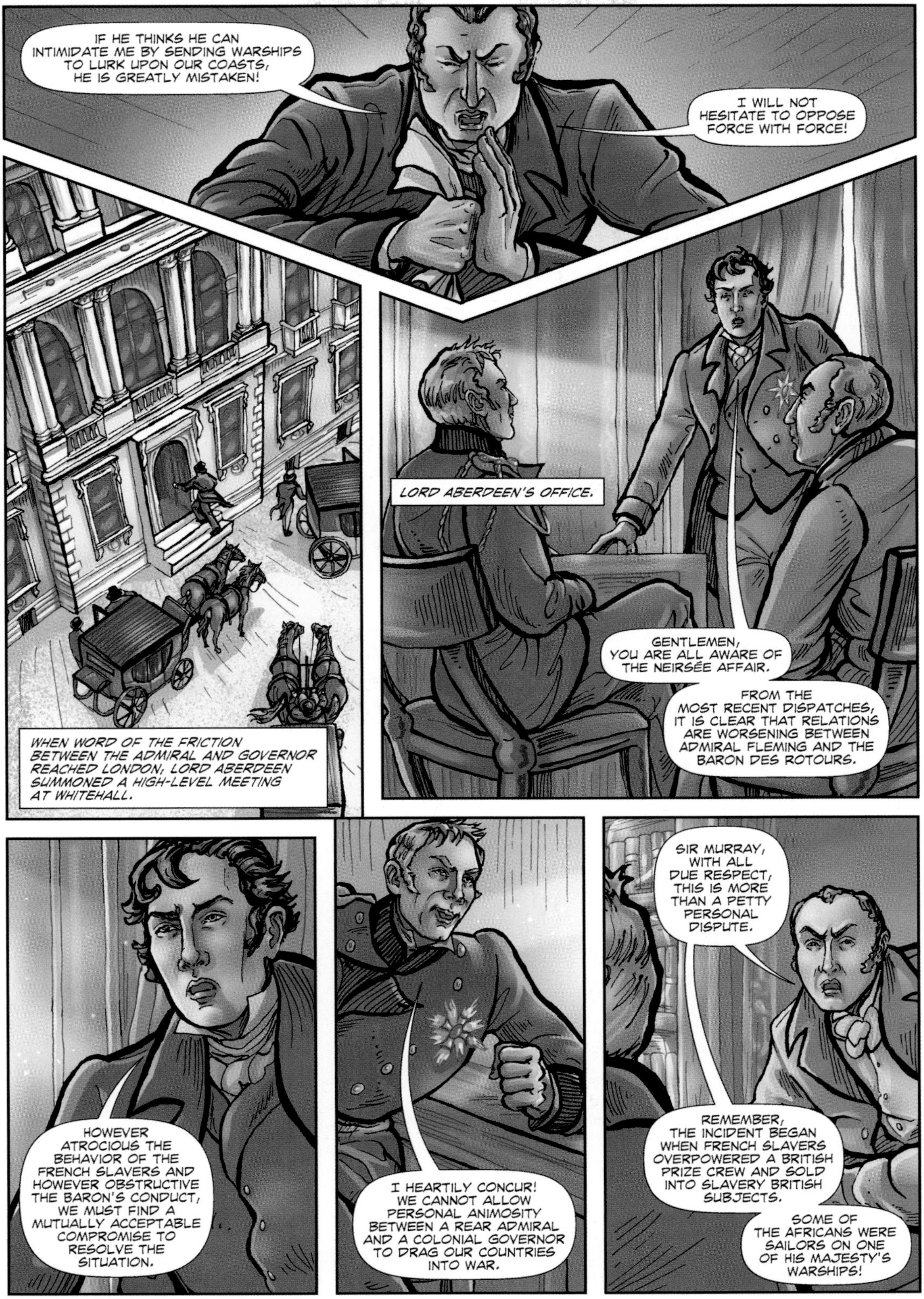
IF HE THINKS HE CAN INTIMIDATE ME BY SENDING WARSHIPS TO LURK UPON OUR COASTS, HE IS GREATLY MISTAKEN!
I WILL NOT HESITATE TO OPPOSE FORCE WITH FORCE!
WHEN WORD OF THE FRICTION BETWEEN THE ADMIRAL AND GOVERNOR REACHED LONDON, LORD ABERDEEN SUMMONED A HIGH-LEVEL MEETING AT WHITEHALL.
LORD ABERDEEN'S OFFICE.
GENTLEMEN, YOU ARE ALL AWARE OF THE NEIRSÉE AFFAIR.
FROM THE MOST RECENT DISPATCHES, IT IS CLEAR THAT RELATIONS ARE WORSENING BETWEEN ADMIRAL FLEMING AND THE BARON DES ROTOURS.
HOWEVER ATROCIOUS THE BEHAVIOR OF THE FRENCH SLAVERS AND HOWEVER OBSTRUCTIVE THE BARON'S CONDUCT, WE MUST FIND A MUTUALLY ACCEPTABLE COMPROMISE TO RESOLVE THE SITUATION.
I HEARTILY CONCUR! WE CANNOT ALLOW PERSONAL ANIMOSITY BETWEEN A REAR ADMIRAL AND A COLONIAL GOVERNOR TO DRAG OUR COUNTRIES INTO WAR.
SIR MURRAY, WITH ALL DUE RESPECT, THIS IS MORE THAN A PETTY PERSONAL DISPUTE.
REMEMBER, THE INCIDENT BEGAN WHEN FRENCH SLAVERS OVERPOWERED A BRITISH PRIZE CREW AND SOLD INTO SLAVERY BRITISH SUBJECTS.
SOME OF THE AFRICANS WERE SAILORS ON ONE OF HIS MAJESTY'S WARSHIPS!

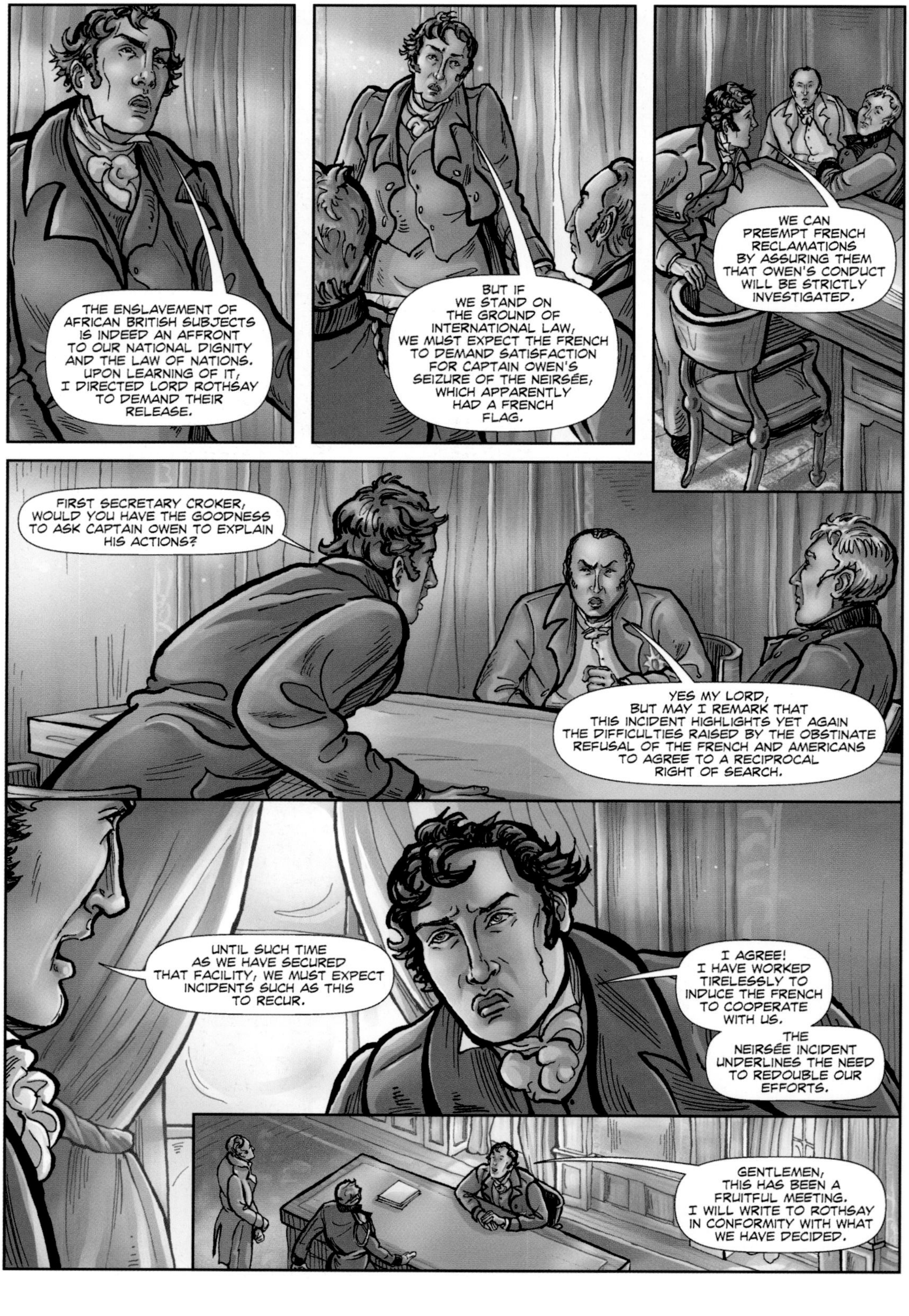

THE ENSLAVEMENT OF AFRICAN BRITISH SUBJECTS IS INDEED AN AFFRONT TO OUR NATIONAL DIGNITY AND THE LAW OF NATIONS. UPON LEARNING OF IT, I DIRECTED LORD ROTHSAY TO DEMAND THEIR RELEASE.
BUT IF WE STAND ON THE GROUND OF INTERNATIONAL LAW, WE MUST EXPECT THE FRENCH TO DEMAND SATISFACTION FOR CAPTAIN OWEN'S SEIZURE OF THE NEIRSÉE, WHICH APPARENTLY HAD A FRENCH FLAG.
WE CAN PREEMPT FRENCH RECLAMATIONS BY ASSURING THEM THAT OWEN'S CONDUCT WILL BE STRICTLY INVESTIGATED.
FIRST SECRETARY CROKER, WOULD YOU HAVE THE GOODNESS TO ASK CAPTAIN OWEN TO EXPLAIN HIS ACTIONS?
YES MY LORD, BUT MAY I REMARK THAT THIS INCIDENT HIGHLIGHTS YET AGAIN THE DIFFICULTIES RAISED BY THE OBSTINATE REFUSAL OF THE FRENCH AND AMERICANS TO AGREE TO A RECIPROCAL RIGHT OF SEARCH.
UNTIL SUCH TIME AS WE HAVE SECURED THAT FACILITY, WE MUST EXPECT INCIDENTS SUCH AS THIS TO RECUR.
I AGREE! I HAVE WORKED TIRELESSLY TO INDUCE THE FRENCH TO COOPERATE WITH US.
THE NEIRSÉE INCIDENT UNDERLINES THE NEED TO REDOUBLE OUR EFFORTS.
GENTLEMEN, THIS HAS BEEN A FRUITFUL MEETING. I WILL WRITE TO ROTHSAY IN CONFORMITY WITH WHAT WE HAVE DECIDED.

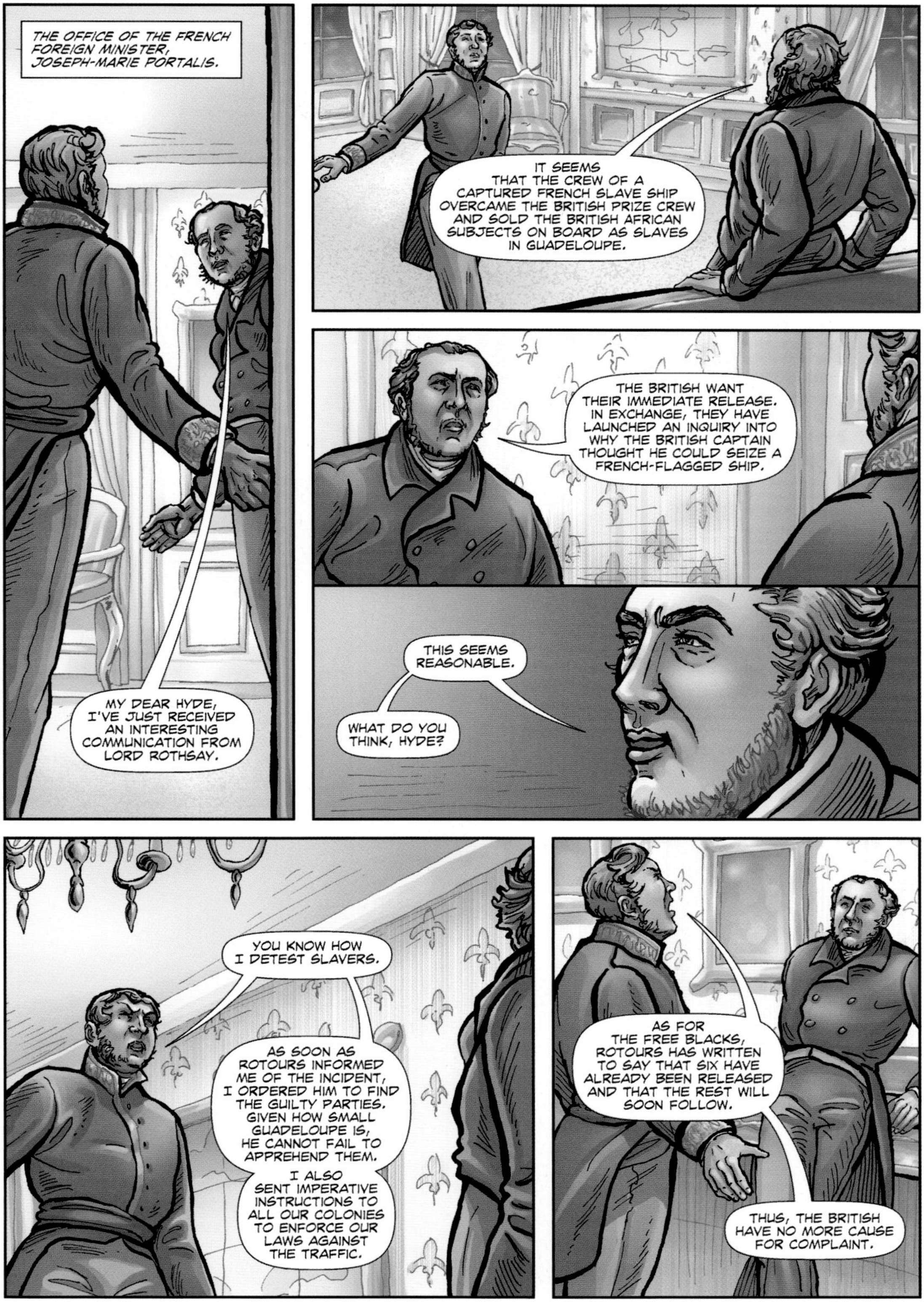
THE OFFICE OF THE FRENCH FOREIGN MINISTER, JOSEPH-MARIE PORTALIS.
MY DEAR HYDE, I'VE JUST RECEIVED AN INTERESTING COMMUNICATION FROM LORD ROTHSAY.
IT SEEMS THAT THE CREW OF A CAPTURED FRENCH SLAVE SHIP OVERCAME THE BRITISH PRIZE CREW AND SOLD THE BRITISH AFRICAN SUBJECTS ON BOARD AS SLAVES IN GUADELOUPE.
THE BRITISH WANT THEIR IMMEDIATE RELEASE. IN EXCHANGE, THEY HAVE LAUNCHED AN INQUIRY INTO WHY THE BRITISH CAPTAIN THOUGHT HE COULD SEIZE A FRENCH-FLAGGED SHIP.
THIS SEEMS REASONABLE.
WHAT DO YOU THINK, HYDE?
YOU KNOW HOW I DETEST SLAVERS.
AS SOON AS ROTOURS INFORMED ME OF THE INCIDENT, I ORDERED HIM TO FIND THE GUILTY PARTIES. GIVEN HOW SMALL GUADELOUPE IS, HE CANNOT FAIL TO APPREHEND THEM.
I ALSO SENT IMPERATIVE INSTRUCTIONS TO ALL OUR COLONIES TO ENFORCE OUR LAWS AGAINST THE TRAFFIC.
AS FOR THE FREE BLACKS, ROTOURS HAS WRITTEN TO SAY THAT SIX HAVE ALREADY BEEN RELEASED AND THAT THE REST WILL SOON FOLLOW.
THUS, THE BRITISH HAVE NO MORE CAUSE FOR COMPLAINT.

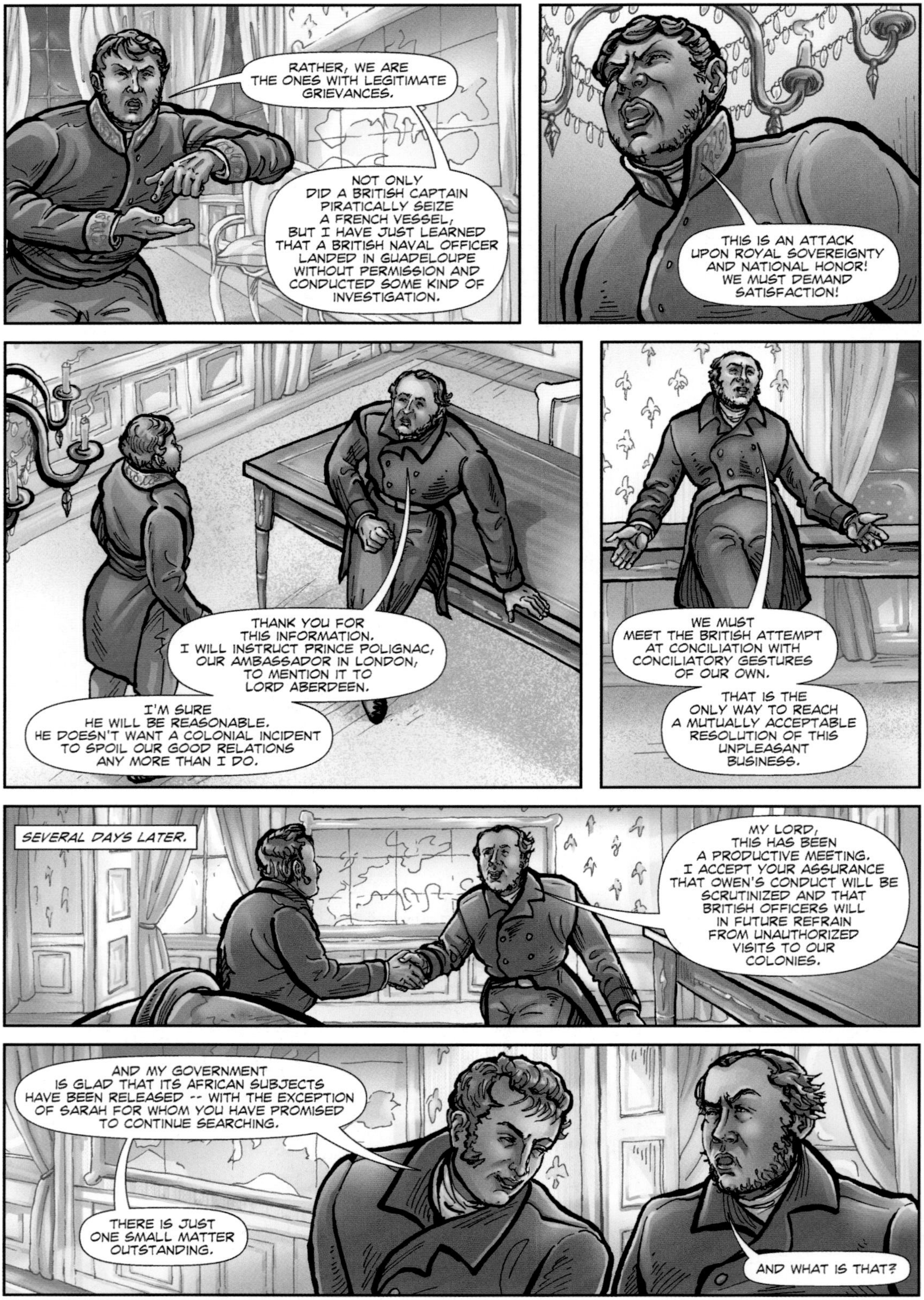
RATHER, WE ARE THE ONES WITH LEGITIMATE GRIEVANCES.
NOT ONLY DID A BRITISH CAPTAIN PIRATICALLY SEIZE A FRENCH VESSEL, BUT I HAVE JUST LEARNED THAT A BRITISH NAVAL OFFICER LANDED IN GUADELOUPE WITHOUT PERMISSION AND CONDUCTED SOME KIND OF INVESTIGATION.
THIS IS AN ATTACK UPON ROYAL SOVEREIGNTY AND NATIONAL HONOR! WE MUST DEMAND SATISFACTION!
THANK YOU FOR THIS INFORMATION. I WILL INSTRUCT PRINCE POLIGNAC, OUR AMBASSADOR IN LONDON, TO MENTION IT TO LORD ABERDEEN.
I'M SURE HE WILL BE REASONABLE. HE DOESN'T WANT A COLONIAL INCIDENT TO SPOIL OUR GOOD RELATIONS ANY MORE THAN I DO.
WE MUST MEET THE BRITISH ATTEMPT AT CONCILIATION WITH CONCILIATORY GESTURES OF OUR OWN.
THAT IS THE ONLY WAY TO REACH A MUTUALLY ACCEPTABLE RESOLUTION OF THIS UNPLEASANT BUSINESS.
SEVERAL DAYS LATER.
MY LORD, THIS HAS BEEN A PRODUCTIVE MEETING. I ACCEPT YOUR ASSURANCE THAT OWEN'S CONDUCT WILL BE SCRUTINIZED AND THAT BRITISH OFFICERS WILL IN FUTURE REFRAIN FROM UNAUTHORIZED VISITS TO OUR COLONIES.
AND MY GOVERNMENT IS GLAD THAT ITS AFRICAN SUBJECTS HAVE BEEN RELEASED -- WITH THE EXCEPTION OF SARAH FOR WHOM YOU HAVE PROMISED TO CONTINUE SEARCHING.
THERE IS JUST ONE SMALL MATTER OUTSTANDING.
AND WHAT IS THAT?

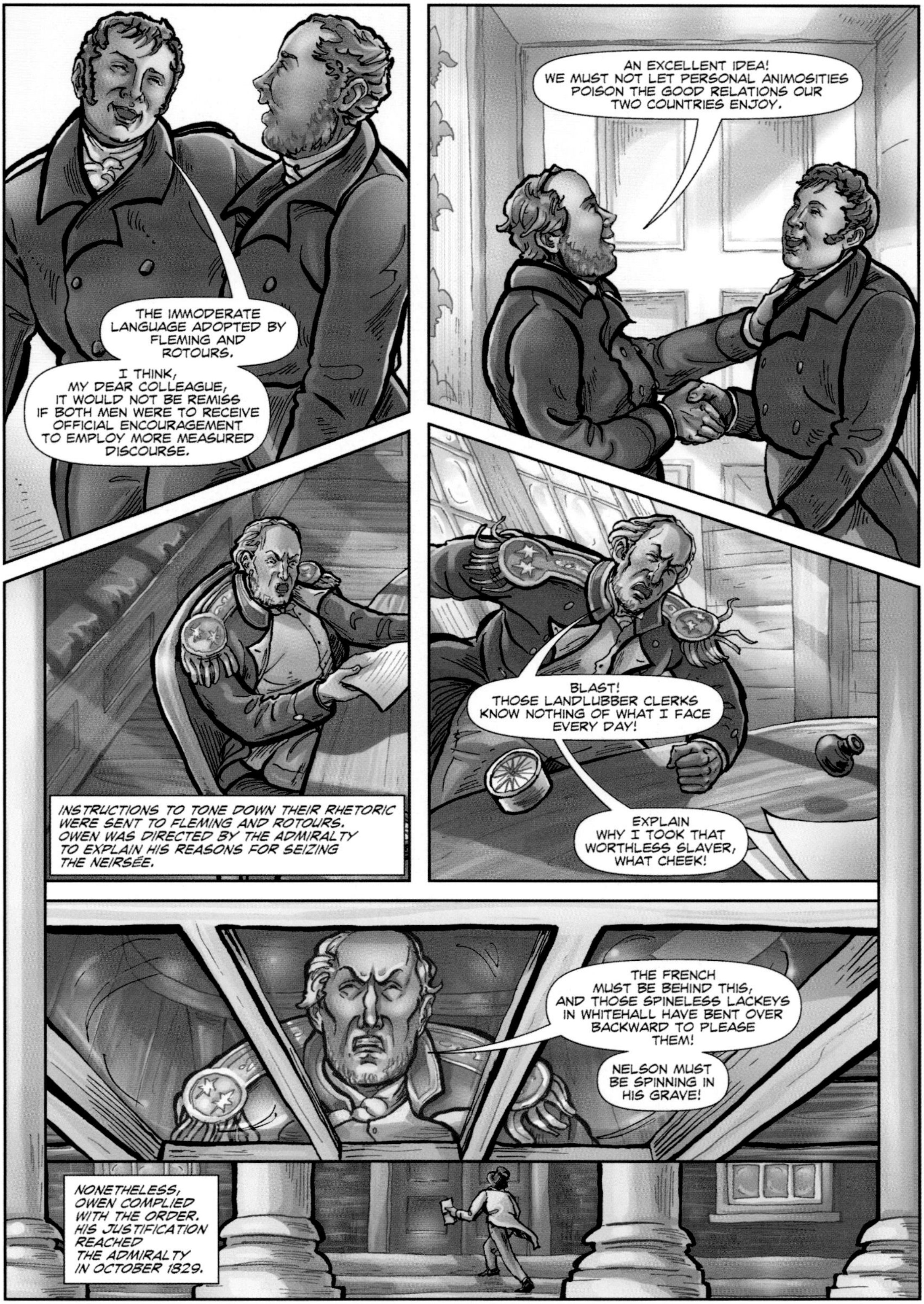
THE IMMODERATE LANGUAGE ADOPTED BY FLEMING AND ROTOURS.
I THINK, MY DEAR COLLEAGUE, IT WOULD NOT BE REMISS IF BOTH MEN WERE TO RECEIVE OFFICIAL ENCOURAGEMENT TO EMPLOY MORE MEASURED DISCOURSE.
AN EXCELLENT IDEA! WE MUST NOT LET PERSONAL ANIMOSITIES POISON THE GOOD RELATIONS OUR TWO COUNTRIES ENJOY.
INSTRUCTIONS TO TONE DOWN THEIR RHETORIC WERE SENT TO FLEMING AND ROTOURS. OWEN WAS DIRECTED BY THE ADMIRALTY TO EXPLAIN HIS REASONS FOR SEIZING THE NEIRSÉE.
BLAST! THOSE LANDLUBBER CLERKS KNOW NOTHING OF WHAT I FACE EVERY DAY!
EXPLAIN WHY I TOOK THAT WORTHLESS SLAVER, WHAT CHEEK!
THE FRENCH MUST BE BEHIND THIS, AND THOSE SPINELESS LACKEYS IN WHITEHALL HAVE BENT OVER BACKWARD TO PLEASE THEM!
NELSON MUST BE SPINNING IN HIS GRAVE!
NONETHELESS, OWEN COMPLIED WITH THE ORDER. HIS JUSTIFICATION REACHED THE ADMIRALTY IN OCTOBER 1829.

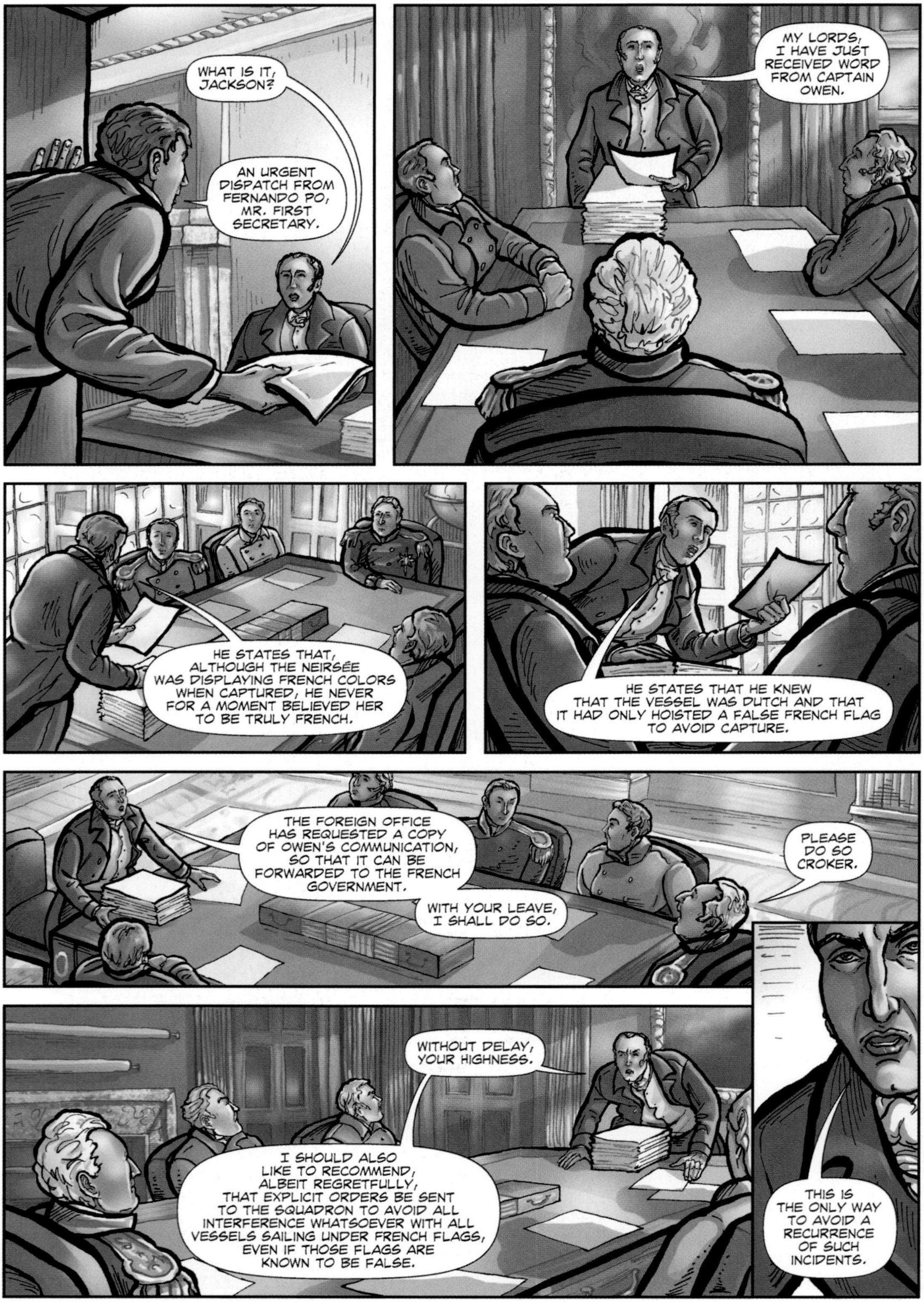
WHAT IS IT, JACKSON?
AN URGENT DISPATCH FROM FERNANDO PO, MR. FIRST SECRETARY.
MY LORDS, I HAVE JUST RECEIVED WORD FROM CAPTAIN OWEN.
HE STATES THAT, ALTHOUGH THE NEIRSÉE WAS DISPLAYING FRENCH COLORS WHEN CAPTURED, HE NEVER FOR A MOMENT BELIEVED HER TO BE TRULY FRENCH.
HE STATES THAT HE KNEW THAT THE VESSEL WAS DUTCH AND THAT IT HAD ONLY HOISTED A FALSE FRENCH FLAG TO AVOID CAPTURE.
THE FOREIGN OFFICE HAS REQUESTED A COPY OF OWEN'S COMMUNICATION, SO THAT IT CAN BE FORWARDED TO THE FRENCH GOVERNMENT.
WITH YOUR LEAVE, I SHALL DO SO.
PLEASE DO SO CROKER.
WITHOUT DELAY, YOUR HIGHNESS.
I SHOULD ALSO LIKE TO RECOMMEND, ALBEIT REGRETFULLY, THAT EXPLICIT ORDERS BE SENT TO THE SQUADRON TO AVOID ALL INTERFERENCE WHATSOEVER WITH ALL VESSELS SAILING UNDER FRENCH FLAGS, EVEN IF THOSE FLAGS ARE KNOWN TO BE FALSE.
THIS IS THE ONLY WAY TO AVOID A RECURRENCE OF SUCH INCIDENTS.

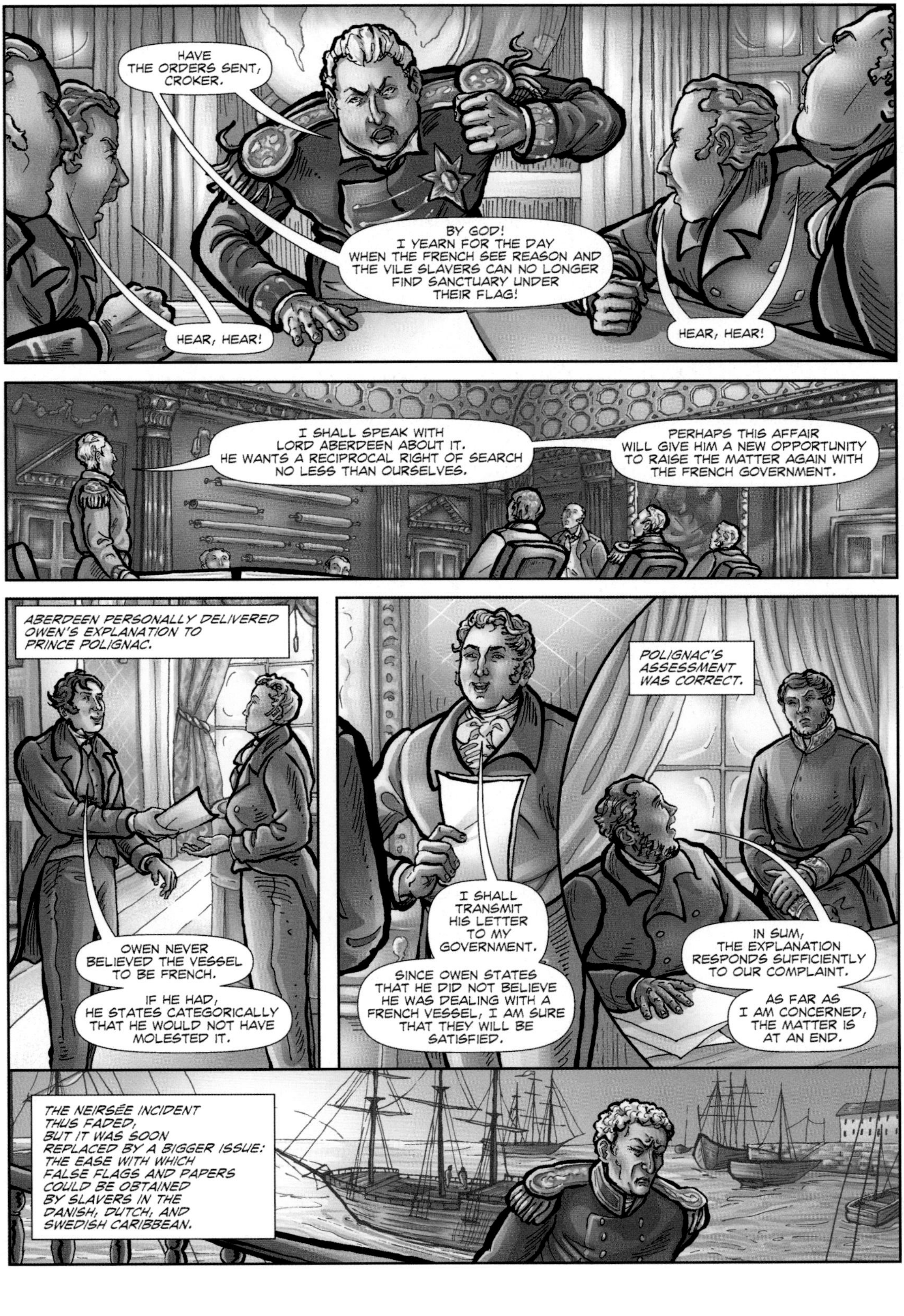
HAVE THE ORDERS SENT, CROKER.
BY GOD! I YEARN FOR THE DAY WHEN THE FRENCH SEE REASON AND THE VILE SLAVERS CAN NO LONGER FIND SANCTUARY UNDER THEIR FLAG!
HEAR, HEAR!
HEAR, HEAR!
I SHALL SPEAK WITH LORD ABERDEEN ABOUT IT. HE WANTS A RECIPROCAL RIGHT OF SEARCH NO LESS THAN OURSELVES.
PERHAPS THIS AFFAIR WILL GIVE HIM A NEW OPPORTUNITY TO RAISE THE MATTER AGAIN WITH THE FRENCH GOVERNMENT.
ABERDEEN PERSONALLY DELIVERED OWEN'S EXPLANATION TO PRINCE POLIGNAC.
OWEN NEVER BELIEVED THE VESSEL TO BE FRENCH.
IF HE HAD, HE STATES CATEGORICALLY THAT HE WOULD NOT HAVE MOLESTED IT.
I SHALL TRANSMIT HIS LETTER TO MY GOVERNMENT.
SINCE OWEN STATES THAT HE DID NOT BELIEVE HE WAS DEALING WITH A FRENCH VESSEL, I AM SURE THAT THEY WILL BE SATISFIED.
POLIGNAC'S ASSESSMENT WAS CORRECT.
IN SUM, THE EXPLANATION RESPONDS SUFFICIENTLY TO OUR COMPLAINT.
AS FAR AS I AM CONCERNED, THE MATTER IS AT AN END.
THE NEIRSÉE INCIDENT THUS FADED, BUT IT WAS SOON REPLACED BY A BIGGER ISSUE: THE EASE WITH WHICH FALSE FLAGS AND PAPERS COULD BE OBTAINED BY SLAVERS IN THE DANISH, DUTCH, AND SWEDISH CARIBBEAN.

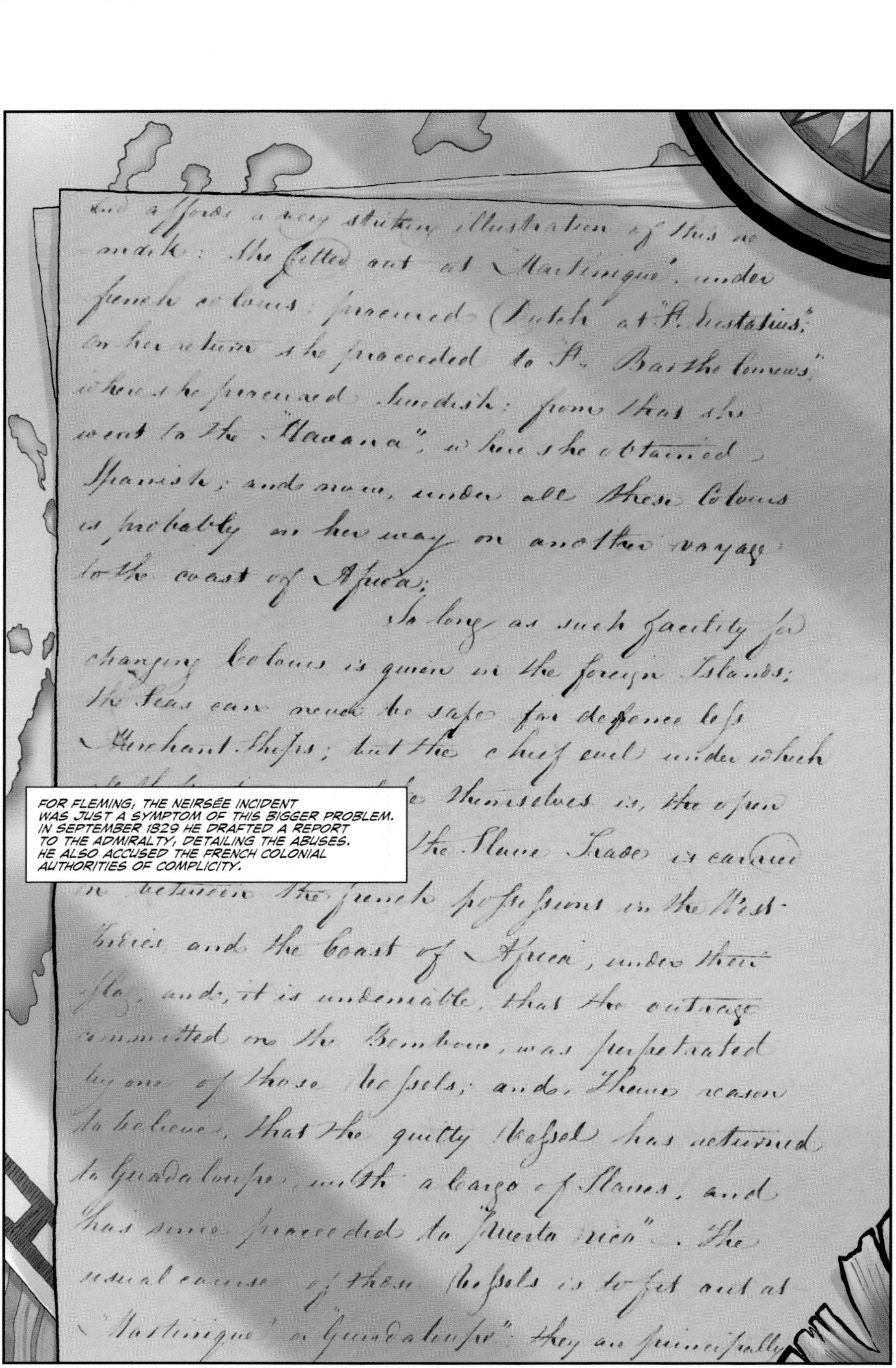
FOR FLEMING, THE NEIRSÉE INCIDENT WAS JUST A SYMPTOM OF THIS BIGGER PROBLEM. IN SEPTEMBER 1829 HE DRAFTED A REPORT TO THE ADMIRALTY, DETAILING THE ABUSES. HE ALSO ACCUSED THE FRENCH COLONIAL AUTHORITIES OF COMPLICITY.
and affords a very striking illustration of this re-
mark: She fitted out at "Martinique", under
french colours: procured Dutch at "St. Eustatius";
on her return she proceeded to "St. Bartholomews",
where she procured Swedish: from that she
went to the "Havana", where she obtained
Spanish; and now, under all these Colours
is probably on her way on another voyage
to the coast of Africa;
So long as such facility for
changing Colours is given in the foreign Islands;
the Seas can never be safe for defenceless
Merchant Ships; but the chief evil under which
themselves is, the open
the Slave Trade is carried
on between the french possessions in the West
Indies, and the Coast of Africa, under their
flag; and, it is undeniable, that the outrage
committed on the Bembow, was perpetrated
by one of those vessels; and I have reason
to believe, that the guilty vessel has returned
to Guadaloupe, with a cargo of Slaves, and
has since proceeded to "Puerto rico". The
usual course of these vessels is to fit out at
"Martinique" or "Guadaloupe": they are principally

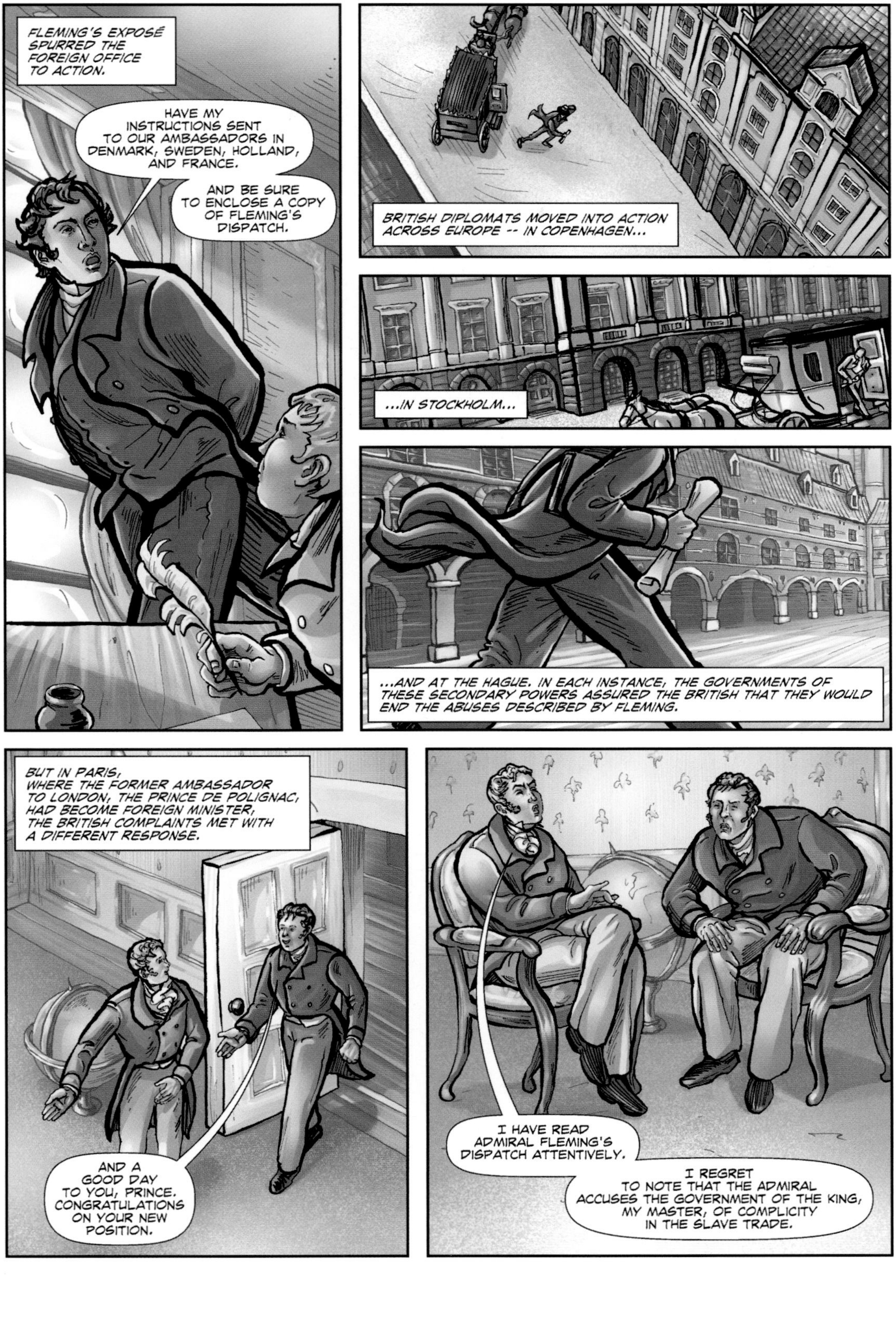
FLEMING'S EXPOSÉ SPURRED THE FOREIGN OFFICE TO ACTION.
HAVE MY INSTRUCTIONS SENT TO OUR AMBASSADORS IN DENMARK, SWEDEN, HOLLAND, AND FRANCE.
AND BE SURE TO ENCLOSE A COPY OF FLEMING'S DISPATCH.
BRITISH DIPLOMATS MOVED INTO ACTION ACROSS EUROPE -- IN COPENHAGEN...
...IN STOCKHOLM...
...AND AT THE HAGUE. IN EACH INSTANCE, THE GOVERNMENTS OF THESE SECONDARY POWERS ASSURED THE BRITISH THAT THEY WOULD END THE ABUSES DESCRIBED BY FLEMING.
BUT IN PARIS, WHERE THE FORMER AMBASSADOR TO LONDON, THE PRINCE DE POLIGNAC, HAD BECOME FOREIGN MINISTER, THE BRITISH COMPLAINTS MET WITH A DIFFERENT RESPONSE.
AND A GOOD DAY TO YOU, PRINCE. CONGRATULATIONS ON YOUR NEW POSITION.
I HAVE READ ADMIRAL FLEMING'S DISPATCH ATTENTIVELY.
I REGRET TO NOTE THAT THE ADMIRAL ACCUSES THE GOVERNMENT OF THE KING, MY MASTER, OF COMPLICITY IN THE SLAVE TRADE.

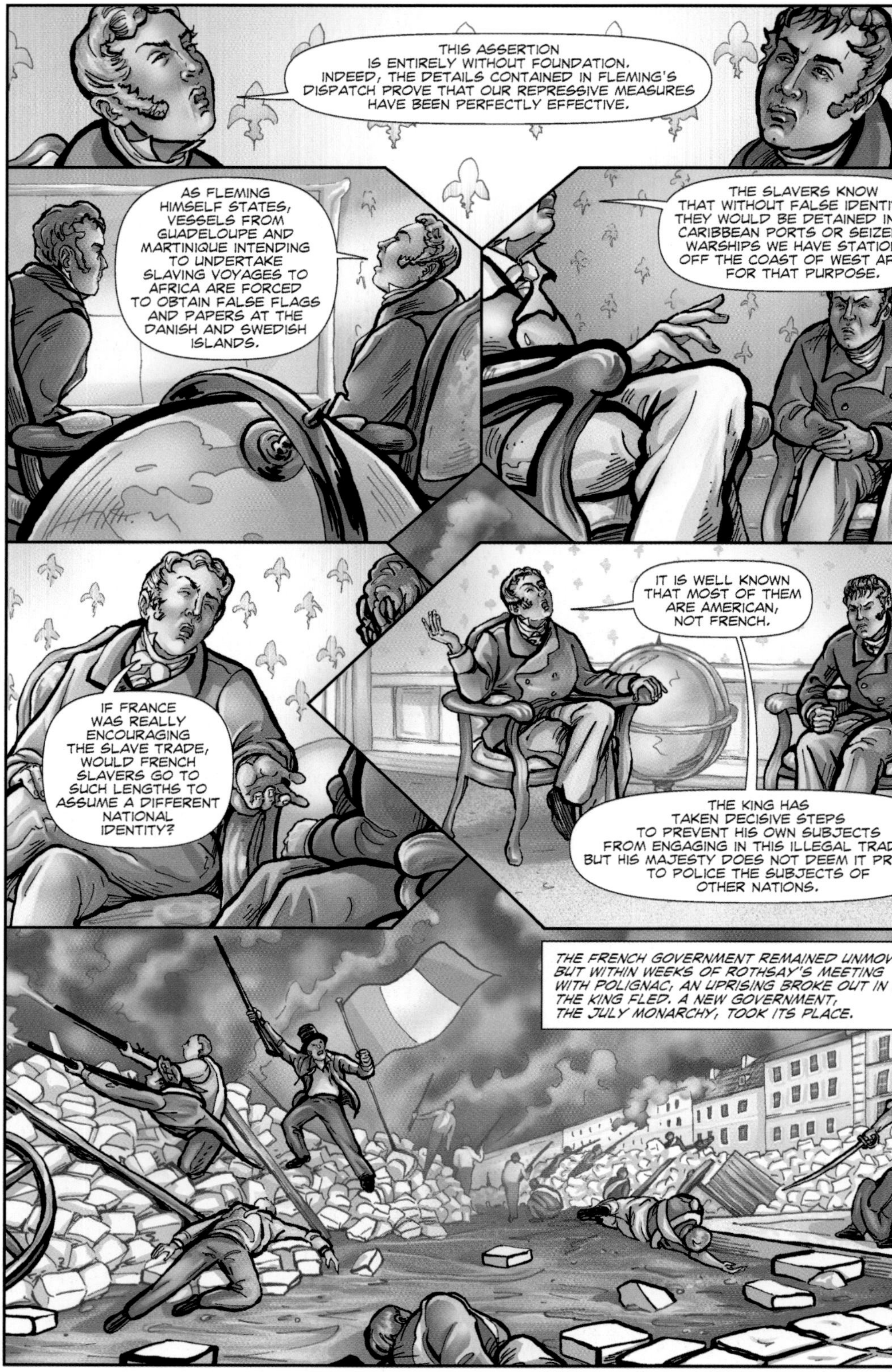
THIS ASSERTION IS ENTIRELY WITHOUT FOUNDATION. INDEED, THE DETAILS CONTAINED IN FLEMING'S DISPATCH PROVE THAT OUR REPRESSIVE MEASURES HAVE BEEN PERFECTLY EFFECTIVE.
AS FLEMING HIMSELF STATES, VESSELS FROM GUADELOUPE AND MARTINIQUE INTENDING TO UNDERTAKE SLAVING VOYAGES TO AFRICA ARE FORCED TO OBTAIN FALSE FLAGS AND PAPERS AT THE DANISH AND SWEDISH ISLANDS.
THE SLAVERS KNOW THAT WITHOUT FALSE IDENTITIES, THEY WOULD BE DETAINED IN OUR CARIBBEAN PORTS OR SEIZED BY WARSHIPS WE HAVE STATIONED OFF THE COAST OF WEST AFRICA FOR THAT PURPOSE.
IF FRANCE WAS REALLY ENCOURAGING THE SLAVE TRADE, WOULD FRENCH SLAVERS GO TO SUCH LENGTHS TO ASSUME A DIFFERENT NATIONAL IDENTITY?
IT IS WELL KNOWN THAT MOST OF THEM ARE AMERICAN, NOT FRENCH.
THE KING HAS TAKEN DECISIVE STEPS TO PREVENT HIS OWN SUBJECTS FROM ENGAGING IN THIS ILLEGAL TRADE. BUT HIS MAJESTY DOES NOT DEEM IT PROPER TO POLICE THE SUBJECTS OF OTHER NATIONS.
THE FRENCH GOVERNMENT REMAINED UNMOVED. BUT WITHIN WEEKS OF ROTHSAY'S MEETING WITH POLIGNAC, AN UPRISING BROKE OUT IN PARIS. THE KING FLED. A NEW GOVERNMENT, THE JULY MONARCHY, TOOK ITS PLACE.

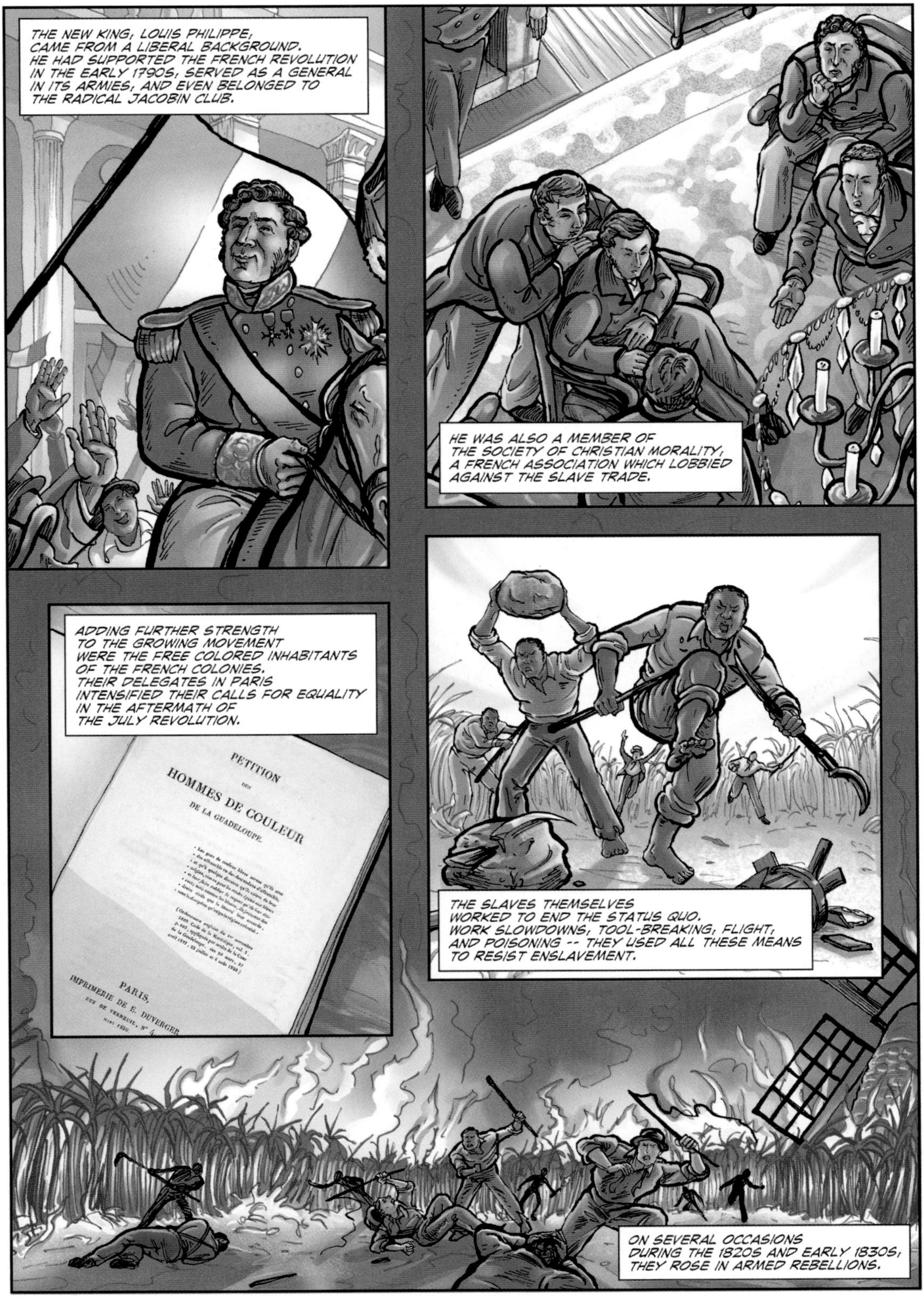
THE NEW KING, LOUIS PHILIPPE, CAME FROM A LIBERAL BACKGROUND. HE HAD SUPPORTED THE FRENCH REVOLUTION IN THE EARLY 1790S, SERVED AS A GENERAL IN ITS ARMIES, AND EVEN BELONGED TO THE RADICAL JACOBIN CLUB.
HE WAS ALSO A MEMBER OF THE SOCIETY OF CHRISTIAN MORALITY, A FRENCH ASSOCIATION WHICH LOBBIED AGAINST THE SLAVE TRADE.
ADDING FURTHER STRENGTH TO THE GROWING MOVEMENT WERE THE FREE COLORED INHABITANTS OF THE FRENCH COLONIES. THEIR DELEGATES IN PARIS INTENSIFIED THEIR CALLS FOR EQUALITY IN THE AFTERMATH OF THE JULY REVOLUTION.
PETITION
HOMMES DE COULEUR
DE LA GUADELOUPE.
PARIS,
IMPRIMERIE DE E. DUVERGER
THE SLAVES THEMSELVES WORKED TO END THE STATUS QUO. WORK SLOWDOWNS, TOOL-BREAKING, FLIGHT, AND POISONING -- THEY USED ALL THESE MEANS TO RESIST ENSLAVEMENT.
ON SEVERAL OCCASIONS DURING THE 1820S AND EARLY 1830S, THEY ROSE IN ARMED REBELLIONS.

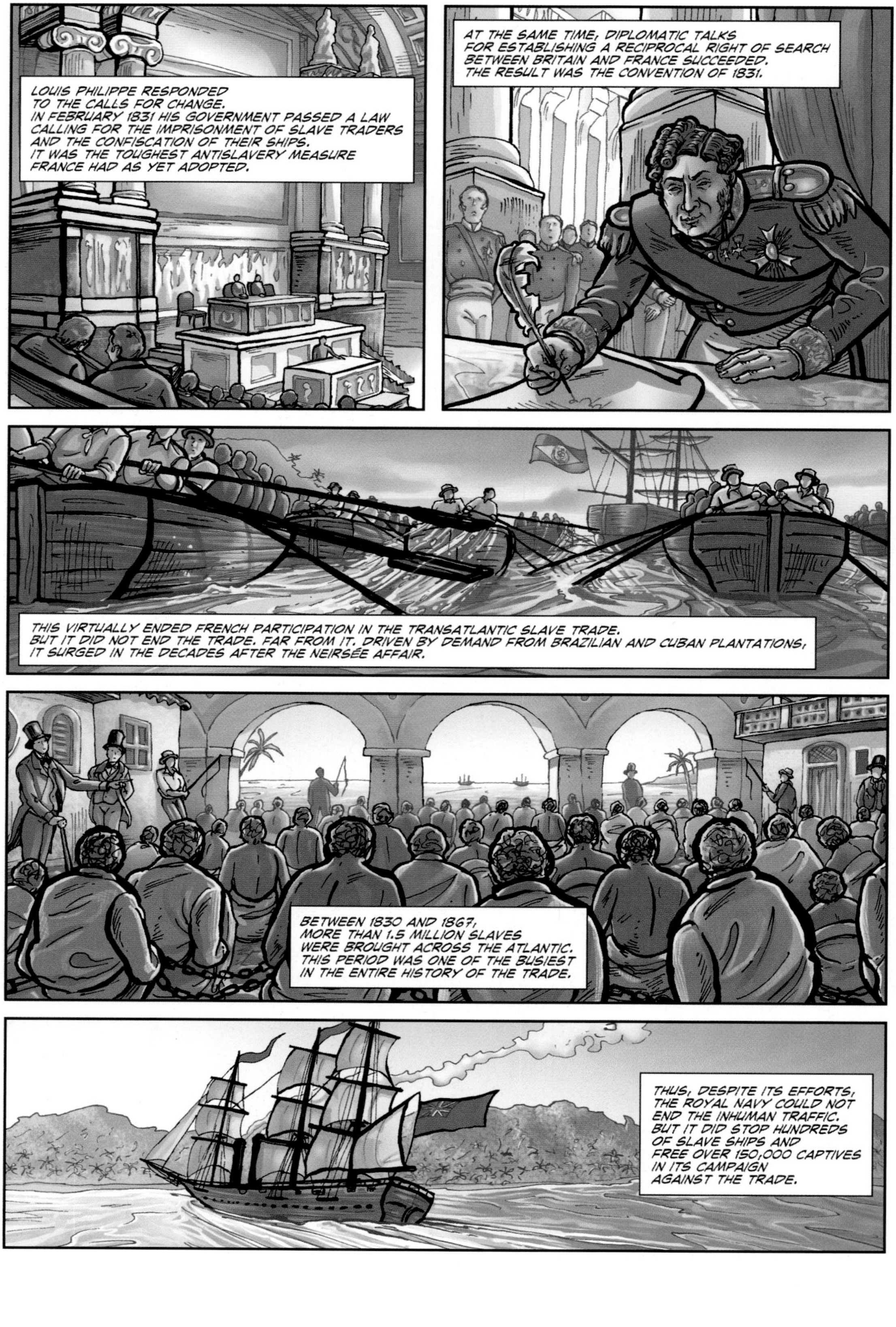
LOUIS PHILIPPE RESPONDED TO THE CALLS FOR CHANGE. IN FEBRUARY 1831 HIS GOVERNMENT PASSED A LAW CALLING FOR THE IMPRISONMENT OF SLAVE TRADERS AND THE CONFISCATION OF THEIR SHIPS. IT WAS THE TOUGHEST ANTISLAVERY MEASURE FRANCE HAD AS YET ADOPTED.
AT THE SAME TIME, DIPLOMATIC TALKS FOR ESTABLISHING A RECIPROCAL RIGHT OF SEARCH BETWEEN BRITAIN AND FRANCE SUCCEEDED. THE RESULT WAS THE CONVENTION OF 1831.
THIS VIRTUALLY ENDED FRENCH PARTICIPATION IN THE TRANSATLANTIC SLAVE TRADE. BUT IT DID NOT END THE TRADE. FAR FROM IT. DRIVEN BY DEMAND FROM BRAZILIAN AND CUBAN PLANTATIONS, IT SURGED IN THE DECADES AFTER THE NEIRSÉE AFFAIR.
BETWEEN 1830 AND 1867, MORE THAN 1.5 MILLION SLAVES WERE BROUGHT ACROSS THE ATLANTIC. THIS PERIOD WAS ONE OF THE BUSIEST IN THE ENTIRE HISTORY OF THE TRADE.
THUS, DESPITE ITS EFFORTS, THE ROYAL NAVY COULD NOT END THE INHUMAN TRAFFIC. BUT IT DID STOP HUNDREDS OF SLAVE SHIPS AND FREE OVER 150,000 CAPTIVES IN ITS CAMPAIGN AGAINST THE TRADE.

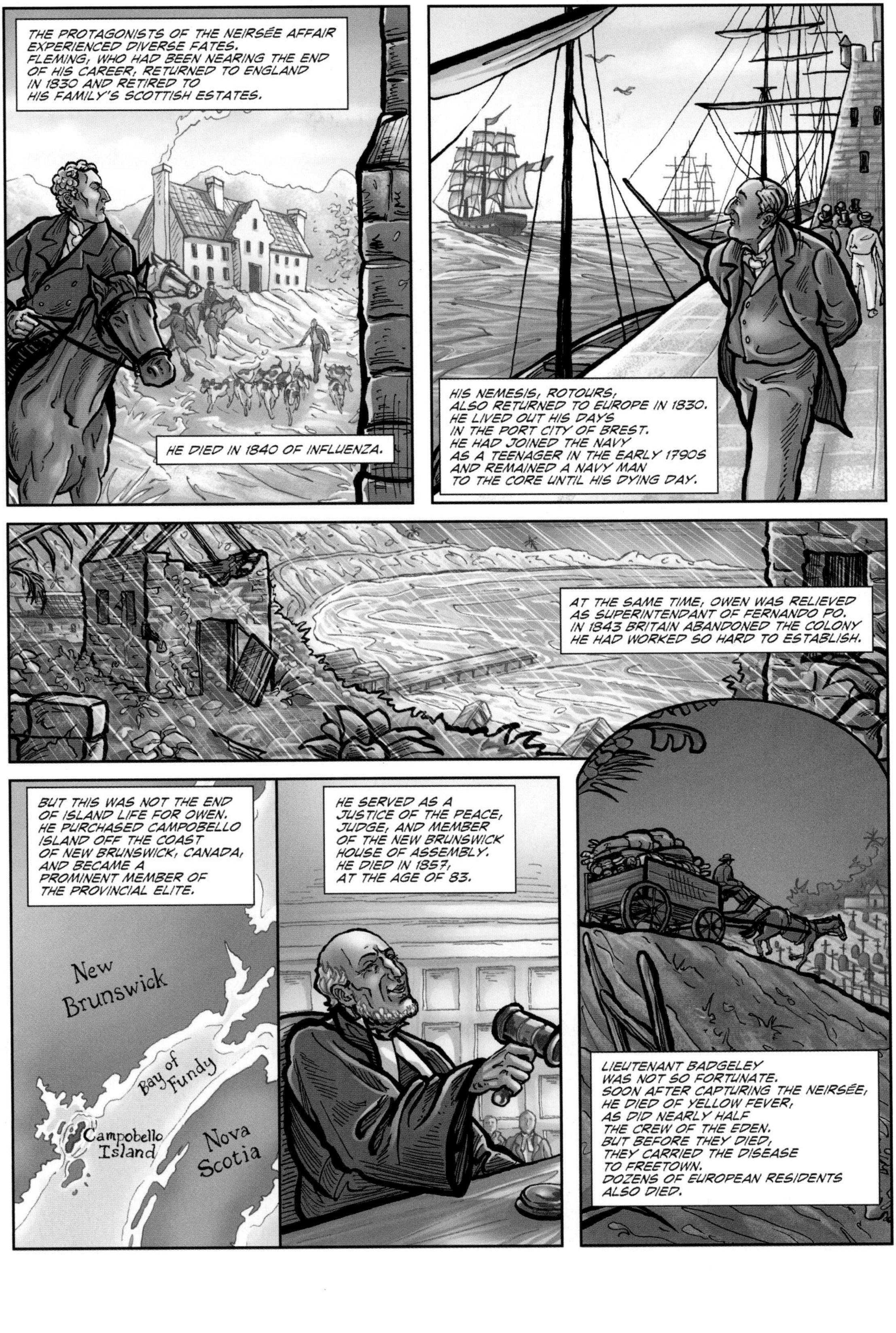
THE PROTAGONISTS OF THE NEIRSÉE AFFAIR EXPERIENCED DIVERSE FATES. FLEMING, WHO HAD BEEN NEARING THE END OF HIS CAREER, RETURNED TO ENGLAND IN 1830 AND RETIRED TO HIS FAMILY'S SCOTTISH ESTATES.
HE DIED IN 1840 OF INFLUENZA.
HIS NEMESIS, ROTOURS, ALSO RETURNED TO EUROPE IN 1830. HE LIVED OUT HIS DAYS IN THE PORT CITY OF BREST. HE HAD JOINED THE NAVY AS A TEENAGER IN THE EARLY 1790S AND REMAINED A NAVY MAN TO THE CORE UNTIL HIS DYING DAY.
AT THE SAME TIME, OWEN WAS RELIEVED AS SUPERINTENDANT OF FERNANDO PO. IN 1843 BRITAIN ABANDONED THE COLONY HE HAD WORKED SO HARD TO ESTABLISH.
BUT THIS WAS NOT THE END OF ISLAND LIFE FOR OWEN. HE PURCHASED CAMPOBELLO ISLAND OFF THE COAST OF NEW BRUNSWICK, CANADA, AND BECAME A PROMINENT MEMBER OF THE PROVINCIAL ELITE.
New Brunswick
Bay of Fundy
Campobello Island
Nova Scotia
HE SERVED AS A JUSTICE OF THE PEACE, JUDGE, AND MEMBER OF THE NEW BRUNSWICK HOUSE OF ASSEMBLY. HE DIED IN 1857, AT THE AGE OF 83.
LIEUTENANT BADGELEY WAS NOT SO FORTUNATE. SOON AFTER CAPTURING THE NEIRSÉE, HE DIED OF YELLOW FEVER, AS DID NEARLY HALF THE CREW OF THE EDEN. BUT BEFORE THEY DIED, THEY CARRIED THE DISEASE TO FREETOWN. DOZENS OF EUROPEAN RESIDENTS ALSO DIED.

CHAPTER 5

FROM HAPPENING TO HISTORY

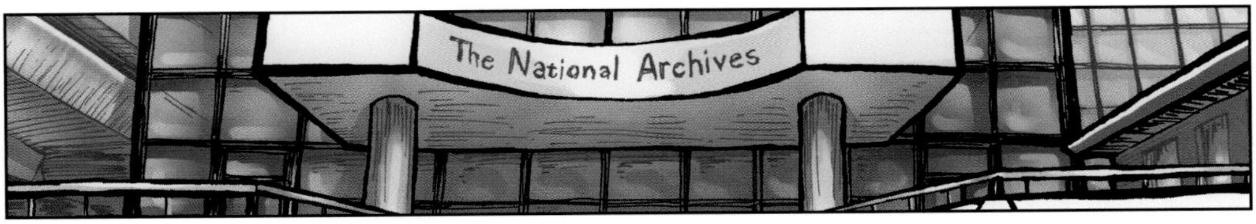
The National Archives

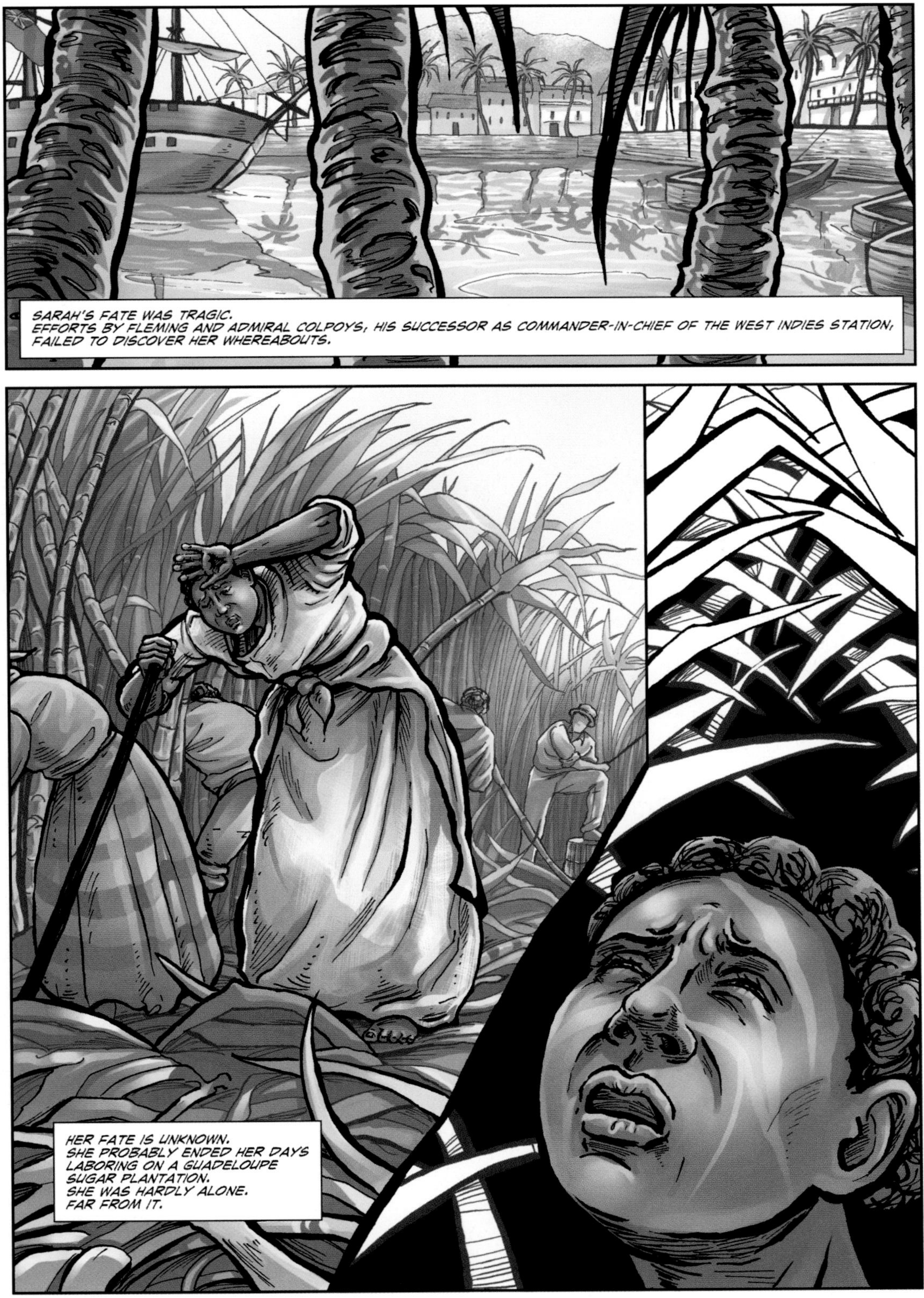
SARAH'S FATE WAS TRAGIC.
EFFORTS BY FLEMING AND ADMIRAL COLPOYS, HIS SUCCESSOR AS COMMANDER-IN-CHIEF OF THE WEST INDIES STATION, FAILED TO DISCOVER HER WHEREABOUTS.
HER FATE IS UNKNOWN.
SHE PROBABLY ENDED HER DAYS LABORING ON A GUADELOUPE SUGAR PLANTATION.
SHE WAS HARDLY ALONE.
FAR FROM IT.

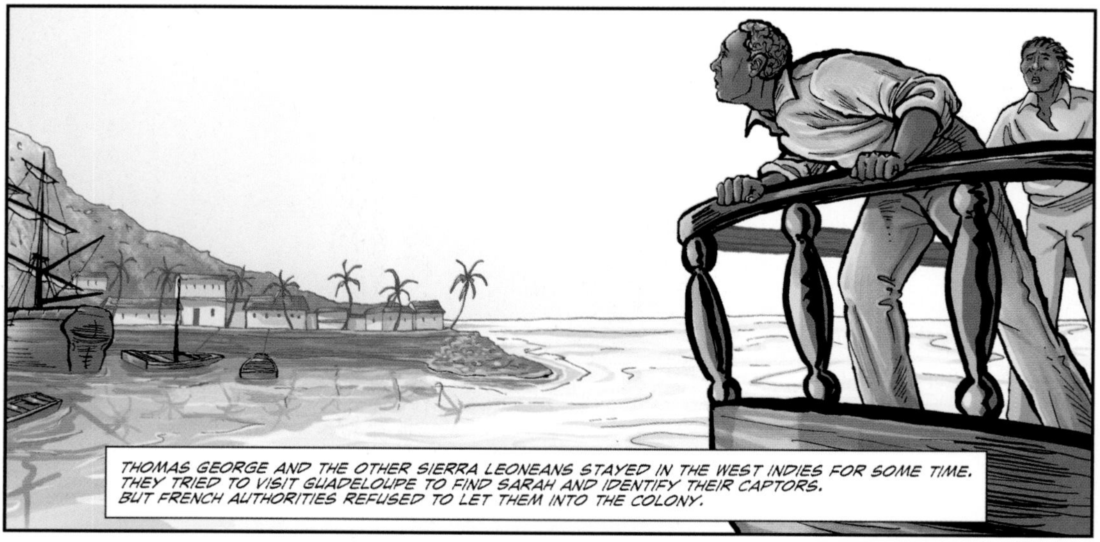
THOMAS GEORGE AND THE OTHER SIERRA LEONEANS STAYED IN THE WEST INDIES FOR SOME TIME. THEY TRIED TO VISIT GUADELOUPE TO FIND SARAH AND IDENTIFY THEIR CAPTORS. BUT FRENCH AUTHORITIES REFUSED TO LET THEM INTO THE COLONY.

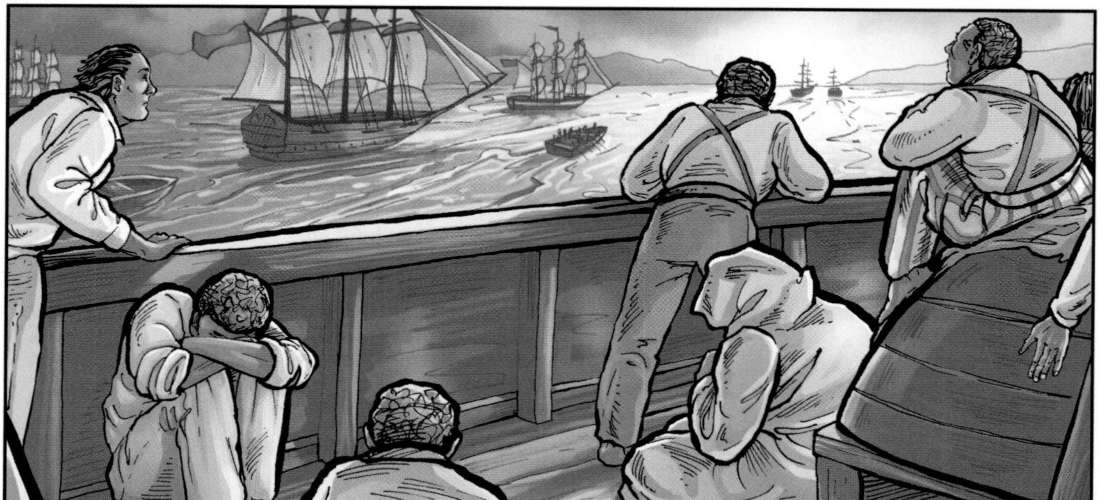
THEY EVENTUALLY GAVE UP HOPE AND TRAVELED TO ENGLAND, ABOARD FLEMING'S FLAGSHIP, WHEN HE ENDED HIS TOUR OF DUTY IN 1830.

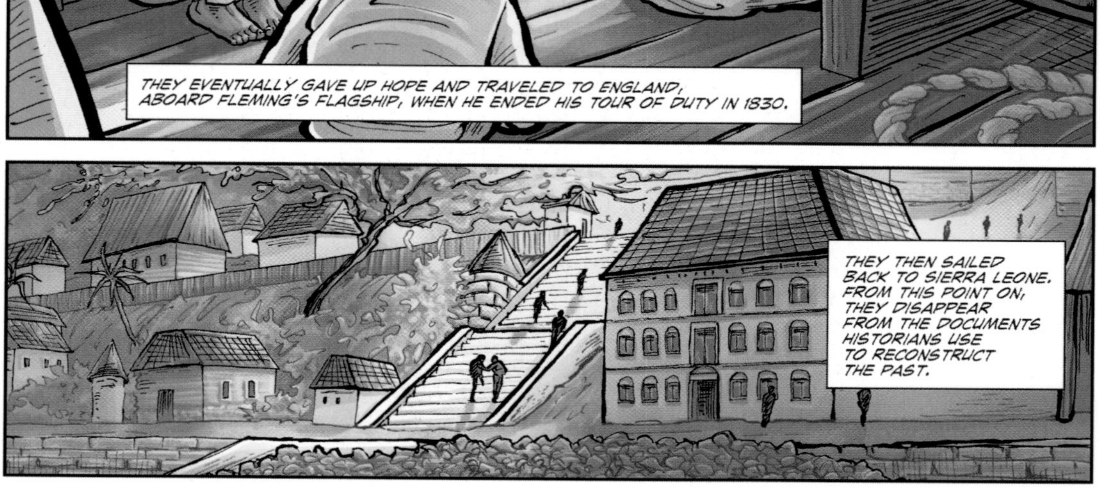
THEY THEN SAILED BACK TO SIERRA LEONE. FROM THIS POINT ON, THEY DISAPPEAR FROM THE DOCUMENTS HISTORIANS USE TO RECONSTRUCT THE PAST.

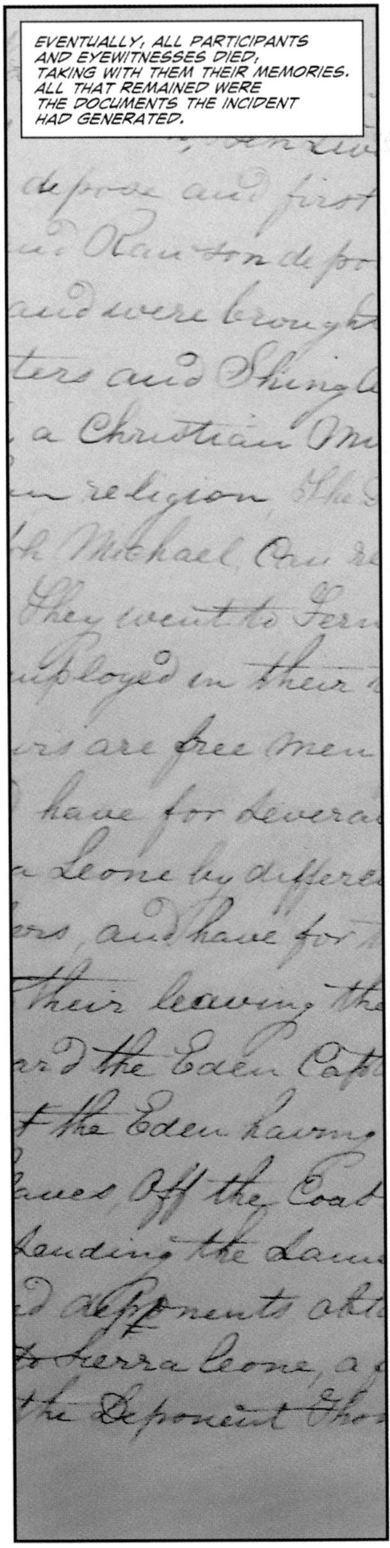
EVENTUALLY, ALL PARTICIPANTS AND EYEWITNESSES DIED, TAKING WITH THEM THEIR MEMORIES. ALL THAT REMAINED WERE THE DOCUMENTS THE INCIDENT HAD GENERATED.
depose and first
Rawson depo
and were brought
ters and Shingle
a Christian
religion
Michael
They went to
employed in their
are free men
have for several
Leone by differe
ers, and have for
their leaving the
the Eden Capt
the Eden having
Off the Coa
Landing the
Deponents
to Sierra leone, a
the Deponent

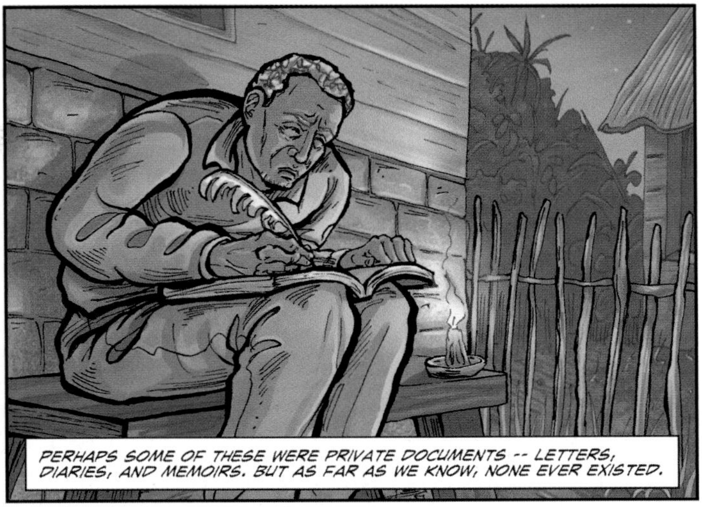
PERHAPS SOME OF THESE WERE PRIVATE DOCUMENTS -- LETTERS, DIARIES, AND MEMOIRS. BUT AS FAR AS WE KNOW, NONE EVER EXISTED.

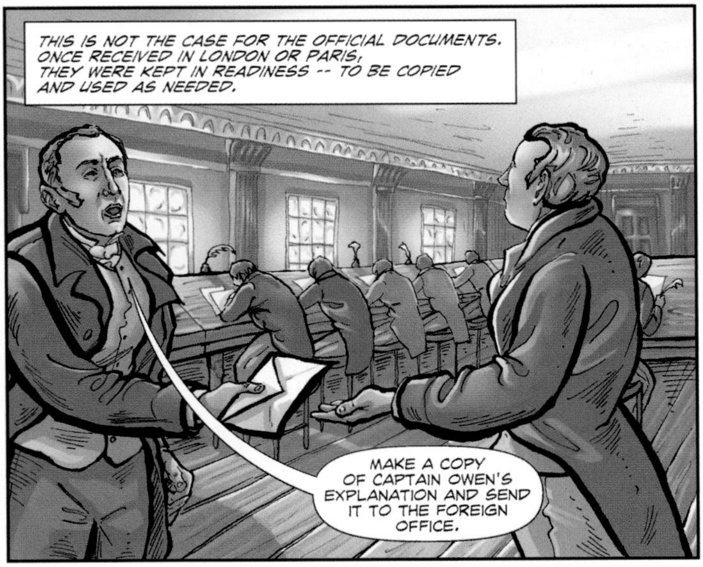
THIS IS NOT THE CASE FOR THE OFFICIAL DOCUMENTS. ONCE RECEIVED IN LONDON OR PARIS, THEY WERE KEPT IN READINESS -- TO BE COPIED AND USED AS NEEDED.
MAKE A COPY OF CAPTAIN OWEN'S EXPLANATION AND SEND IT TO THE FOREIGN OFFICE.

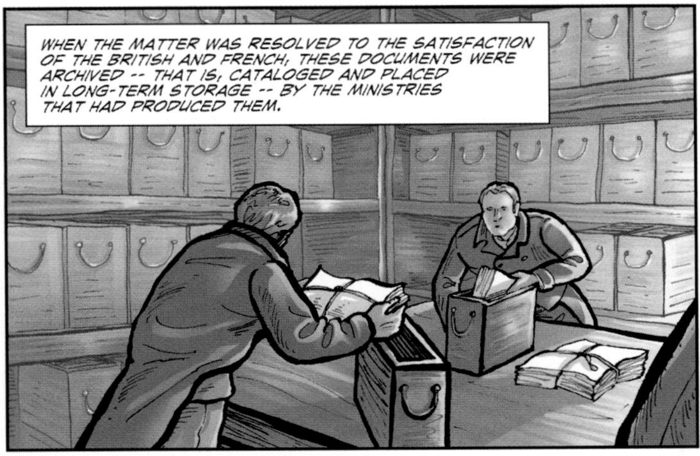
WHEN THE MATTER WAS RESOLVED TO THE SATISFACTION OF THE BRITISH AND FRENCH, THESE DOCUMENTS WERE ARCHIVED -- THAT IS, CATALOGED AND PLACED IN LONG-TERM STORAGE -- BY THE MINISTRIES THAT HAD PRODUCED THEM.

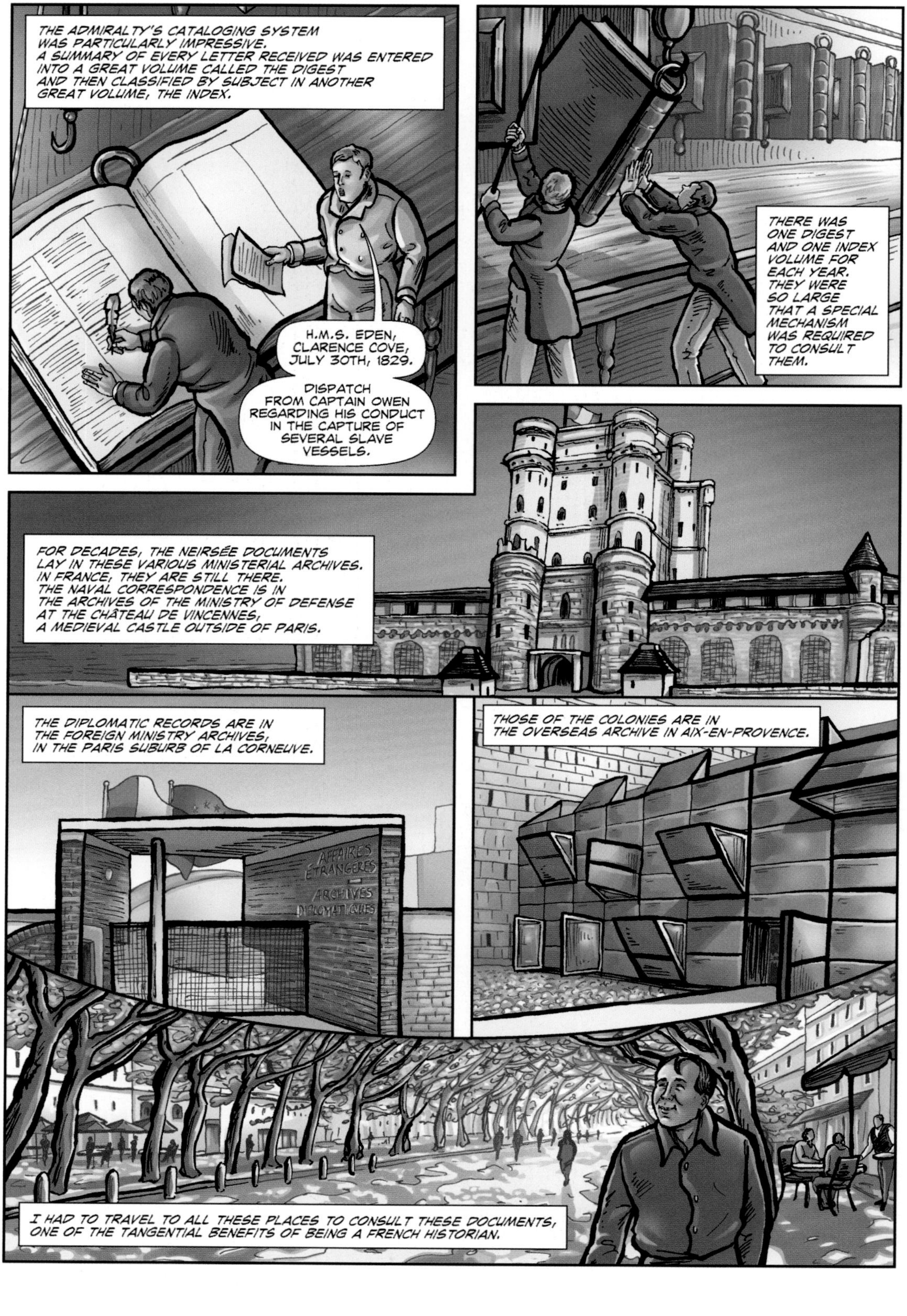
THE ADMIRALTY'S CATALOGING SYSTEM WAS PARTICULARLY IMPRESSIVE. A SUMMARY OF EVERY LETTER RECEIVED WAS ENTERED INTO A GREAT VOLUME CALLED THE DIGEST AND THEN CLASSIFIED BY SUBJECT IN ANOTHER GREAT VOLUME, THE INDEX.
H.M.S. EDEN, CLARENCE COVE, JULY 30TH, 1829.
DISPATCH FROM CAPTAIN OWEN REGARDING HIS CONDUCT IN THE CAPTURE OF SEVERAL SLAVE VESSELS.
THERE WAS ONE DIGEST AND ONE INDEX VOLUME FOR EACH YEAR. THEY WERE SO LARGE THAT A SPECIAL MECHANISM WAS REQUIRED TO CONSULT THEM.
FOR DECADES, THE NEIRSÉE DOCUMENTS LAY IN THESE VARIOUS MINISTERIAL ARCHIVES. IN FRANCE, THEY ARE STILL THERE. THE NAVAL CORRESPONDENCE IS IN THE ARCHIVES OF THE MINISTRY OF DEFENSE AT THE CHÂTEAU DE VINCENNES, A MEDIEVAL CASTLE OUTSIDE OF PARIS.
THE DIPLOMATIC RECORDS ARE IN THE FOREIGN MINISTRY ARCHIVES, IN THE PARIS SUBURB OF LA CORNEUVE.
AFFAIRES ÉTRANGÈRES
ARCHIVES DIPLOMATIQUES
THOSE OF THE COLONIES ARE IN THE OVERSEAS ARCHIVE IN AIX-EN-PROVENCE.
I HAD TO TRAVEL TO ALL THESE PLACES TO CONSULT THESE DOCUMENTS, ONE OF THE TANGENTIAL BENEFITS OF BEING A FRENCH HISTORIAN.

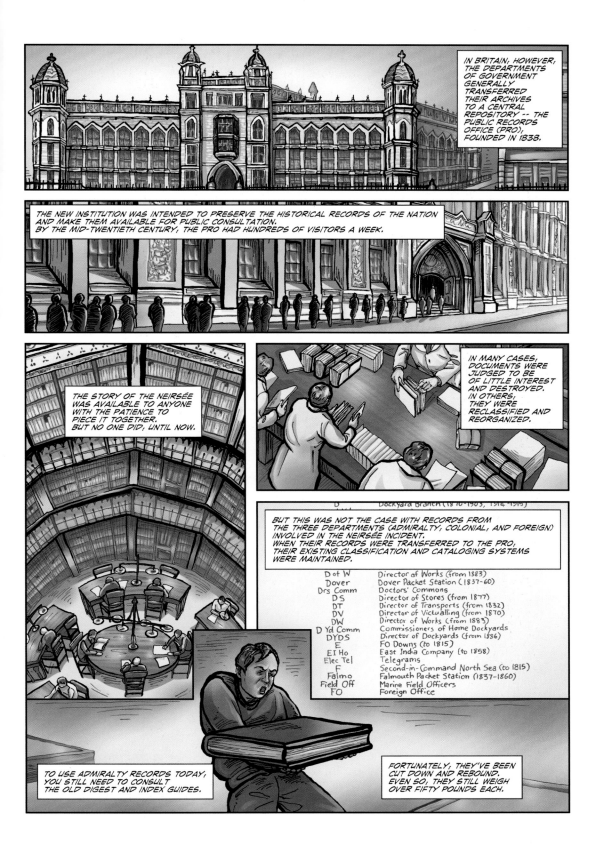

IN BRITAIN, HOWEVER, THE DEPARTMENTS OF GOVERNMENT GENERALLY TRANSFERRED THEIR ARCHIVES TO A CENTRAL REPOSITORY -- THE PUBLIC RECORDS OFFICE (PRO), FOUNDED IN 1838.

THE NEW INSTITUTION WAS INTENDED TO PRESERVE THE HISTORICAL RECORDS OF THE NATION AND MAKE THEM AVAILABLE FOR PUBLIC CONSULTATION. BY THE MID-TWENTIETH CENTURY, THE PRO HAD HUNDREDS OF VISITORS A WEEK.

THE STORY OF THE NEIRSÉE WAS AVAILABLE TO ANYONE WITH THE PATIENCE TO PIECE IT TOGETHER. BUT NO ONE DID, UNTIL NOW.

IN MANY CASES, DOCUMENTS WERE JUDGED TO BE OF LITTLE INTEREST AND DESTROYED. IN OTHERS, THEY WERE RECLASSIFIED AND REORGANIZED.

BUT THIS WAS NOT THE CASE WITH RECORDS FROM THE THREE DEPARTMENTS (ADMIRALTY, COLONIAL, AND FOREIGN) INVOLVED IN THE NEIRSÉE INCIDENT. WHEN THEIR RECORDS WERE TRANSFERRED TO THE PRO, THEIR EXISTING CLASSIFICATION AND CATALOGING SYSTEMS WERE MAINTAINED.

	Dockyard Branch (1870-1903, 1914-1915)
D of W	Director of Works (from 1883)
Dover	Dover Packet Station (1837-60)
Drs Comm	Doctors' Commons
DS	Director of Stores (from 1877)
DT	Director of Transports (from 1832)
DV	Director of Victualling (from 1870)
DW	Director of Works (from 1883)
D Yd Comm	Commissioners of Home Dockyards
DYDS	Director of Dockyards (from 1886)
E	FO Downs (to 1815)
EI Ho	East India Company (to 1858)
Elec Tel	Telegrams
F	Second-in-Command North Sea (to 1815)
Falmo	Falmouth Packet Station (1837-1860)
Field Off	Marine Field Officers
FO	Foreign Office

TO USE ADMIRALTY RECORDS TODAY, YOU STILL NEED TO CONSULT THE OLD DIGEST AND INDEX GUIDES.

FORTUNATELY, THEY'VE BEEN CUT DOWN AND REBOUND. EVEN SO, THEY STILL WEIGH OVER FIFTY POUNDS EACH.

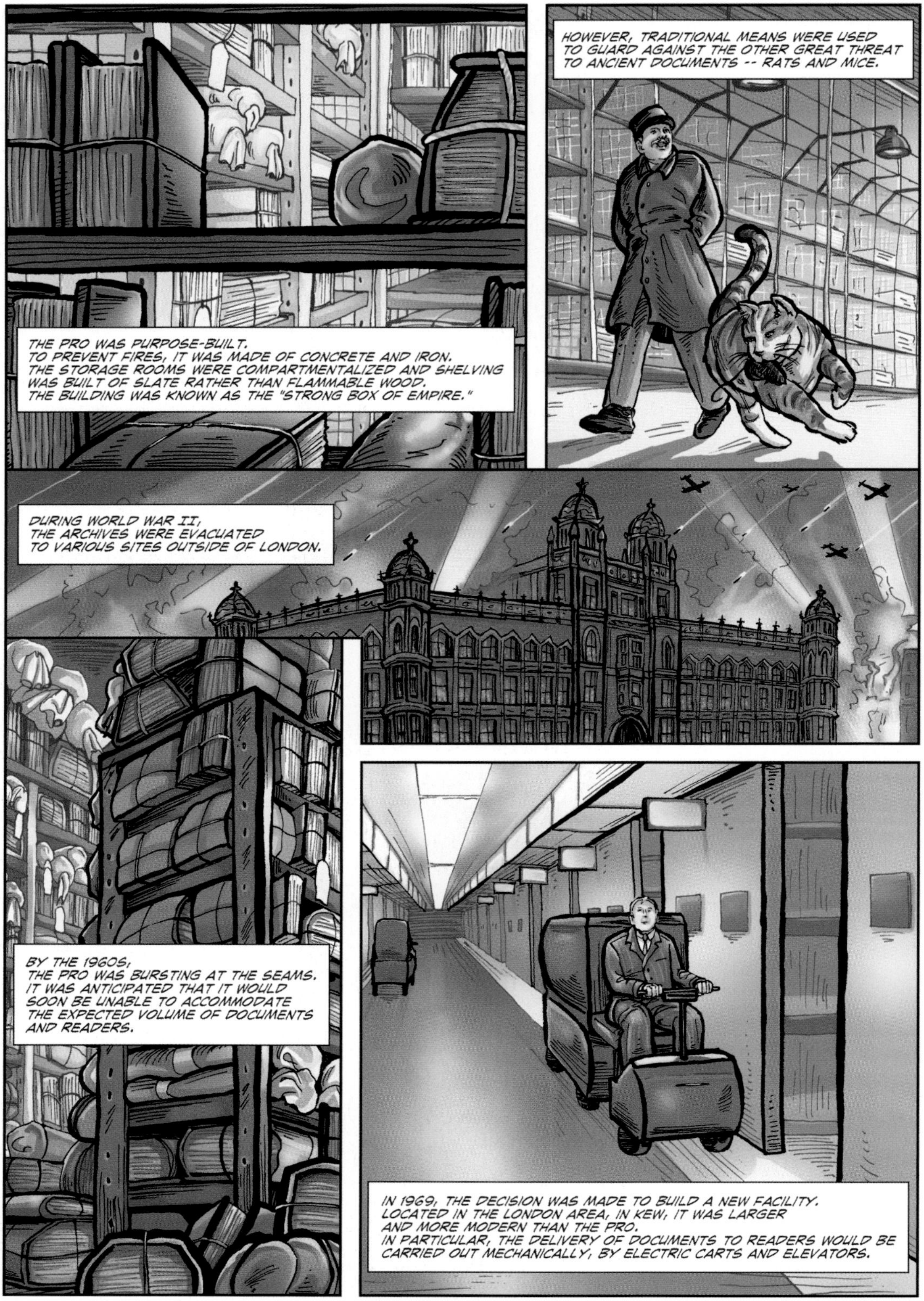
THE PRO WAS PURPOSE-BUILT. TO PREVENT FIRES, IT WAS MADE OF CONCRETE AND IRON. THE STORAGE ROOMS WERE COMPARTMENTALIZED AND SHELVING WAS BUILT OF SLATE RATHER THAN FLAMMABLE WOOD. THE BUILDING WAS KNOWN AS THE "STRONG BOX OF EMPIRE."
HOWEVER, TRADITIONAL MEANS WERE USED TO GUARD AGAINST THE OTHER GREAT THREAT TO ANCIENT DOCUMENTS -- RATS AND MICE.
DURING WORLD WAR II, THE ARCHIVES WERE EVACUATED TO VARIOUS SITES OUTSIDE OF LONDON.
BY THE 1960S, THE PRO WAS BURSTING AT THE SEAMS. IT WAS ANTICIPATED THAT IT WOULD SOON BE UNABLE TO ACCOMMODATE THE EXPECTED VOLUME OF DOCUMENTS AND READERS.
IN 1969, THE DECISION WAS MADE TO BUILD A NEW FACILITY. LOCATED IN THE LONDON AREA, IN KEW, IT WAS LARGER AND MORE MODERN THAN THE PRO. IN PARTICULAR, THE DELIVERY OF DOCUMENTS TO READERS WOULD BE CARRIED OUT MECHANICALLY, BY ELECTRIC CARTS AND ELEVATORS.

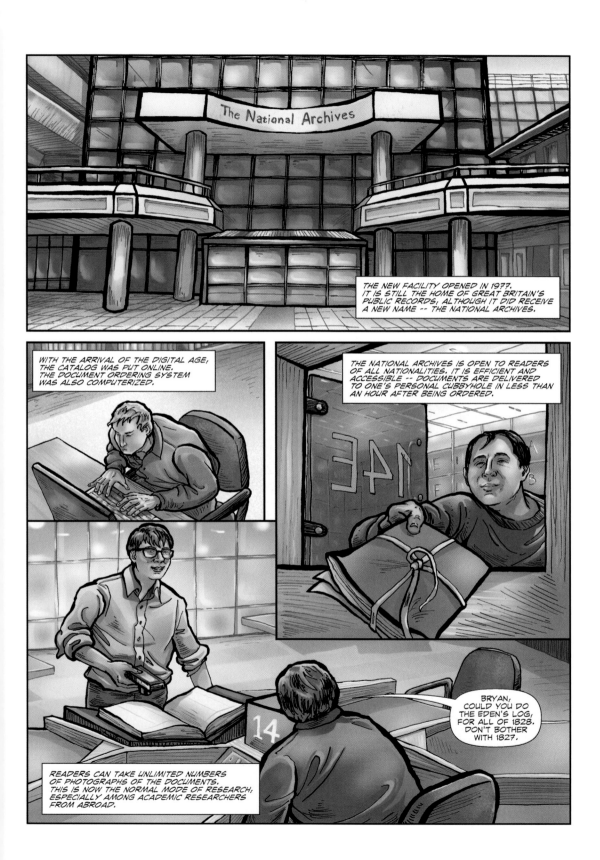

The National Archives

THE NEW FACILITY OPENED IN 1977.
IT IS STILL THE HOME OF GREAT BRITAIN'S
PUBLIC RECORDS, ALTHOUGH IT DID RECEIVE
A NEW NAME -- THE NATIONAL ARCHIVES.

WITH THE ARRIVAL OF THE DIGITAL AGE,
THE CATALOG WAS PUT ONLINE.
THE DOCUMENT ORDERING SYSTEM
WAS ALSO COMPUTERIZED.

THE NATIONAL ARCHIVES IS OPEN TO READERS
OF ALL NATIONALITIES. IT IS EFFICIENT AND
ACCESSIBLE -- DOCUMENTS ARE DELIVERED
TO ONE'S PERSONAL CUBBYHOLE IN LESS THAN
AN HOUR AFTER BEING ORDERED.

BRYAN,
COULD YOU DO
THE EDEN'S LOG,
FOR ALL OF 1828.
DON'T BOTHER
WITH 1827.

READERS CAN TAKE UNLIMITED NUMBERS
OF PHOTOGRAPHS OF THE DOCUMENTS.
THIS IS NOW THE NORMAL MODE OF RESEARCH,
ESPECIALLY AMONG ACADEMIC RESEARCHERS
FROM ABROAD.

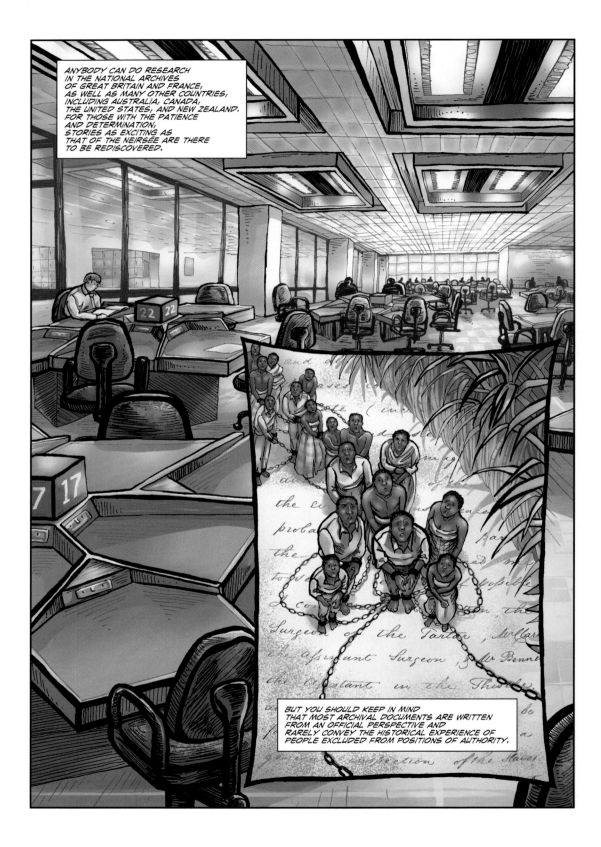

ANYBODY CAN DO RESEARCH IN THE NATIONAL ARCHIVES OF GREAT BRITAIN AND FRANCE, AS WELL AS MANY OTHER COUNTRIES, INCLUDING AUSTRALIA, CANADA, THE UNITED STATES, AND NEW ZEALAND. FOR THOSE WITH THE PATIENCE AND DETERMINATION, STORIES AS EXCITING AS THAT OF THE NEIRSÉE ARE THERE TO BE REDISCOVERED.

BUT YOU SHOULD KEEP IN MIND THAT MOST ARCHIVAL DOCUMENTS ARE WRITTEN FROM AN OFFICIAL PERSPECTIVE AND RARELY CONVEY THE HISTORICAL EXPERIENCE OF PEOPLE EXCLUDED FROM POSITIONS OF AUTHORITY.

PART III
THE PRIMARY SOURCES

This graphic narrative is based on unpublished, archival documents. There are many other kinds of historical sources, such as autobiographies and newspapers, but archival documents are of special importance to historians. They often reveal things that published sources do not. For example, there are no newspaper accounts of the *Neirsée* affair. In order to reconstruct what had happened, I read many archival documents—dispatches, depositions, ships' logbooks, and even a physical description of the perpetrators. What follows is a selection of the ones most important to the story.

I chose to include these documents because they form the backbone of the graphic narrative. I left out documents that did not advance this narrative. This process of selection highlights what historians really do. We do not find preexisting stories in the archives waiting to be discovered and told. Rather, we build narratives using information gleaned from masses of documents that could be used to tell all sorts of different stories. The documents I did not include in the selection—as well as some of those I did—could be used to tell alternative stories. A few of the histories I chose not to tell include: Argentine privateering during the war between Buenos Aires and Brazil (1826–1828), the culture of the aristocratic diplomatic corps in Restoration-era Europe, the resettlement of recaptives in Sierra Leone, and the economic and political agency of African and Eurafrican slave-trading merchant elites in the Bight of Biafra. I chose not to tell these stories here because, in my opinion, the most historically significant and dramatic narrative I could build from the documents was that of the enslavement and liberation of the Africans aboard the *Neirsée*.

WEST AFRICA: SEIZURE OF THE *NEIRSÉE*
DOCUMENT 1. CAPTAIN WILLIAM FITZWILLIAM OWEN TO JOHN WILSON CROKER, FIRST SECRETARY OF THE ADMIRALTY (Sierra Leone, 14 July 1828).

His Majesty's Ship *Eden*[1]
Sierra Leone, 14 July 1828
Sir,

His Royal Highness the Lord High Admiral may possibly expect from me such observations as I have made on the present state of the Slave Trade in the Rivers in my immediate vicinity, and on the advantages which may result from our occupation of Fernando Po. Although the theatre for my observations has (from my vessels being confined to one spot) been necessarily very limited, yet I feel it my duty to offer such as have occurred. My boats have visited only the St. John's, the Bonny, New Calabar, Old Calabar, Bimbia, and Cameroons. . . .

There is in no part of the Coast within the limits mentioned any extended single Government, but the whole is broken into isolated tyrannies of Petty Chiefs, who all of them are the traders for all articles and particularly for Slaves. It therefore will be impossible to put down that traffic in the said region but by one of these modes: either by absolute subjugation and conquest, dictating our will, or by treaty with each of the Chiefs, leaving our agents or the visits of Ships of War to see the said treaties executed, or lastly as is now done by treaty with those European Powers whose subjects engage in it to enable us to seize the fruits.

The first method is perhaps the only sure one. The second might, if zealously undertaken and executed, be equally successful, but by the last we shall surely never utterly destroy this trade, and yet viewing it as a British Seaman, this method has the advantages of continually keeping a part of our navy employed, and its energies always in exercise, ready for more important action when required; and this method would probably in the present state of Europe have no objection, did not its rewards arise from our own funds and if it did not load us with a dead weight of useless Negroes to take care of and provide for. I have not mentioned the means aimed at by Christian Philanthropists, by enlightening and civilizing Africa.

I believe this to be impossible by any mundane means until those multitudes now separated into invisible communities be forcibly subjugated to single rule, or formed into nations of importance by their magnitude and population.

In all the regions on which I presume to offer any observations, the trade in slaves is their principal; the second in importance in their own estimation is our Palm oil trade, which embraces also some trifling exchanges for Gold and Ivory. The effects of our palm oil trade carried on as it is by old slave traders rather tends to encourage than discourage the Slave Trade. The ships employed in it bring out many more goods than are necessary to purchase their cargo which they sell for cash. Many of the slavers therefore come with cash only to Bonny, the Old Calabar, and Cameroons, and get their cargoes of slaves with scarcely any delay at all, the Chief being always the agent through whom all business is conducted. . . .

The Chief of the most extensive dominion in the part I speak of is Duke Ephraim, who is the Chief, or as he is called, King of the Calabar. His authority is assumed to extend on both sides the river from its bar for a hundred miles into the interior, in all which distance the river is navigable for large vessels, there he says begins a new tongue, and he knows nothing of the country beyond. . . .

The general character of vessels trading for slaves at these rivers is from two hundred to sixty tons, brigs and schooners, under Spanish colors and papers, under French colors with simulous French papers, having also Spanish or Netherland documents; and Brazilians; and a few small craft from the Portuguese Islands of Princes and St. Thomas's. The whole number of slaves exported from the three rivers may be taken at twelve thousand a year, certainly not more.

When circumstances permitted me to detach one boat only from my ship, with a small vessel as a rendezvous, I was able so completely to blockade Old Calabar, Cameroons, and Bimbia as to leave but little chance of escape to any slaver, and one Spanish vessel was obliged to sell her cargo of four hundred to a French vessel, and to sail empty to cruise as a pirate, in consequence of my placing my pinnace within the bar of Old Calabar to blockade her. . . .

Of Fernando Po and its eminent situation for commanding both bights, it will be superfluous to offer a word, further than to explain that the removal of the Court of Mixed Commission to Clarence will have the immediate effect of more than trebling the power of the vessels employed to put down the traffic. Of nine vessels I have sent to Sierra Leone, their voyages have been of four of them, more than six weeks, two one month, and two fifteen days; whereas from all parts from the Congo to Cape Coast, eight days or less will suffice generally for a voyage to Fernando Po and from the ports to windward. The wind is always fair for Fernando Po with numerous refreshing stations intermediate; so that in no case need the cargoes of slaves suffer, as in many cases they have done in the voyage to Sierra Leone.

> I have the honor to be
> Sir,
> your humble
> and obedient servant
> WFW Owen   captain

[1]*Source:* The National Archives (TNA), Admiralty (ADM) 1 2273.

DOCUMENT 2. OWEN TO LIEUTENANT BADGELEY (Clarence Cove, Fernando Po, 17 January 1828).

Having certain information by the Margaret of Liverpool that there are in New Calabar River several vessels ready for taking in slaves and with their cargoes ready for embarkation and being also desirous of opening a communication with New Calabar, Bonny, and Old Calabar to make our arrangements for supplies of live stock, articles of provisions, and free native labor.[2]

It is my direction that you take command of the Royal Admiral (the Eden's pinnace), manning her with 11 seamen, 4 marines, Mr. Mercer mid-shipman, and yourself, also ten Kroo and Fishmen whom you will vict-ual for fourteen days. With whom you will repair on board the Africans schooner and take command of her likewise, having engaged her as my tender, Mr. Smith, her master, being appointed to act as master of the Eden for the purpose of this expedition only and his crew having engaged for this specific service.

With the Royal Admiral and the African, you are to proceed and exam-ine all the three rivers before named, and obtain for my examination every Spanish, Portuguese, and Netherland vessel you may find therein, either with slaves on board or with indubitable evidence of their being engaged in the traffic for slaves in contravention of the treaties between Great Britain and their nations respectively, and you will bring them to this anchorage with as little delay as possible for my said examination.

You will take advantage of this service to make arrangements with the chief authorities in each place for collecting for the service of this establishment:

1. Live cattle and live stock of all description
2. Other articles of victualing, such as cassava, rice, maize, etc.
3. To hire for the establishment such free laborers as can be procured.

[2]*Source:* TNA, ADM 1 2273.

DOCUMENT 3. RICHARD CUMMINS, CAPTAIN OF THE *KENT*, TO BADGELEY (Old Calabar, 26 January 1828).

Sir, I understand you will leave this in the morning. I am sorry for it, but at the same time if you remained here, it would be the same regarding our vessel and trade.[3] I feel quite safe while on board, but it is of consequence to our trade for me to be ashore during the day three or four times, as the principal part of our cargo is received there. But when Frenchmen come to our oil house and when we are in the act of taking our cargo fired on our people, as last night they unfortunately shot our second officer. I cannot be safe and I am informed they are not at all well disposed towards myself. Duke Ephraim I know would protect me and every person in the Kent, but he cannot protect me from such rascals who may do me or any of my crew an injury, when we least expect it, when passing such narrow paths or straits, or coming near our oil house. We cannot defend ourselves, nor know when they are coming. I have been long here in the Calabar trade when there have been many slave vessels, but never before saw them in-sult any person belonging to the palm oil ships. I have not the hopes that the Duke's doctor people have of our second mate's speedy recovery. A shot passing through a person's belly is a serious thing and requires skill, attention, etc. I am unprovided with a surgeon unfortunately, but all we can do we will for him.

[3]*Source:* TNA, ADM 1 2273.

DOCUMENT 4. OWEN TO CROKER (Clarence Cove, 25 November 1828)

I have the honor to report that having dispatched the Horatio and Cornelia to the Old Calabar River to procure and settle for supplies of meat for this establishment . . . the Cornelia brought me certain information that the Estafette alias the Nirzee, a pretended French brig under fictitious papers would sail immediately with a cargo of slaves, I dispatched Lieutenant Badgeley immediately in the Cornelia to coast for her on the bar.[4] Her captain has sent a private message to offer me a thousand guineas to let him pass. The Cornelia left this anchorage on the 22nd and on the 24th returned with the vessel sought with two hundred and eighty slaves on board. I shall take this occasion to discharge a number of the African mechanics, the time for which they were engaged having expired and they have requested to return to their families at Sierra Leone. I have also so many prisoners, viz., about a hundred and fifty, as to inconvenience us to feed them, I shall therefore send them off also or as many of them as we can.

[4]*Source:* TNA, ADM 1 2274.

CARIBBEAN: ENSLAVED ON GUADELOUPE
DOCUMENT 5. WILLIAM NICOLAY, GOVERNOR OF DOMINICA, TO SIR GEORGE MURRAY, SECRETARY OF STATE FOR WAR AND THE COLONIES (Roseau, Dominica, 2 February 1829).

It is notorious that, notwithstanding the laws established in France for the abolition of the slave trade, great numbers of African slaves are continually imported into the colonies of Guadeloupe and Martinique.[5] I have now to report a most flagrant case of this illicit traffic, which has recently occurred under very extraordinary circumstances.

In the month of November last, a brig having on board 280 slaves was captured off the coast of Africa by His Majesty's ship Eden. Mr. Davies, Master's Assistant, with five English seamen and eight free black men, were sent onboard the prize to conduct it to Sierra Leone for the purpose of adjudication. While on the voyage thither, these men were surprised and overpowered by part of the original crew of the slave vessel, who carried it to Guadeloupe, where, on the night of the 23rd ult. [last], the whole of the slaves, all the free black men aforementioned, and a free black woman, wife of one of them, were promiscuously landed in the most expeditious and methodical manner. It was understood that the brig sailed immediately afterwards for Martinique. The officer and the five English seamen, belonging to the Eden, were put into an open boat, and, fortunately, they reached this island. I have the honor to transmit, enclosed, the deposition of Mr. Davis, taken before the Chief Justice, and which will put you more minutely in possession of the particulars of this transaction.

I have applied to the Governor of Guadeloupe for the restitution of the eight men, and the woman, free blacks and British subjects, who were all forced on shore with the slaves, and I have written to the Governor of Martinique representing that as the brig was found actually employed in the illegal transport of slaves, and that she was proceeding to Sierra Leone, in order to fair trial and adjudication, she ought still to be considered a British prize, but if any doubt should exist on that head, I requested that the vessel, if at Martinique, might be detained until the case should be referred to higher authority for decision. The result shall be reported to you by the first possible opportunity after my receipt thereof.

From the atrocious instance herein brought to your knowledge and from many other well known facts, it is not to be doubted that a regular system for the importation of African slaves into the French colonies is carried on to an enormous extent, and which could surely not take place were the local authorities sincere and active in the enforcement of the French laws relative to the abolition of the slave trade.

I have transmitted to the officer commanding His Majesty's Naval Forces on this station a full account of all that has passed upon this subject, requesting at the same time to know his wishes with regard to the disposal of the officer and seamen belonging to the Eden. It is however impossible for my letter to reach him before the departure of the mail, about to proceed to England; and I therefore beg to submit that the substance of this my dispatch to you may be communicated to the Lords of the Admiralty, to remove the anxiety which must naturally be felt respecting the fate of the brig and of the persons sent on board her from the Eden.

[5] *Source:* TNA, Colonial Office (CO) 71 67.

DOCUMENT 6. DEPOSITION OF JAMES DAVIES, MASTER'S ASSISTANT OF H.M.S. *EDEN* (Roseau, 28 January 1829)

Before the Honorable Robert Jameson, Chief Justice of the Supreme Court of Judicature held in and for the said Island of Dominica

Appeared James Davies, Masters Assistant of His Majesty's Ship of war, the "Eden," who being duly sworn upon the holy evangelist of Almighty God, deposeth and saith, that, on or about the eighteenth day of November last past, the "Eden," Captain Owen, captured the French Brig commanded by one Tiran, and bound to Guadeloupe, whilst she was at anchor off Calabar, in the Bight of Biafra, with two hundred & eighty African slaves on board.[6] The brig by the ship's papers was called the "Neirsee" and her company consisted besides her commander of thirty three men, including a captain in second and two mates. The brig was taken with her cargo to Fernando Po and kept there until the twenty seventh day of November aforesaid, when deponent was directed to proceed with the Brig to Northwest Bay, distant about twenty miles, to purchase yams for the use of the crew and of the African slaves on board (the quantity found on board at the time of the capture not being deemed sufficient) and there to await the arrival of the "Horatio" tender, to proceed to Sierra Leone for the adjudication of the brig and cargo. On the second of December, the Brig sailed from Northwest Bay in company with the "Horatio" tender, having on board besides deponent five seamen of the Eden's crew, two marines (invalids), five free black men (known upon the African Coast by the name of Kroo men) belonging to the Eden and *entered on the ship's books*, besides three other free black men, passengers going to Sierra Leone. There were also on board, of the original French crew, the captain in second, the two mates, and fifteen men, the rest of the crew having been landed at Fernando Po, with the exception of the commander Tiran, who was on board the tender. Some days after they had been at sea, two of the seamen of the Eden's crew fell sick. Deponent sent them on board the tender, and received in return two Spaniards who had previously been taken on board slave vessels and had volunteered to serve on board the tender. On the morning of the nineteenth of December, about two o'clock, the Brig parted company with the tender in a tornado. This was in sixty miles south latitude and six degrees east longitude. On the morning of the twenty fourth of December, about half past eleven o'clock, as deponent was lying in his cot taking his usual rest from the fatigues of the preceding night, he heard the report of a pistol, when he immediately got up, and was at the same moment fired at by one of the French crew. He was then ordered by the French captain in second to go below. One of the Spaniards (who had joined the French and ultimately remained with them) at the same time seized deponent by the back and forced him down the hatchway. Two of the seamen of the Eden's crew were wounded, one in the head and the other stabbed and cut in two different places. The three seamen, the eight free black men, and two marines were all put in irons on the same day; and were allowed for eight or ten days the use of the forecastle, but on some alleged suspicion on the part of the Frenchmen that the Eden's crew intended retaking the Brig, they were ordered and kept below during the rest of the voyage, with the exception of the two marines, who were relieved for two or three days on account of illness. Deponent further saith that at the commencement of the revolt and on the firing of the pistols, the eight free black men, instead of coming to the assistance of this deponent, took alarm and ran down below. During the rest of the voyage nothing particular occurred. They arrived at the French island of Deseada distant from Guadeloupe about fifteen miles and went into port under Dutch colors about eleven o'clock in the forenoon of Friday the twenty third day of January instant, where she remained at anchor and in communication with the shore, until about five o'clock in the afternoon when she got under weigh and proceeded to Guadeloupe, which they reached about eleven o'clock at night, and anchored. They immediately commenced landing the Africans which occupied them until about two o'clock the following morning. The eight free black men were landed also promiscuously with the slaves, and deponent saith that the landing of the slaves was carried on without any apparent attempt at secrecy, there being a large fire upon the shore and at least twelve large boats assisting, and this deponent as far as he could judge from the myriad lights, believes that the place of landing was in the vicinity of some town which from its situation he believes to have been that of Point-à-Pitre. Two hours after the landing was completed, they made sail for Martinique (to which island this deponent was informed the brig belonged and was one of several ships which annually brought cargos of slaves to the French islands) leaving the captain in second on shore there, and having previously thrown overboard their two remaining great guns, their musketry and small arms, the pistols belonging to the men of the Eden, were given the pilot who conducted the brig from Deseada to Guadeloupe. Deponent together with the three seamen and two marines were put into an open boat and informed that the island in sight was the British island of Dominica and that himself and men might make the best of their way there. Deponent reached Prince Rupert's Bay in this island on the same day about five o'clock in the afternoon and came up to Roseau the following day, Sunday morning the twenty fifth of January. Deponent further saith that though by the ship's papers the brig's name appeared to be Neirsee, yet he was given to understand she went on the Coast by the name of the Estafette, that the deponent has no doubt but that he could identify the said vessel, and the several individuals who formed the crew, and also the several free black persons landed among the slaves, and lastly deponent was informed by the mate of the brig that it was the custom of the French slave ships to call at one of the small French islands, either Deseada or Marie Galants, and there to take instructions as to the place of landing the cargo.

[6]*Source:* TNA, ADM 1 280.

DOCUMENT 7. DEPOSITION OF DANIEL WILSON, HUGH JONES, AND JOSEPH ROLFE, SEAMEN, AND JAMES MOORE, MARINE, OF H.M.S. *EDEN* (Roseau, 29 January 1829)

Daniel Wilson, Hugh Jones, and Joseph Rolfe, the three seamen, and James Moore, one of the two marines referred to by the Deponent James Davies (the other marine being too ill to attend) were severally examined by me upon oath respecting the facts detailed in the above deposition and confirmed so far as they were concerned every circumstance therein stated with the addition that there were in fact *nine* free Africans (eight male and a female) carried away among those who had been made slaves by the French, the female being the wife of one of the three passengers.[7] They further stated that these nine persons had been long in the service of the English upon the African Coast (having been to the examinants' own knowledge nearly two years employed on board the Eden, and three as carpenters or shingle makers at Fernando Po), and that they all spoke English very well. All the examinants agreed that they could easily identify these several persons.

Mr. Davies was again examined respecting the fact of there being a female free African also. He stated that the information was true, but that it had escaped his memory at the time of making his deposition.

[7]*Source:* TNA, ADM 1 280.

DOCUMENT 8. NICOLAY TO MURRAY (Roseau, 10 March 1829)

In my dispatch of the 2nd ult., I reported to you that a brig (La Neirsee) having on board 280 slaves, was captured in the month of November last by His Majesty's Ship Eden, and that the prize was retaken and carried into Guadeloupe, where all the slaves and several free Africans were forcibly landed.[8] I likewise informed you that Mr. Davis, Master's Assistant, and five English seamen belonging to the Eden, who had been taken to Guadeloupe in the slave brig, had arrived here. The particulars of this transaction were fully detailed in Mr. Davis's deposition which accompanied my report.

The enclosed papers, nos. 1 and 2, are copies of my letters to the Governors of Martinique and Guadeloupe, and of their replies, which I did not receive until after the sailing of the packet bearing my dispatch of the 2nd ult.

I have now the honor to communicate to you the subsequent occurrences relative to this subject.

On the 14th ult. six of the free Africans who had been landed with the slaves reached this island, having been embarked at Guadeloupe in a sloop from which they were removed to an open boat in the channel between that island and Dominica.

On the 17th Captain Deare, Commander of His Majesty's Sloop Grasshopper, arrived here, and after ascertaining that the brig, La Neirsee, had not been at Martinique, as was supposed, he took on board with him Mr. Davis, the five English seamen, and the six free Africans aforementioned, and sailed on the 19th for Guadeloupe with instructions from Vice Admiral Fleming to demand the restitution of the slaves who had been landed there from the brig, as also of the rest of the free Africans who were forced on shore with them. Mr. Robe, my Secretary, accompanied Captain Deare, and on this occasion I again wrote to the Governor of Guadeloupe. No. 3 contains a copy of our correspondence, by which you will perceive that, in the reply to my letter, no notice is taken of that part touching the bringing to justice the persons who had been concerned in compelling the free Africans to work as slaves.

On the 21st ult., the remainder of the free black men reached this island in an open boat. They were sent from Guadeloupe previously in the same manner as the other six, evidently from alarm on the part of the persons by whom they had been unlawfully detained. Thus, all the free Africans who had been sent from the Eden, to the slave brig, have been recovered, except the woman; and I trust that she will shortly be restored.

The accompanying papers, nos. 4 and 5, are the depositions of the nine African men, and which are in perfect accordance with the statement formerly made by Mr. Davies. . . .

Vice Admiral Fleming called here on the 5th. He had been at Guadeloupe; but did not receive from the Governor of that Island any satisfactory reply to the representations he had made with respect to this important subject.

The several circumstances brought to light in the investigation of this extraordinary case afford ample evidence of innumerable acts of a most cruel and atrocious nature, having been committed in the instance of the brig Neirsee; and there is, moreover, incontestable proof that, in violation of all laws and treaties, the slave trade is carried on with the French colonies in the most inhuman manner, and to an enormous extent; which undoubtedly could not happen without the tacit assent of the local authorities.

[8]*Source:* TNA, CO 71 67.

DOCUMENT 9. DEPOSITION OF JAMES PATTERSON, THOMAS GEORGE, JOSEPH MICHAEL, JAMES RAWSON, BEN LIVERPOOL, AND JACK DAVIES (Roseau, 18 February 1829)

James Patterson, Thomas George, Joseph Michael, James Rawson, Ben Liverpool, and Jack Davies respectfully depose and first the said Patterson, George, Michael and Rawson depose that they are native Africans and were brought up at Sierra Leone as carpenters and shingle makers.[9] They were instructed by a Christian Minister and profess the Christian religion. The deponents James Patterson and Joseph Michael can read; the former of these also writes. They went to Fernando Po for the purpose of being employed in their trade. The deponents Liverpool and Davis are free men of the Korou or Kroo nation, and have for several years been employed at Sierra Leone by different persons as laborers and jobbers, and have for the last fifteen months (previous to their leaving the African Coast) been serving on board the Eden, Captain Owen. The deponents say that the Eden having captured a French brig laden with slaves off the coast of Calabar, Captain Owen was sending the same to Sierra Leone. The four first named deponents obtained a passage in order to return to Sierra Leone. A female named Sarah, the wife of the deponent Thomas George was also a passenger. She had formerly been taken on board a Spanish slave ship and liberated upon the condemnation of the vessel at Sierra Leone. After the deponents had been some days at sea, the crew of the French brig rose against the English and retook the vessel, and put the deponents and the English seamen in irons. This the deponent Paterson says took place as he believes about the 24th Dec. last. They then sailed to Guadeloupe where upon their arrival about midnight the whole cargo of slaves were landed together with these deponents and three other free men of the Kroo nation serving on board the Eden and who with the deponents Liverpool and Davis had been put on board the brig to assist in navigating her to Sierra Leone and also the said Sarah. The next day they were all marched in a line in the broad day light to a plantation about three miles from the shore. The slaves together with the woman Sarah were put into a large room or boiling house and the deponents and the said three other Kroo men were confined in a sort of loft adjoining. During the first seven days all the slaves together with the free woman Sarah were sold to different purchasers who came to the place in great numbers, some purchasing five others ten, fifteen, or twenty at a time. The deponents and their three other countrymen were also exposed to sale, and many persons were brought by the captain of the French brig to buy them. They were kept apart from the other Africans because the French captain said they were his own private property, his "prize money." The French captain spoke English as did several of the persons who came to purchase. Deponents protested against being sold and stated that they were free men and subjects of the King of the England. They had for the same reason protested against the sale of Sarah, particularly the deponent Thomas George, who entreated that they would not sell his wife. The French captain struck him upon the head and said he should certainly sell them all. The deponents declared their freedom whenever purchasers came and they believe that persons for that reason were deterred from buying them. The French captain was very angry, and struck the deponent Patterson several times; he behaved very outrageously and threatened to shoot them all if they prevented their own sale. After all the cargoes of negroes had been sold, the deponents were taken to an adjoining sugar plantation belonging to a person named Sergente (whether purchased by him or not they do not know) and were there compelled by him to work. The four first named deponents labored at their trade and made during their abode there several carts and wheels for their estate. The Kroo men were made to work at the mill or to assist those who were making rum or sugar. The deponents further say that late in the night of Friday the 13th February inst., Mr. Sergente and another gentleman came to the deponents and told them they were to be sent back to the English. They were brought to the shore and put on board a small sloop, except three of the Kroo men who were told by some of the French slaves, several of whom could speak English, that they were only to be taken to some other island to be sold, and refused to enter the sloop. The deponents embarked about midnight, accompanied by ten or eleven Frenchmen; and at half past five or six o'clock in the morning of Saturday, appeared to be about midway in the Channel between Guadeloupe and Dominica. Then they were put into a small boat with three oars, they had three loaves, some salt fish and a flask of water given them, and were directed to make the best of their way to this island. The deponents enquired whether there was a harbor and were told they must find one as they could. Deponents reached Prince Rupert's Bay in this island about eleven o'clock in the morning of Sat Feb. 14th instant. Deponent Patterson saith that one Sunday he was permitted to go in company with one of Mr. Sergente's servants to the Church of a large town within a short walk from the place where the sale of the negroes was held. He does not know the name, but there were several merchant ships and a few schooners lying close to the town.

The before named persons who have sworn to the truth of this deposition are very intelligent Africans and speak English remarkably well (especially James Patterson) and have been instructed in the principles of Christianity which they profess. Upon re-examining the other two, Liverpool and Davies, they did not appear to have had the same advantages or to be sufficiently sensible of the nature of an oath which I have therefore refrained from administering. Robert Jameson.
[9]*Source:* TNA, ADM 1 280.

DOCUMENT 10. DEPOSITION OF YELLOW WILL, DICK WILSON, AND PRINCE WILL (Roseau, 23 February 1829)

The three Kroo men calling themselves Yellow Will, Dick Wilson, and Prince Will, referred to in the deposition of James Paterson and others dated the 18th Feb inst and who arrived in this island on the evening of Saturday the 21st inst were this day examined by me.[10] They stated that they are all free Africans who have for several years been laborers employed by the English at Sierra Leone and elsewhere. They have never been instructed in any religion. During the last two years of nearly that time, they have been acting as hired assistants to the crew of the Eden, stationed at Fernando Po. They gave the same account of the circumstances of taking the French slave ship and its being retaken by a conspiracy of the French captain and seamen as has been given by Mr. Davis and by their own countrymen. The examinant Yellow Will had upon the last mentioned occasion received two stabs from a large knife, one on his thigh and one on his hand (still very apparent). They state that the brig, on board which they were, arrived at the French island in the night and anchored. That a large fire was kindled upon the beach and a great number of boats were immediately ready and employed in landing the slaves, and that they (the examinants) were landed at the same time, but kept apart from the others by the captain of the French brig. That about seven o'clock in the morning of their landing all the slaves, together with the examinants, were conducted in a body to a plantation not far from the shore. The examinants were backed up together and several persons were brought by the French captain to purchase them. They could see the sale of the slaves going on and saw a free woman named Sarah, the wife of George, one of their free companions, sold along with them. George had cried out against her being sold and was kicked by the French captain. When persons came to look at them, they all cried out against being sold and laid that they were free and "Englishmen." Upon an occasion of this kind a French man who was bargaining with the captain for some of them kicked the examinant Yellow Will and said he should buy them notwithstanding if he liked. He did not however buy any of them. They told everyone they saw that they were free men and many of the French purchasers understood them. The French captain threatened "to kill them like sheep if they spoke English." The examinants believe that they were at last sold. The person who bought them spoke English and told them that he was an Englishman, and therefore that he had a right to buy them. By this person they were carried away from the place where the sale was carried on. George, whose wife had been sold resisted and was handcuffed. They were conducted to a plantation very near the place of sale and were made to work among the slaves and in all respects treated as such and fed with them upon yams and salt fish in the negro huts. They worked from five o'clock in the morning until eight at night when they were always locked up by themselves in a house adjoining the boiling house. They believe they were working twenty two days. The examinants and two others named Ben Liverpool and Jack Davies assisted the men at the still carrying water and fuel and filling the hogsheads with sugar. The other four free men worked at their trades. Three were carpenters and one a mason.

They further stated that one evening about six or seven days since "two fine men came from the big town" and that same night the person who brought the examinants informed them they were to be sent to an English country. They were all taken to the beach, but on their way they were told by a French slave who spoke English that they were only to be taken to another French island to be sold. The examinants therefore escaped and ran back to their former abode. The master asked why they had returned. They gave their reason. The master said they need not be afraid, for the two gentlemen from the town would take care of them. One of these two gentlemen spoke English to them and told them they could not be sold but might be quite sure they were only going back to the English. On the following night, they left the French island in a sloop. When they got so near the island that they could row to land, they were put into a small boat and the French sloop sailed away.

[10] *Source:* TNA, ADM 1 280.

CARIBBEAN: COLONIAL AUTHORITIES IN ACTION
DOCUMENT 11. NICOLAY TO THE BARON DES ROTOURS, GOVERNOR OF GUADELOUPE (Roseau, 28 January 1829)

I have the honor to address your Excellency upon a subject of very great importance, which has just been brought to my knowledge.[11] The circumstances are as follows:

In the month of November last, a brig, having on board 280 slaves, was captured off the coast of Africa by the Eden, a British man of war. The name of the brig was stated in the ship's papers to be La Neirsee, but there is reason to believe that she had previously been called L'Estafette.

An officer of the Eden, with five English seamen and eight black men (all free British subjects) were sent on board the prize to conduct it to Sierra Leone for the purpose of adjudication before the proper tribunal. While on the voyage thither, these men were surprised and overpowered by part of the original crew of the slave vessel, and who carried it to Guadeloupe, where, on the night of the 23rd instant, the whole of the slaves and all the free blacks aforementioned were landed in so expeditious and methodical a manner as clearly to evince that the arrival of the brig was not unexpected. Immediately afterwards she sailed for Martinique. The English officer and the five seamen were put into an open boat and fortunately they reached this island.

The enclosed documents being evidence taken on oath before the Chief Justice of Dominica will put your Excellency more minutely in possession of the particulars of this case.

I am persuaded that Your Excellency will be anxious to bring to justice the persons concerned in this flagrant infraction of the laws and regulations acceded to by the French government for the abolition of the slave trade, and that you will feel highly indignant at the fact of eight free blacks (British subjects) having been forcibly and clandestinely landed at Guadeloupe.

From the well-known vigilance and activity of the Police under Your Excellency's government, it is not to be doubted that these men will readily be
found. And I confidently rely on Your Excellency's justice that you will be
pleased to give directions to that effect, and cause them to be duly restored.

P.S. I am just informed that a free black woman (the wife of one of the eight
free men) was also put on shore at Guadeloupe.

[11]Source: TNA, CO 71 67.

DOCUMENT 12. ROTOURS TO NICOLAY (Basse-Terre, Guadeloupe, 14 February 1829)

I received the letter that Your Excellency did me the honor to write on the
28th of last month, together with the attachment concerning the supposed
landing on the coast of Guadeloupe of a cargo of Blacks from a French vessel which, detained on the African coast by a British warship, is supposed
to have been retaken by the French crew and taken to this island, after
having landed at Dominica the prize captain and his crew.[12] Monsieur
Governor, I have not yet been able to obtain sufficiently accurate information on the landing to be able to respond categorically. By my orders, the
coast of Guadeloupe is under the strictest surveillance, both to stop the
landing of slaves and to interdict contraband trade; but it is possible that
some slavers manage to evade this surveillance, just the same as the pur-
veyors of prohibited merchandise from Dominica and the other colonies
of His Britannic Majesty succeed in landing their goods. But you can rest
assured, Monsieur Governor, that if I find any trace of the vessel, I will do
everything I can to fulfill your request.

[12]Source: TNA, CO 71 67.

DOCUMENT 13. FLEMING TO CROKER (Carlisle Bay, Barbados, 18 February 1829)

I request you will be pleased to acquaint my Lords Commissioners of the
Admiralty, that I arrived here on the 13th instant, and found the Grasshopper and Arachne.[13] Captain Crawford being appointed to act in the
Magnificent has proceeded to join that ship by the Cygnet, packet, being
superseded by acting commander Deare.

On the next day, I received a letter from the Governor of Dominica, a
copy of which I enclose; and in consequence I detached the Grasshopper to
that Island, to receive on board the officer and men belonging to the Eden;
and proceed with them to Guadeloupe and Martinique; and I have written
to the Governors of these Islands, requesting that the Crew belonging to
the Neirsée may be given up to be tried by the competent authority for the
piracies they have committed. I have claimed the British subjects; as well

as the Africans, which by the laws of both countries, must now be free. The Eden's people will be enabled to identify the British subjects, and the pirates; and perhaps a number of the unfortunate Negroes. Commander Deare is directed to join me at Antigua; where I shall proceed tomorrow; and if I find it necessary, I shall go to Point-à-Pitre (Guadeloupe) from that port; and from there to Trinidad, unless my presence may be necessary at any of the other Islands.

By what I understand the French law to be respecting persons connected with the slave trade, the authorities in Guadeloupe and Martinique will have sufficient power to punish them; We shall judge therefore of their sincerity in putting down the horrible traffic by their conduct on this occasion.

[13]*Source:* TNA, ADM 1 280.

DOCUMENT 14. FLEMING TO ROTOURS (Carlisle Bay, 14 February 1829)

I have the honor to transmit Your Excellency a copy of a letter from Major General Nicolay, Governor of Dominica, together with a declaration from an officer and five men belonging to His Britannic Majesty's Ship Eden, by which it appears that a most daring act of piracy has been committed by the crew of the French brig "Neirsée" alias "Estafeta," accompanied by great inhumanity and atrocity; and, as it appears, that all the Africans on board that vessel, together with his Britannic Majesty's subjects, described by the said officer and men, are in Guadeloupe.[14]

I have to request you will cause them forthwith to be delivered up and taking such measures as Your Excellency may think proper for bringing the persons connected with receiving and detaining those unfortunate beings to justice.

The officer who is charged with the honor of delivering this dispatch to Your Excellency has been directed to receive on board the officer and men belonging to the Eden, for the purpose of identifying His Britannic Majesty's African subjects and any of the crew who have been guilty of the above piracy; the former of whom I demand may be instantly set at liberty as justice requires; reserving the right of indemnification against all persons who have been guilty of the injustice towards them, by depriving them of their liberty and other illegal acts; and I request that the pirates who can be identified may be given up, in order that they may be brought to a competent tribunal to answer for their crimes.

[14]*Source:* TNA, ADM 1 280.

DOCUMENT 15. ROTOURS TO FLEMING (Point-à-Pitre, Guadeloupe, 22 February 1829)

I received the letters and diverse pieces that you did me the honor to address to me on the 19th of this month.[15] There is no doubt that the landing on the shore of Dominica of the six men of color, demanded as subjects of His Britannic Majesty, was the result of measures I took to discover their whereabouts, as well as those of the people who, according to what you say, had taken possession of them. . . .

In conformity with your desires, I am giving the most rigorous orders to search in all the parts of the island, as well as in its dependencies, for the four men that you request. However, I must let you know, Monsieur Admiral, that the localities present obstacles that will make these investigations very difficult; I would have immediately accepted the offer that Captain Deare made to leave here two of the men returned to Dominica and come back with him if the commander of the Gendarmerie, whom I had summoned in person, had not observed that, in addition to the difficulty he would have had in answering for men likely to escape, their presence would awaken the disquiet of runaways and thus become more dangerous than useful.

[15]*Source:* TNA, ADM 1 280.

DOCUMENT 16. CAPTAIN DEARE, H.M.S. *GRASSHOPPER*, TO FLEMING (English Harbor, Antigua, 23 February 1829)

I have the honor to inform you that in obedience to your order dated the 13th inst. I proceeded to sea in his Majesty's Sloop under my command on the evening of that day, and anchored off the town of Roseau the next night.[16] I delivered the dispatches I was charged with to His Excellency General Nicolay the following morning and was informed by him that six free black men, who had landed from the "Neirsee" at Guadeloupe had arrived at Prince Rupert's Bay and that he had sent orders for them to be forwarded to Roseau. At His Excellency's suggestion, I weighed the same evening (having first received on board Mr. Davis, three seamen, and two marines belonging to His Majesty's Ship Eden) and proceeded to Fort Royal, Martinique, where I arrived on Wednesday afternoon, and delivered the dispatches I was charged with, and also the deposition of the Eden's men, according to your direction. I was informed by the Naval Commanding officer there (the commander of a schooner) that your letter to Admiral Bergeret would be answered by the Governor in his letter to you, which I herewith forward.

On my way to Fort Royal, I hove to off the town of St. Pierre's, and landed there at General Nicolay's request, for the purpose of ascertaining whether the Neirsee was in that harbor, which I found she was not, and from what I heard on shore am induced to believe that she had not been there. I left Fort Royal the same evening after receiving the Governor's answer to your letter, and anchored at Roseau on Thursday morning, when I received on board the six free black men who had arrived from Price

Rupert's Bay and of whose deposition as to what had occurred to them and their companions I have the honor to forward you a copy.

I was informed by General Nicolay that in consequence of information he had received, he was inclined to think that the Neirsee or l'Estafette, instead of going to Martinique as was reported, went from Guadeloupe to St. Eustatius; then took out papers for St. Bartholomews and again took out papers at that island and proceeded to the Havana for sale. It was further reported that the circumstances of the revolt and the capture of the Neirsee was the public talk at St. Bartholomews.

On Thursday evening last, I left Roseau and proceeded to Basse-Terre, Guadeloupe, having been requested to do so by General Nicolay, who had been informed that the Governor of that Island was there. I was however told by Rear Admiral Bergeret, who was laying in the road with his flag on board the Jean d'Arc that His Excellency had left Basse-Terre a few days before for Point-à-Pitre. I accordingly weighed immediately and anchored off that port the following morning when I delivered the dispatch I was charged with to him, together with the deposition of the Eden's men (which I enclosed as directed by your instructions) the description of the Neirsee's crew, and al the deposition of the four free black men, copies of all which I have the honor to enclose for your information.

I was informed by His Excellency the Governor that he would do all in his power to recover the three free British subjects, whom you will perceive by the deposition of the three others had been detained there, but that it was out of his power to recover the negroes who had been landed; nor could he give any account of the Neirsee or her crew.

[16]Source: TNA, ADM 1 280.

DOCUMENT 17. DEARE TO FLEMING (Port of Spain, Trinidad, 12 March 1829)

In pursuance of your orders dated the 5th instant, I left the anchorage of the town of Roseau, Dominica, the next morning at one o'clock, and arrived at Point-à-Pitre, Guadeloupe, at nine the same day.[17] I immediately went on shore for the purpose of delivering the letter you did me the honor to charge me with to His Excellency, the Governor of that island. I was, however, informed by the general commanding the troops that the governor was not in town, nor was it known when he would be. He however took charge of your dispatch which I accordingly left with him. On returning to my boat, I was informed by Mr. Davis (late prize master of the Neirsee) whom I had brought with me, that a schooner, which he pointed out close to the wharf, was owned and commanded by the man (Janoel by name) who piloted that vessel into the anchorage at Deseada, and whose son conveyed her afterwards from thence to that part of the coast of Guadeloupe, on which her cargo was landed. I immediately went alongside the schooner, to ascertain if Mr. Davis was right, which I was convinced he was by their telling me on my asking the question the master's name. On my asking for him, which I said with the intention of prevailing either on him (or his son whom I thought it likely would be with him) to go to sea with me as pilot, I was informed he was on shore. I made endeavors to find him, but without success. I then returned to the general, to whom I mentioned the circumstance and requested he would send a police officer with me to find him, or at least to make some enquiries that might throw a light on the subject of the Neirsee. He accordingly begged a French naval officer, the commandant of the "Topaze" schooner to go with me, and gave me to understand that I might speak to the man "Janoel" in his presence. I accordingly proceeded on board the "Topaze" with this officer who sent for "Janoel" to meet me there. He however was not to be found and the person who came from his schooner ("Le Frelon") said that he had gone out into the country, and that his son was laying sick at Port La Mole; concluding from what I heard that it was not likely I should see this man, I thought my best chance of success in the object I had in view was to proceed as directed by you to the island of Deseada, which I accordingly did, and arrived there at 10 o'clock on Saturday morning; when I landed, and in answer to my enquiries was informed that there was not a pilot in the place; nor had they ever known a vessel laden with Negroes to approach the anchorage. This was of course an untruth, as Mr. Davies point out to me a man (whose name I believe is "Francois Myer") who came off to the Neirsee while she was lying there.

I also made enquiries of these people respecting "Janoel" and his son, both of whom they appear to know and told me that the latter was on board with his father six days before, but that it was likely he was taken ill since, and might have gone to Port La Mole. Finding I could obtain no further intelligence that could be useful to me, I determined to run the coast down with a pilot, and take the chance of Mr. Davis or some of the Negroes recognizing the spot on which the latter had been landed. I accordingly bore up for that purpose and when running along the south coast of Guadeloupe, and about four miles from the east land, I was informed by Mr. Davis that a sandy beach we were abreast of was the place where the Neirsee had discharged her cargo; I immediately hove to with our head off shore and landed in the gig and cutter with Mr. Davis and all the Negroes. After I had done this, I proceeded with Lieut. Mayne (who was of great assistance to me by his knowledge of the French language) and Thomas George (the husband of the woman Sarah) only; thinking I stood a better chance of succeeding by doing so than if they had all been with me. I had met several people on the beach who professed to be the proprietors of small estates close to, and who invited me to their houses, to which we went. When I questioned them on the subject of the Neirsee, of which they pretended ignorance, but appeared however to be sensible of the cruelty of keeping the woman from her husband; and were or pretended to be affected at the poor fellow's evident anxiety and distress respecting her. In the course of conversation, I gathered from them that if a cargo of Negroes had been landed, they were certainly marched off to a distant part of the island, which I am induced to think might have been Port La Mole. I was informed afterwards by Thomas George that he saw one of the men I had been talking to purchase several Negroes, after they were landed from the Neirsee. He also pointed out a man to me whom he had seen at the place he was forced to work at; but I could not learn his name or that of the estate on which they were, but it was about half a mile from the coast, and three miles to the eastward of Bourg Francois, to which we afterwards visited in company with the commandant, who overtook us on our way there, having left his house, as I understood, for the purpose of finding out the object of my visit. Thomas George, the negro, could not point out to me the exact place he was working at, but from his manners, I am fully convinced he was well acquainted with the neighborhood, and would have found out the spot, had we not been overtaken by the commandant, who expressed very great surprise at our having landed on the coast; and on my explaining my business, informing him that I was merely obtaining information which I intended to give to the governor of the island, respecting the outrage that had been committed, he denied all knowledge of the transaction, and gave me to understand (although in a polite and gentlemanlike manner) that he expected I would discontinue my search. As I did not conceive myself at liberty to continue it in defiance of him, I acceded to his request, and embarked in the boats, which I had ordered to follow me round to the town. While on the beach before getting into the boats, I was informed by Mr. Davis that he had recognized one of the owners of the "Neirsee" who left the beach immediately on perceiving him. I mentioned the circumstance to the commandant, who told me it was quite out of his power to interfere. On my return on board, I wrote an account of what I had done to the governor of Guadeloupe and sent my letter to the commandant, who had offered to take charge of it.

[17]*Source:* TNA, ADM 1 280.

DOCUMENT 18. FLEMING TO CROKER (Trinidad, 13 March 1829)

I have the honor herewith to transmit for the information of the Lords Commissioners of the Admiralty, copies of a correspondence relative to the Brig Neirsee alias L'Estafette, together with the copy of a letter I have written to the British Ambassador at Paris.[18]

The conduct of the Governor at Guadeloupe appears to me most singularly insincere. Notwithstanding my repeated applications, and having been there myself, he has not delivered up all the British subjects; nor do I understand that any measures whatever have been taken for recovering the Africans. Commander Dear went on shore at the place where these people were landed, not far distant from Bourg Francois. Many of those present were recognized by the men of the Eden, as well as by the black men, who had been in captivity there, as having been accessory to this disgraceful transaction.

The Island lawyers differ in opinion as to the seizure of the Neirsee by the former crew being piracy; as she had Dutch papers and came to Guadeloupe under Dutch colors, contrary to the treaty with the King of the Netherlands, it appears to me that the French authorities can have no right to admit either the ship or cargo; and their being sold does not relieve them from the responsibility of permitting such a transaction, illegal by the laws of France, as it is inconsistent with the rights of Nations.

I shall not relax in my endeavors to procure the restitution of these unfortunate persons; and more particularly the British subjects, for which purpose I shall send the first disposable ship again to Guadeloupe; and I intend to retain on this part of the station the people belonging to the Eden, as well as the Black Men, for the purpose of identifying the crew of the "Neirsee," and to serve as witnesses should the French authorities think proper to proceed against the parties connected with this affair.

You will perceive by Captain Deare's report that this vessel went to the Dutch part of St. Martins. As her papers were all taken out by the Eden, she could not be legally entered at that port. Nevertheless with that disgraceful facility which has lately been afforded at all those islands, she was enabled to proceed to St. Bartholomews with some sort of document (and there it is not necessary to be very correct) where she was sold and hoisted Swedish colors.

The conduct of the Swedes surpasses all others in openness of protecting every sort of irregular transaction. Their slave vessels (the ground work of all piracies) are openly fitted out; changing their names or colors at their will, and publicly arming and shipping men. Every difficulty is at all times thrown in the way of British officers in recovering property seized by, or tracing pirates. His Swedish Majesty's dominions in these seas is preeminently conspicuous for the protection afforded to vagabonds of all nations, driven by their crimes from all others. Here the infamous Almeida found an asylum, and there his family now are. There too he found ready associates for the disposal of His Brazilian Majesty's subjects stolen from that coast.

I am very credibly informed that more than two hundred seamen, American and British, have been at times detained in that island, many of whom leave their ships in hopes of getting better employment; but when once on shore there can never be embarked until the debt incurred to a set of men who make it a business to supply their wants is discharged, as well as a dollar and a half claimed by the government for a passport. Thus the slavers and pirates by discharging the debt become in a certain degree the Masters of these people, by which means they are enables to carry on their nefarious practices.

I have great reason to believe that American and even British capital is employed in this horrid traffic, although so covered as to practice, that it is next to impossible to bring forward proof thereof. It is however very evident that piracy will never cease so long as the slave trade exists; and that the former can never be put down without the honest exertions of the European governments.

His Danish Majesty's late decree will tend much to narrow the extent of this evil; but while France so openly violates her own laws and treaties, and the Dutch and above all the Swedes are permitted to continue their present conduct, the safety of all property on the seas must remain in its present precarious state. It is right, however, to mention that the Dutch have been lately more circumspect, it having been rumored that a Frigate was coming from Europe, having on board a commission to enquire into the conduct of their officers.

[18]*Source:* TNA, ADM 1 280.

DOCUMENT 19. FLEMING TO ROTOURS (H.M.S. *Barham*, off Point-à-Pitre, 3 March 1829)

It is with extreme regret, I observe the indifference with which your Excellency has thought proper partially to notice in that letter the piracy committed by the crew of the brig "La Niersee" or "L'Estafette" who, after the cruelties practiced on His Britannic Majesty's subjects by wounding them, confining them in irons, exposing their lives in an open boat; and atrociously disposing of those of color for slaves, found an asylum in the Island of Guadeloupe and a ready market for those unfortunate people; by which conduct many of the inhabitants of that Island have incurred the penalty attached to piracy by all nations; and which I thought it only necessary to mention to Your Excellency to ensure your ready co-operation in seizing and delivering up the pirates, releasing His Britannic Majesty's subjects and free Africans; and bringing to punishment all those connected with these foul and scandalous proceedings.[19]

That the African slave trade has been carried on openly and to a great extent in this Island is well known to all, and His Britannic Majesty's Government has been duly informed thereof; it forms no part of my duty, however, to expostulate with Your Excellency on this subject. The infracture of the French laws and the failure of His Most Christian Majesty's stipulations in the treaty of the 30th May 1814 will no doubt be promptly alluded to by the British Government; but the effect of this infamous practice, by the demoralization of the inhabitants, is now obvious by the ready protection to the pirates and the participation in their infamous practices, which in the present instance has taken place.

I assure Your Excellency that this is no common case, that it will not be looked on as such by the British Government who will not relax in their exertions until all the pirates and those connected with them are duly punished and all his Britannic Majesty's subjects, as well as the Africans, set at liberty. This it is in your Excellency's power immediately to effect; and by doing so, you will save to those unfortunate people several months of misery, for it must be recollected, part of the crew of the "Estafette" with all her papers are in the possession of the ship which captured that vessel, by virtue of the treaty between His Britannic Majesty and the King of the Netherlands. These, with the people now here, will substantiate the facts. The latter will prove the pirates having been received at the little island of Deseada; they will point out the place where they landed the Africans, the estates they have been since seen on, where they were themselves confined, and confirm every other particular relative to this atrocious transaction.

I have the honor herewith to transmit to Your Excellency the depositions of the men of color who were sent to Dominica under the circumstances therein detailed. These, as well as the Eden's crew, are at the disposal of Your Excellency as witnesses, either to proceed against the pirates or those equally guilty with them, by the purchase of the persons above mentioned.

Your Excellency will perceive that part of the crew of the pirate brig Niersee were left at Guadeloupe, and I have reason to believe that when the Grasshopper was here, one of those persons was at Basse-Terre. I have further to acquaint your Excellency that I have received intelligence that "La Niersee" or "L'Estafette" has been at St. Eustatius whither she proceeded after landing the people here; and that under apprehension of her being seized by the Dutch government, she had gone to St. Bartholomews, leaving part of her crew who are natives of that place at that island; these I have sent to reclaim, as well as the vessel.

[19]*Source:* TNA, ADM 1 280.

DOCUMENT 20. DESCRIPTION OF THE SECOND CAPTAIN, TWO OFFICERS AND SEVEN SEAMEN BELONGING TO THE BRIG NEIRSEE OR ESTAFETTE

NAME	QUALITY	AGE	STATURE	COMPLEXION	REMARKS
Richard	2nd Captain	56	5'6	dark	Has been thirty years employed in privateering and in the slave trade.[20] Speaks good English
Miller	2nd Mate	30	5'8	fair	A Dane by birth, speaks English, has never before been in the slave trade. Was formerly Captain of a French ship trading from Bordeaux to the West Indies
Sicard	Surgeon	26	5'9	dark	A Frenchman; although called 3rd mate yet is no sailor. Is marked with the small pox; has a scar on left cheek; speaks English
Cornish	Seaman	20	5'6	dark	Said to be a Dutch Creole of Curacao. Speaks English and French
Antonio	ditto	30	5'6	dark	A Spaniard, had been taken in a Spanish slaver, and afterwards volunteering for the service was put on board the Neirsee as one of the prize crew; when the prisoners rose he joined them, also
Manuel	ditto	28	5'9	dark	A Portuguese; under similar circumstances as the preceding
Heneque	ditto	26	5'10	dark	A Dutch Creole, speaks English and French
Alfred	steward	28	5'6	dark	A French Creole, speaks English
Alexander	seaman	26	5'4	dark	A French Creole, speaks English
Battie	ditto	36	5'7	dark	A French Creole, blind of his left eye, speaks English

[20]*Source:* TNA, ADM 1 280.

EUROPE: A DIPLOMATIC INCIDENT
DOCUMENT 21. FLEMING TO LORD STUART DE ROTHSAY, BRITISH AMBASSADOR TO FRANCE (H.M.S. *Barham*, off Martinique, 5 March 1829)

I avail myself of the opportunity of being off this island to send your Excellency a copy of a correspondence which has taken place respecting a vessel detained by His Majesty's Ship Eden, on the coast of Africa, and carried off by a part of the crew left in her, after firing at the people of the Eden, whom they treated with great inhumanity, confining them in irons below during the passage and afterwards putting them at the risk of their lives into a very small boat in which they reached the island of Dominica with difficulty.[21]

The Governor of Guadeloupe does not appear to be inclined to separate this case from those of slave vessels which very frequently repair to that island; where establishments are formed along the coast for facilitating the disembarkation of the unhappy people they contain; and although the Negroes belonging to the Eden called Kroomen and the artificers have been sent back at different times in the same inhuman manner; yet the free woman Sarah (the wife of one of the latter) and all the Africans are still detained, having been publicly sold to the different planters, and it appears very clearly to have been the intention of those concerned in this nefarious transaction that these men should have followed the same fate; they were obliged to work without pay, beaten and ill treated when they refused, the Kroomen being employed in grinding canes, and the others at their trades; the last three who reached Dominica were put into a rotten canoe so leaky as to require one man to be constantly bailing and altogether in so bad a condition as to warrant the supposition that they never were intended to reach the land.

It appears that this vessel was originally fitted out at Martinique under French colors; but subsequently procured Dutch papers which appears to have been the cause of her detention by Captain Owen of the Eden; her name has been so frequently changed that it is difficult to trace whether she procured those papers at St. Eustatius or not; part of her crew however were from that island and some creole Spaniards shipped there. On their arrival at Deseada, they came in under the Dutch flag and were allowed to proceed in the evening to land the Negroes although the papers were all taken out of her by the Eden. Your Excellency will perceive that she has since proceeded to St. Bartholomews where she hoisted Swedish colors. I regret to say that not any of her crew have been arrested, and that the French authorities in Guadeloupe have done nothing whatever towards liberating the people, those who have returned having been sent back by the planters in consequence of the appearance of the British ships of war off Guadeloupe, and the rumors which have been spread in consequence. As this disgraceful transaction arises entirely out of the horrid traffic in Negroes, so openly carried on in the island of Guadeloupe, and not infrequently in Martinique, I think it right to acquaint your Lordship that since I have commanded the British Naval force in this country, I have not heard of one single slave vessel being either captured or detained by any French authority; and that although it is well known that all these vessels touch at Deseada or Marie Galante for orders, and there are no less than five armed vessels stationed at Guadeloupe, not one of them have ever been employed in giving force to the French laws, when by stationing one at each of the above mentioned islands, an end would be put to these expeditions.

[21]*Source:* TNA, ADM 1 280.

DOCUMENT 22. ROTOURS TO HYDE DE NEUVILLE, MINISTER OF THE NAVY AND COLONIES (Basse-Terre, 2 March 1829)

Despite the active and determined surveillance of the local navy, Gendarmerie, and police, the lure of immense profit, on the one hand, and the need for labor, on the other, lead to the landing of negroes from time to time in the colonies.[22] Moreover, the nature of the coasts of Guadeloupe unfortunately offer too great a chance of success to this deplorable traffic.

A landing of this type seems to have occurred last December, and it involves circumstances that, to the extent that I become able, I will hasten to bring to Your Excellency's attention. They have given rise to an exchange of correspondence between the Governor of Dominica and me; they have also been the object of a letter that Admiral Fleming, commander of His Britannic Majesty's forces in these seas, to me.

Here are the facts that result from the depositions of the English who were momentarily imprisoned by the slaver crew.

On November 2nd, a brig loaded with 280 negroes was captured at anchor before Calabar, in the Bight of Biafra, by a vessel of the English royal navy, the Eden, captain Owen. This officer took his prize to Fernando Po. It remained there until the 27th, when the brig was sent to Bathurst to obtain food supplies and wait for the Horatio, tender, which was to escort it to Sierra Leone.

On December 2nd, the brig departed together with the Horatio. Its prize crew consisted of an officer, five sailors, and eight colored individuals. Fifteen members of the French crew, the second captain, and two master artisans were also on board. The slave ship's commander, Captain Feraud, was on the Horatio.

A few days later, the weather became heavy and these two vessels were separated. Seizing this opportunity, the crewmen of the slaver got the English sailors drunk, confined them in the hold after a struggle that did not result in any serious wounds, although several pistol shots were fired, seized the officer and forbade him from going onto the bridge. At the start of the fight, the eight men of color fled into the hold.

According to these same depositions, the vessel steered a course for this colony, and the landing, which the inhabitants seemed to expect, took place at a spot the deponents could not identify. After having unloaded its cargo, the slave ship departed and, while passing Dominica, placed in a canoe the English officer and men, who arrived safely at Prince Rupert Bay.

A few days later, I received from Monsieur the Governor of Dominica, together with the deposition of the captured English officer, a letter by which he demanded, on the grounds that they were British subjects, the release of the eight free blacks who had been part of the prize crew and who appeared to have been landed and sold along with the African blacks.

Your Excellency will not doubt the seriousness with which I undertook the most rigorous investigation to discover the whereabouts of these eight individuals.

The most precise orders were given to the Gendarmerie and police. While their searches were unsuccessful, I have no doubt that they were not entirely fruitless, for I soon received from Monsieur the Governor of Dominica and Monsieur the Admiral Fleming communications which, while announcing the return of six of these individuals, demanded the restitution of the two others. Investigations are being conducted with the same energy as before, and I have no doubt that the fear now being felt by those who took part in this apparent violation of human rights will soon lead to—if it has not already done so—the return of the two individuals who did not come back with the others.

Although the landing took place some time ago and although I have little hope that the judicial investigation will reveal if the outfitters of this expedition belong to the colony of Guadeloupe, I have nonetheless invited the attorney general to take all necessary measures.

[22]*Source:* Archives Nationales d'Outre Mer (ANOM), Fonds Ministériel (FM), Série Géographique (SG), GUA/Corr/78.

DOCUMENT 23. HYDE DE NEUVILLE TO ROTOURS (Paris, 28 April 1829)

I received your letter of March 2nd by which you informed me of the correspondence that has taken place between you and the British authority in the Antilles concerning a slave-trading ship indicated as French which, after having been captured by an English warship, was retaken by its original crew and conducted to Guadeloupe with a cargo of blacks.[23]

The English ambassador has informed the government that information was going to be obtained without delay in order to gain an exact understanding of the circumstances surrounding the intervention of a warship of His Britannic Majesty in the capture.

But today we must address the British demand for the release of the free blacks taken to Guadeloupe by the slave ship.

The supplemental depositions taken by the magistrates of Dominica indicate that these blacks numbered nine, eight negroes and one negrese.

You informed me that six of these individuals had been delivered to this foreign colony, and your letter gives me reason to believe that the other blacks will have also been allowed to follow the same route. If not, you will have to take all necessary steps to satisfy the demand that has been made to you on that subject.

You have already received the most formal instructions to ensure in Guadeloupe the execution of the laws concerning the repression of the trade in blacks. These instructions should have served to govern the conduct of the public authorities in the present affair. It is hard to believe that, in such a small country, their efforts to discover the authors or accomplices of a crime such as this could have been fruitless, given that it concerns a landing of an entire cargo of blacks that took place at a time, according to the depositions, that only goes back to the 23rd of last January.

Any laxity in the measures to be taken against the guilty parties would provoke the discontent of the government, and I would be forced to inform His Majesty of it.

[23]*Source:* ANOM, Fonds Ministériel (FM), 1 CORR/118.

DOCUMENT 24. ROTOURS TO HYDE DE NEUVILLE (Basse-Terre, 10 May 1829)

I had the honor to inform Your Excellency . . . of diverse circumstances that accompanied and followed the landing of a cargo of black slaves on the coast of Guadeloupe, in the Saint Francis district.[24] Given that six of the free men whose release he was demanding arrived in Dominica and given that I had assured him that I would devote all of my efforts to finding the two others, I thought that the Governor of that colony would be satisfied and that this case would finally be closed. But when I arrived at Point-à-Pitre, General Vatable told me that Vice-Admiral Fleming, commander of British naval forces in these seas, after having waited several days for me on his flagship, had left, asking him to deliver a letter to me. I greatly regretted not have seen Admiral Fleming; the explanations that I would have given him would have doubtlessly made it unnecessary to write to me in terms so disrespectful toward the King and so unmeasured toward me personally, as Your Excellency will see from reading this letter.

It had just been given to me when I received another from the commander of the Saint Francis district informing me that Captain Deare of the corvette Grasshopper, after having anchored off shore and landed with one or two officers, had entered a plantation and then gone to the burg, where he was probably preparing to conduct some sort of investigation, perhaps even a house-to-house search, when the commander, who had hastened there upon hearing of his landing, asked him to re-embark. This he did, after having addressed me a letter to inform me of what he had just done, as if it was most simple and natural thing imaginable. This is not how I saw it.

Assuming that Captain Deare had acted in this way on Admiral Fleming's orders, I wrote to the Admiral to complain of this territorial violation and of several facts that had just been reported to me about his own conduct and of Captain Deare's at Désirade. At the same time I forcefully protested about the expressions I mentioned above. In effect, I had the right to be shocked at such proceedings when, having accepted the complaints of the Governor of Dominica, I had done everything possible to satisfy them, which neither he nor Admiral Fleming can doubt, given the results already produced by the measures I ordered. What more can I do? Do the English intend to arrogate to themselves the right of conducting searches upon French territory? My duty was not only to oppose this, but also to complain and demand explanations. Admiral Fleming's response to my letter, and Captain Deare's, are no more than the denials and word games typical of the English, who make everything conditional and always reserve the right to go back on what they say, from whatever angle that suits them. Nonetheless, it is clear that . . . despite General Vatable's injunctions, this captain landed at Saint Francis, interrogated the negroes of a plantation to learn about its interior regime, went to the burg where, I repeat, he conducted a sort of investigation without any authorizations whatsoever. . . .

As for Admiral Fleming, Your Excellency will sufficiently appreciate, without my calling further attention to them, the reflections contained in his letters. To say that the King of France has violated treaties because several renegade outfitters still carry out the commerce in slaves is to forget, in a very serious manner, the respect due to His Majesty when addressing one who has the honor to represent him in the colony. I cannot oppose this with too much indignation. As for what regards me personally, to claim that the commerce in blacks from Africa is carried out openly at Guadeloupe is to make its director or accomplice. The unconditional denial that I gave Admiral Fleming will have made him understand that you do not attack a French officer's honor with impunity. . . .

He claims to be well informed about what happens in Guadeloupe. We know that with their gold, the English easily find spies everywhere. But if those they employ here served them better, they would know that the most active surveillance is maintained over the coasts of the colony to oppose the landing of cargoes of black slaves, that these landings are rare, and that the Gendarmerie and the justice have always done their duty in such cases, if not efficiently because of the inadequacy of the laws, at least with the zeal expected of them.

I do not think that the Admiral Fleming's assertions require me to justify myself. Even so, Your Excellency . . . should be aware that my vigilance extends far beyond the coasts of Guadeloupe. I should add that these coasts, 80 leagues in length, double the length of the other French possessions, offer more than any other bays and inlets suited to fraudulent landings. But Admiral Fleming prefers to ignore these facts, and it would be useless to try to change his mind. I did not feel myself obliged to respond to his last letter, especially since the Governor of Dominica has since informed me that the last two negroes he was demanding had been landed on that island, thus completing the liberation he demanded.

Given this state of things, what more can the English Government want and what are His Majesty's rights?

Admiral Fleming demands that the cargo of blacks landed at Saint Francis be handed over to him. But, first, under what flag had the captured vessel been sailing? The Admiral does not say, doubtless because this slave ship was flying the flag of France and that, in this case, the English did not even have the right to inspect, let alone seize it. . . . And second, how to find these negroes among the 80,000 slaves who people the colony?

Thus, on the one hand, Admiral Fleming has received all the satisfaction he can reasonably demand, and, on the other, to the contrary, the King's Government has the right to demand satisfaction for Captain Deare's territorial violation.

[24]*Source:* ANOM, FM, SG, GUA/Corr/78.

DOCUMENT 25. ROTOURS TO HYDE DE NEUVILLE (Basse-Terre, 25 June 1829)

The eight free blacks demanded by Admiral Fleming were taken to Dominica by their criminal purchasers, who were afraid of the measures I had taken to discover them.[25] One must rejoice at such a result, when one considers that these measures, like all those taken in similar cases, would have usually been useless; for how can one find eight blacks distributed across so many plantations, in a country measuring 80 leagues around, which is crowned with impenetrable forests, and whose plains are covered with more than 400 sugar or other plantations.

Your Excellency ends his dispatch of April 28th by saying that it is hard to believe that a cargo of blacks can be concealed from the pursuit of justice on such a small island. I have the honor to observe that Guadeloupe is by far the largest in the Antilles; thus, if its size and the facilities the shores of this colony offer for fraudulent landings are taken into consideration, I cannot fear that Your Excellency takes for laxity the lack of success that I might have in my investigations. . . .

The eight free blacks demanded by Admiral Fleming had been dropped off at Dominica; as for the negresse Sarah, Your Excellency will judge, since I said it to the Admiral, that she is only a pretext he is using to prolong this affair. It is obvious that this negresse was part of the cargo and that she was the wife of one of the free negroes only for the duration of the crossing, as is often the practice on slave ships. It is thus disingenuously that Admiral Fleming insists on her restitution. In any case, it would not be any easier than the restitution of the cargo for the reasons I have just mentioned. These very plausible reasons and the frank and open manner with which I have interacted with Admiral Fleming should have satisfied him . . . especially since it is he who owes an explanation for the conduct of Captain Deare, of the Grasshopper corvette, who took the liberty of making a sort of investigation or, at the very least, a search on the territory of the King of France. It seems that at this point, we both ought to await the orders of our governments. What does Admiral Fleming want to accomplish when he says that his corvette will periodically visit the coast of Guadeloupe until the cargo of blacks is delivered up to him? Who is he blaming for the excesses that he claims were committed on the subjects of His Britannic Majesty? I feel that I answered him, on these points, as I should have, always acting with uprightness and frankness. If the corvette with which Admiral Fleming is threatening me commits some depredations, lands spies, and assumes a hostile attitude, it will not do so without impunity on these shores.

Admiral Fleming cites a Monsieur Sergente, inhabitant of Le Moule, who allegedly subjected the free blacks, during the time he detained them, to slave labor. Searches were made of his property, but without result. To undertake new ones, should I use these same free blacks, subjects of the King of England? I did not think I ought to do it. In this regard, Your Excellency will give me the orders that he thinks proper, but, in my opinion, the kind of confrontation that would result from the resulting searches and judicial proceedings would have serious drawbacks, among others to cause the government to lose respect in the eyes of colonists by an act which they would regard as extremely abject.

[25] *Source:* ANOM, FM, SG, GUA/Corr/78.

DOCUMENT 26. FLEMING TO CROKER (Curaçao, 7 September 1829)

From the frequent changes of colors, names, and masters [of illicit slave ships], it becomes extremely difficult to identify individuals and vessels of this description.[26]

The case of the Niersee alias Estafeta is already before their Lordships and affords a very striking illustration of this remark. She fitted out at Martinique under French colors, procured Dutch at St. Eustatius. On her return she proceeded to St. Bartholomews where she procured Swedish; from that she went to the Havana where she obtained Spanish, and now, under all these colors is probably on her way on another voyage to the coast of Africa.

So long as such facility for changing colors is given in the foreign Islands, the seas can never be safe for defenseless merchant ships, but the chief evil under which all the pirates now clothe themselves is the open manner in which the slave trade is carried on between the French possessions in the West Indies and the Coast of Africa, under their flag; and it is undeniable that the outrage committed on the Benbow was perpetrated by one of those vessels; and there is reason to believe that the guilty vessel has returned to Guadeloupe with a cargo of slaves and has since proceeded to Puerto Rico. The usual course of those vessels is to fit out at Martinique or Guadeloupe; they are principally American-built, having been privateers under various flags; from one of these islands they proceed to St. Thomas's and purchase the requisite goods for the Coast; clear out for Cuba and under pretence of protection from pirates get permission to land; but lately the Danish authorities have been more circumspect and this part of their equipment has generally been done at St. Bartholomews where a depot of seamen of all nations has hitherto been kept, on pretence of their being in debt, as already noted in my letter No. 69 of the 23rd of March last, and having Danish, Dutch, or Swedish subjects on board as supercargoes, surgeons or stewards, these act occasionally as the master of the colors they think proper to display.

The remedy for these evils can only come from Europe. The Dutch, Danish and Swedish governments have instructed their authorities in the West Indies not to be too strict; under a false notion of encouraging trade and getting back to their islands that which is irrevocably lost since the Revolution which has taken place in Spanish America and in which the islands of Jamaica and Trinidad have borne their full share. The establishment of free ports here, at St. Bartholomews and at St. Thomas's all originate from the same desire; that instead of being beneficial to their own governments, with the exception of St. Thomas's they are only useful to the individuals of all nations of the worst possible description; ready to enter into any desperate undertakings, and thus may be found in this island Corsicans, Genoese, Sardinians, French, English, American, Brabants, etc. etc., outlaws of their own country and of many others; but there from the false grounds above stated they find protection.

Since I have been in this port, vessels have arrived under the Columbian flag, sailed again under Dutch colors, and returned under Spanish. Americans likewise have become Danes and Columbians Spaniards.

A privateer which appears here with a prize has only to complain that she requires some repair; when she is immediately permitted to sell her without condemnation to pay the expenses. The remainder is deposited for 6 sometimes 12 months for claims; and none being lodged (the owners being ignorant of the fate of their vessels) the balance is paid over to the captain of the privateer; and thus he is enabled to cheat the crew and appropriate to himself property which never would have been condemned to him in a regular court.

Soon after my arrival at Curacao, I found a vessel called the Cubana from Cuba and Jamaica under Sp colors had been taken by the noted "Bernard Ferrero" who instead of sending her over to Columbia, sent her to Aruba where she was permitted to change her colors to Dutch and under which she arrived here with the Columbian crew still in possession. Under a supposition that there might be Brit prop on board, I applied to the government to have this vessel detained and wrote to Jam for info. But none having been obtained after a delay of 6 weeks, the Gov sent the crew over in a Dutch man of war to Puerto Cabello. Soon afterwards "Bernard" arrived, claimed the vessel, and she sailed from this under Columbian colors; but I have strong reason to believe the Dutch would be used as a protection to some other part and thus a vessel without any legal condemnation falls a sacrifice to persons who are literally pirates.

During the last year, a person calling himself "Fournier" arrived at St-Eustatius from Boston in a vessel called the 25th of May (Neustro 25 de Mayo), said to be a BY man of war, having on board a quantity of blank commissions from that government, dated the 1st of Jan 1828, to be in force for one year, which were disposed of to all persons who chose to become purchasers. The colonel, by authority which he pretended to have, extended the time from the day on which they were bought. This person got possession of a vessel which had been under the BA flag and had been seized at St. Thomas for some irregularity. He brought her over to St Eustatius and there fitted her out as a privateer; putting on board a person in possession of a very old BA commission with a crew of all nations. She proceeded to the coast of Africa and on the 5th of Feb last captured a large Port ship which had sailed from Rio de Janeiro in the month of Dec; after the term allowed by the Treaty bet Brazil and Buenos Aires had elapsed, she returned to St. Eustatius with this vessel and off the little island of Saba disposed of all the cargo. Soon after His Netherlands Majesty's ship Falcon, Capt Van Ness, arrived and detained both vessels. They have been carried up to Surinam where they are still under litigation and I understand very likely to be liberated.

In consequence of the failure of many of the foreign speculators in Cuba, the price of slaves has fallen very considerably in that island; and as that race do not decrease in the Spanish Islands, as is the case of those of France, there appears no doubt that if the French Government would honestly and seriously put down the slave trade, it would fall altogether in a few years.

[26]Source: TNA, ADM 1 281.

DOCUMENT 27. LORD ABERDEEN, FOREIGN SECRETARY, TO ROTHSAY (London, 3 April 1829)

I herewith transmit to Your Excellency the copy of a communication which I have received from the Colonial Dept., stating that a Brig named "Neirsee" or "Estafette," laden with slaves, was detained off Calabar by H.M.S. "Eden"; that the vessel in question was taken first to Fernando Po; and that in proceeding from that Island to Sierra Leone, where it was intended that the circumstances attending her detention should be submitted to the Court of Mixed Commission for investigation; the crew, aided by other individuals on board of the vessel, rose upon the persons at the time in charge of her, and carried the vessel to Guadeloupe, at which place having landed the slaves reported to be 280 in number together with nine free Africans, who had been placed on board by the British authorities in possession, the vessel made sail for Martinique, and in her way thither, landed at Dominica the British officers and men who had originally be placed on board when she was detained by H.M.S. Eden.[27]

H.M.'s Govt. animated with the same spirit of frankness and good faith by which all their communications with the Govt. of His Most Christian Majesty are dictated have no desire to conceal from the latter any of the circumstances which have come to their knowledge upon this transaction, nor do they hesitate to avow, that those circumstances, so far as H.M.'s Government are yet apprised of them, do appear to make out against the commander of one of H.M.'s cruisers a case of interference with a vessel suspected to be French, which not when the traffic in which she was engaged, can justify.

Upon this part of the case, His M's Govt. can at present only assure the Govt. of H.M.C. Majesty that enquiries will be instituted without delay by the proper Department of H.M.'s Govt. with the view of obtaining the fullest explanation upon the questionable circumstances here adverted to.

In the mean while, H.M.'s Government deem it to be their duty to communicate without reserve to the Government of H.M.C. Majesty the statement which has reached them upon this transaction: and entertain no doubt that the French Govt. of whose humane anxiety to put down the hateful traffic in slaves H.M.'s Govt. are fully assured will institute immediate enquiries into the illegal proceedings in which their subjects appear to have been engaged on this occasion, with the view of punishing the transgressors, and of preventing in future the successful prosecution of undertakings proscribed by the laws of every nation of Europe.

H.M.'s Govt. request that the French Govt. will give directions that the free Africans who were put on board of the vessel in question by British officers may be delivered up to the Governor of Dominica to be transported back to their native country.

[27]*Source:* TNA, CO 71 68.

DOCUMENT 28. HYDE DE NEUVILLE TO PORTALIS, MINISTER OF FOREIGN AFFAIRS (Paris, 22 April 1829)

By your letter of the 14th of this month, you did me the honor to inform me of a communication from Monsieur the English ambassador concerning a ship employed in the slave trade and thought to be French, which, after having been captured by a warship of His Britannic Majesty in the Bay of Biafra (west coast of Africa), was retaken by its original crew and taken to Guadeloupe.[28]

I see from the copy of the ambassador's letter that the English government disapproved that a warship of his nation intervened in the present case and that he has announced that information will be obtained without delay, in order to gain an exact knowledge of the facts accompanying the capture.

Your Excellency will doubtlessly think it necessary to ask to be informed of the result of these investigations. I would like you to share it with me. Until that time, I think I should reserve my opinion on this part of the affair.

As Your Excellency notes, the principal object of the English ambassador's demand is the return to the Governor of Dominica of the free blacks taken to Guadeloupe by the slave ship.

Depositions taken before the judicial authority of Dominica reveal that these blacks numbered nine, eight negroes and one negrese.

The Governor of Guadeloupe informed me, by his letter of March 2nd, that six of these individuals arrived at Dominica, and I have reason to think, according to the terms of his letter, that the other blacks will have also been enabled to follow the same route. I also directed him to neglect none of the measures necessary to satisfy, on that point, the English government's demand.

The colonial authority has received the most severe orders to assure, in our overseas establishments, the execution of the laws on the repression of the slave trade. Nonetheless, I addressed to the governors of Martinique and Guadeloupe new orders in this vein, on the occasion of the present affair.

[28] *Source:* Archives des Affaires Etrangères (AAE), Affaires Diverses Politiques (ADP) 30.

DOCUMENT 29. HYDE DE NEUVILLE DE PORTALIS (Paris, 3 July 1829)

However you regard what took place, it is beyond doubt that a vessel under the French flag and presumed to be French was search at sea and detained by ships of His Britannic Majesty and that officers of the English Royal Navy undertook, on the shores of a French possession and without permission from the local authorities, incursions and illegal investigations totally contrary to the friendly relations existing between the two powers.[29] Your Excellency cannot fail to appreciate the importance of these facts.

[29] *Source:* AAE, ADP 30.

DOCUMENT 30. HYDE DE NEUVILLE DE PORTALIS (Paris, 24 July 1829)

I send you, together with diverse attachments, a report from Monsieur the Governor of Guadeloupe on the landing and the events that followed.[30] I hope these documents will convince Your Excellency that, far from having the right to complain, the English government actually owes His Majesty an apology, not only for the search and illegal detention of a French-flagged ship, but even more so for the reprehensible acts that officers of His Britannic Majesty permitted themselves to commit on French territory. Whatever the English government decides to do, I think that His Majesty has every right to insist that the conduct of Admiral Fleming and the investigations undertaken at his orders by Captain Deare on the territory of Guadeloupe be genuinely disavowed.

[30]*Source:* AAE, ADP 30.

DOCUMENT 31. PORTALIS TO HYDE DE NEUVILLE (Paris, 31 July 1829)

I have asked the chargé d'affaires at London to make protests against the conduct of the English officers which will prevent the repetition of the acts of which we are complaining.[31] I have every reason to believe that they will be heard and that, in reminding the leaders of the English navy of the respect and harmony which Admiral Fleming appears to have forgotten, the English minister will understand how important it is to make sure, as you have noted, that a kind of bitterness injects itself in the relations between the respective commanders. Not that I presume to blame the entirely natural vivacity with which Monsieur des Rotours rejected the insinuations that attacked his character as a subject and representative of His Majesty as much as his personal honor. But even while giving his conduct the praise it merits, you will perhaps judge it necessary to invite him to bring to the relations that circumstances might create between Admiral Fleming and himself the moderation that is in the spirit of the two governments.

[31]*Source:* AAE, ADP 30.

DOCUMENT 32. OWEN TO CROKER (Clarence Cove, 21 June 1829)

I beg to acknowledge the receipt of your letter of the 7th April last, relative to the "Estafette" or "Niersee," said to be French.[32] I cannot allow the Lord Suffield to sail for England without seizing a moment from incessant occupation in delivering up this establishment, and in repairing as far as I can the evil done by the Sierra Leone Fevers, to inform you that the Estafette was never even suspected to be French, that she was known to be Dutch; that her Captain was known by the name of Feraud, had some property at Martinique, but he stood on his false articles by the name of Castagnet.

He declared her to be a Netherlands vessel and even after it was suspected that she might have been seized by her crew, he offered his testimony to the same effect to the Court of Mixed Commission at Sierra Leone, when it was refused, as the vessel itself did not appear. He had before capture, with others at Old Calabar, sent to tempt me by the offer of a sum of money to let him pass. She had Dutch Colors and but wore a French Flag to deter my boats from seizing her.

Captain Badgeley, who boarded her is, I grieve to say, dead, so that I cannot, at this moment, enter further into the case; but he moment I shall be able to enter upon the explanation of this and other points referred to you from the Foreign Office, I promise myself the honor of entering on their full detail.

[32]*Source:* TNA, Foreign Office (FO), 146 107.

DOCUMENT 33. OWEN TO CROKER (H.M.S. *Eden*, at sea, 30 July 1829)

By the Eden and Champion in the middle of last month, I received various dispatches from His Majesty's Secretary of State for the Colonies, from the Secretary of His Majesty's Treasury, and from yourself.[33]

To those which regard my conduct in the capture of several slave vessels; in the cases of the Nirzee alias Estafette, the Moskito, Voadora, and Felix Victoria, I have been unable to make the necessary answers owing to the continued occupation furnished me 1st by the change of government at Clarence, 2nd by the yellow fever imported in the Champion and Eden from Sierra Leone by which most of my time was demanded for the care of my people and my ship, 3rd by my own sickness which added to that of my people has obliged me to quit Clarence, leaving its affairs and accounts still unsettled, and 4th by the continued sickness on board my ship, which includes the surgeon who has done no duty whatever since the first week of his embarkation, thus throwing the whole weight and care of the sick entirely upon myself and my lieutenant. I am now however so far recovered as well as most of my men that I shall be able to consider and answer the several documents in question.

In the case of the Nirzee, alias Estafette, I have the honor to enclose two afadavits, one by the late acting commander Badgeley, who was the officer that boarded and detained her, and one by acting lieutenant Mercer. Although these afadavits were made for a different purpose, at times when I could hardly have had a suspicion of the fact that has since transpired, namely the recapture of that vessel by the part of her crew left on board her; it will be perceived by them that with the officers in question there was no suspicion whatever intimated that she might be French; but in obedience to the command you have done me the honor to communicate, I will give a detail of the circumstances which led to the detention of the Nirzee and such a detail of the others assuming a French character as you desire.

In February 1828 I reported the circumstance of a master of a slaving vessel under a French flag having shot the mate of a palm oil ship (the Kent of Liverpool) through the body, and the demand for protection made in consequence by Mister Richard Cummings, master of the Kent. I also reported that in consequence of this circumstance, and the necessity of putting myself in communication with the Chief of Old Calabar to procure supplies for our new settlement, I visited that place in the Felix Victoria, and influenced by the statement of Mr. Cummings, the master of the Kent, I told the chief that if the man who shot the mate, whose name was Feraud (at least that was the name he was known by) should ever return to Old Calabar, I should expect such information from his as would enable me to get possession of Mr. Feraud. In November 1828, my communications with Old Calabar informed me that there were lying there and under French flags, notoriously known to have been assumed to prevent my boarding them, the Coquette, alias Brutus alias Venus; les Deux Freres; Les Freres; the Bolivar alias Pinchincha alias Frederick alias the Arrogante Barcelonese; the Nirzee; the Jules; and Jeune Eugenie, at least these were their assumed names. Two of those vessels were known to be commanded by two brothers calling themselves by the name of Feraud and one was the person who committed the act of violence in January preceding, but which of the two I could not know, and was the more alert in consequence to let neither of them escape me. In the mean time, I informed myself of the actual equipment of the vessels in question by the correspondence found in some of my previous captures, by several of the officers who had thus fallen into my hands, and by direct communication with the officers of the vessels themselves at Old Calabar, through the medium of the late acting commander Badgeley. This information was so positive and precise in every case that it could not be questions and was that the Bolivar was a Spanish vessel from Puerto Rico (whose case has been reported), that the Nirzee was properly named the Estafette and had been fitted out at St. Eustatius; that the Jules and Jeune Eugenie had also Dutch names and had been equipped from, and belonged to, the same place; and moreover that all of them had false French papers procured at St. Thomas's from which port they last sailed on their voyage. The Nirzee was taken on the 23rd of November when her master believed all my vessels and boats away. The Bolivar was taken on the 17th December knowing that I had no vessels watching the bar, but I had precise information of her master's intentions; and the other two were taken in the first days of January under a similar belief that I had no force near the place. One of these was commanded by the Mr. Feraud I wanted to answer for his violence to an Englishman lawfully employed, and was put into my hands by the Chief of Old Calabar, and did so answer before a Court of Magistrates at Clarence, where he perfectly cleared himself as has been reported.

When the Nirzee arrived at Clarence, her master did present to me a set of French papers, and I found it was his brother who was then at Calabar in the Jules who had committed the act of violence before alluded to. In examining the French papers that had been presented to me, they bore throughout such manifest proofs by internal evidence of their falsehood that on them only she must have been condemned in any Admiralty Court in Europe; and although false, the term of her passport had expired and had been renewed by extending the term by a notorious erasure. None of the descriptions or measures in the false passport or register corresponded at all to the vessel, and Mr. Feraud himself stood on her papers under the name of Castagnet; in short, seeing that the falsity of the papers was manifest, Mr. Feraud then avowed his true character and declared his vessel to be what I knew she was, a Netherland vessel, but I have since learnt that some merchants of Martinique had some shares in her, but have no certain evidence of that.

I have since found that all the vessels in question whilst at Old Calabar doubting the possibility of their escape did arrange that such of the officers and crews as were left in them should use all means by the aid of bribing and liquor to recover their vessels on the voyage to Sierra Leone; and the Coquette, the Bolivar, and the Nirzee did all essay to do so, the last succeeded I presume by the use of the means indicated, and the prize master, being a young man, a master's assistant, and the only officer I had at that time on board that could be detached. Could I however have had any suspicion of their ever resorting to the diabolical means they all used, I would certainly not have sent an officer or man of their own crews in them. . . .

The lamented sickness and death of acting commander Badgeley has prevented my getting the Nirzee's French papers, but they are still, I hope, in the hands of my agent at Sierra Leone, and shall be forwarded to you if I procure them with such remarks as it may be proper to make on them. . . .

Having thus given in addition to my former reports a full detail of the material facts of every case of my detention of vessels assuming a French character, I shall endeavor to answer that part of my Lord Aberdeen's letter which demands it, viz.: "His Majesty's Government animated with the same spirit of frankness and good faith by which all their communications with the Government of His Most Christian Majesty are dictated have no desire to conceal from the latter any of the circumstances which have come to their knowledge upon the transaction, nor do they hesitate to avow that those circumstances, so far as His Majesty's Government are yet apprised of them, do appear to make out against the Commander of one of His Majesty's cruisers a case of interference with a vessel suspected to be French, which not even the traffic in which she was engaged can justify."

My present answer to the opinion of my Lord Aberdeen, founded on a report of circumstances, which report has never reached me, must be confined to its precise expression, which is that the report in question does appear to make against me "a case of unjustifiable interference with a vessel *suspected to be French* etc. etc."

Now, Sir, so far from acting on the suspicion that the vessel in question, the Estafette or Nirzee, <u>was French</u>, my whole conduct with respect to her, and all the others, was founded on the belief, nay, conviction, that both she and they were *not French*, and the results have in every case where they were brought to trial proved that they were *not so*; and in the case of the Estafette, even after *he* was convinced of her recapture, her master offered his testimony to the Courts of Mixed Commission to prove her Netherland character, which, as will be seen by Lieut. Mercer's affidavit, was not received because the vessel herself had not arrived.

[33]*Source*: TNA, ADM 1 2274.

DOCUMENT 34. OWEN TO CROKER (H.M.S. *Eden*, at sea, 2 August 1829)

I have received from Commodore Collier under whose orders I am now placed an extract copy of a secret order without date to the follow effect, viz:

"You are however to abstain and positively to direct the commanders of His Majesty's Ships under your orders to abstain, from all interference on account of slave trading with vessels under the French flag or any other which you are not authorized by your instructions to interfere with, though you are to transmit home all the information you may obtain respecting the participation of French subjects or others in that traffic."[34]

Had this order been sooner conveyed to me through any channel, it would certainly have altered my position very materially with respect to the vessels which I have detained and captured, notwithstanding they had assumed the French flag and character, although it is possible I might still in effect have done as I have done, for to transmit home all the information I might obtain respecting the participation of French subjects or others in that traffic, it would be necessary that I should acquire such information by all legitimate means, which, as it enjoins the right of examination, would probably have led to similar results, since the examination of every of the ten cases in question shewed clearly that although under a French flag and assuming a French character, they had every one of them rendered themselves subject to the terms of the treaties between Great Britain, Spain, and the Netherlands, and were therefore subject to the particular instructions relative to the vessels of those nations. Yet, Sir, the positive order to abstain from all interference with vessels under any other flag than those of the Netherlands, Spain, or Portugal would have placed me in a dilemma, as it has done every commander of His Majesty's vessels on this station, which might indeed have been removed by a single qualification in the order; if, for example, the order had run thus, "to abstain from all interference with vessels under the French flag or others" (*those flags being legally assumed and worn*, and the vessel being legitimately employed according to the terms of their passports which must be absolutely respected) "which you are not authorized by your instructions to interfere with etc etc." Such a qualification as that I have presumed to offer to notice would have removed the seeming contradiction and difficulty which its present wording offers, and that this must have been the meaning and intent of the order appears to me clear, for if by examining vessels under another flag for the information which the same order enjoins, I find that she is subject to the instruction I am acting under by having assumed another national character; it becomes a manifest duty to detain her, although in apparent contradiction to the terms of the first part of the order, and this principle does appear the only one on which officers can continue to act, with all proper caution, until further orders may more clearly define the line of conduct to be followed on such occasions as those I have reported.

It never could have been the intention of their Lordships by the order in question to allow the vessels of Spain, the Netherlands, Brazil, or Portugal to cover their slave transactions by hoisting a table cloth or anything else which might bear a resemblance to the flag of some other nation; if otherwise (I speak with all humility), it would be impossible ever to succeed in putting down that diabolical traffic, which by the existing laws of nations, treaties, and our own force and activity, we are now fully equal to, if we do not suffer ourselves to be turned aside from the right line of public duty by the grave but jealous and petulant sensitiveness of France, who assumes a right principle to cover wrong transactions, and carries the principle itself much beyond reason and beyond her own practice.

Many of the merchants and planters at Martinique and Guadeloupe have very considerable shares in most of the vessels from St. Thomas', but that the present state of French laws rendering the voyage to Africa absolutely illegal and impossible from the West Indies with regular papers, which moreover in case of capture would compromise the parties, it has become a part of the system to furnish all such vessels with simulous papers procured for the most part at St. Thomas'.

It has also long been the practice to cover themselves also with Dutch papers, and some with Spanish, but the persons who sold Netherland papers have lately so much risen the price (even in some cases to two thousand dollars) that this expense does now in many cases prevent the practice.

[34]*Source:* TNA, ADM 1 2274.

DOCUMENT 35. HYDE DE NEUVILLE TO PRINCE POLIGNAC, MINISTER OF FOREIGN AFFAIRS (Paris, 4 June 1830)

Prince, you did me the honor by your letter of the 17th of last month to keep me abreast of the communications which the English ambassador made to Your Excellency on the subject of the grave inconveniences which result from the ease with which ships sailing in the Antilles and off the West African coast can change their nationality.[35]

I received with this letter the translation of a report sent to the British government by Monsieur the Vice-Admiral Fleming [Document 26], which tends to establish that these sorts of changes are done with the aim of committing acts of piracy and of evading the penalties pronounced against the slave trade.

Your Excellency informed me that Lord Stuart demanding, in the name of his Court, that appropriate measures be taken to extirpate these abuses.

Before examining to what degree it is possible to remedy them, I must reject several inexact allegations contained in Admiral Fleming's report.

We read in this document that "the chief evil under which all the pirates now cloak themselves is the open manner in which the slave trade is carried on between the French possessions in the West Indies and the coast of Africa."

This assertion is partially disproven by the very terms of the report, which announce that ships outfitted at Martinique and Guadeloupe for the trade, most of which are American, go to St. Thomas to get permission to fit out and to obtain cargoes. It is obvious that the owners of these ships would have no reason to seek these sorts of facilities in foreign possessions if it were true that slave-trading expeditions were tolerated in our colonies.

As for the operations of this nature which take place on the coast of Africa, the exactitude with which the French station in those waters fulfills the service entrusted to it is attested to by the care taken by the captains of slave-ships to disguise themselves, in its presence, with a foreign nationality, by means of sea papers obtained in the Danish, Swedish, or Spanish isles.

Admiral Fleming adds that since "the price of slaves has fallen very considerably in Cuba; and as that race do not decrease in the Spanish Islands, as is the case of those of France, there appears no doubt that if the French Government would honestly and seriously put down the slave trade, it would fall altogether in a few years."

Such an allegation is insulting to the government of His Majesty and Your Excellency will doubtless judge it proper to respond to it, since it is expressed in such a formal manner in an official diplomatic communication.

Today, there should be no doubt whatsoever about the commitment of France to end the slave trade.

A severe law has been passed against this criminal traffic. The administration devotes itself with perseverance to gathering and forwarding to the government all clues which can be brought to the tribunals, and its zeal in this regard has not limits but those which it cannot cross without interfering with the liberty of judgments.

Numerous cruisers on the west coast of Africa, the Antilles, and in the Indian seas are charged with searching and detaining French ships employed in the trade.

We know that, to escape the penalties pronounced by the law, French ships intended for this shameful traffic are sent to foreign countries where they receive their special equipment and from which they are sent to the African coast. This outfitting takes place, in appearance, on the account of foreign subjects after the simulated sale of the ship. The captains and principal investors receive pro forma naturalization and sea papers of diverse nations. It is by means of maneuvers such as these that their operations are accomplished. It is in the same foreign colonies to which the ships are returned, whether to be employed again in the trade or to be dismantled.

Thus, it is certainly not in France where we should today expect to see guilty verdicts returned in the matter of the slave trade.

As for our colonies, it is difficult, given this state of things, for the repression of the trade to be effective. In effect, without the presence of the slave ships and their crews, the tribunals of these establishments can only act upon public rumor, upon vague clues, for the furtive landing of blacks.

We cannot expect to see this situation improve in our overseas possessions as long as slave traders continue to find protection with the foreigners. For a long time, the Department of the Navy has deplored the fatal impunity and criminal acts that result from this, and it has on many occasions informed the predecessors of Your Excellency of it. Thus, I can only desire that you decide, together with the British government, to make new protests to the Courts of Denmark, Sweden, and Spain so that they put an end to the abusive facilities offered by their colonies to slave ships.

I must inform Your Excellency that many of the French papers found aboard slave ships have been shown to be false. It must be presumed that the same will be true of foreign sea papers, once the captains of slave ships cease to be able to procure authentic ones easily. But at least the measures I would like to see adopted would have stripped crime of the appearance of legality with which it still manages to mask part of its activities.

I do not know if, in requesting that steps be taken to guarantee the security of the seas and to ensure the execution of the laws against the trade, the ambassador of England wants France to adopt the principle which would accord to the warships of both nations the right of search and detention over merchant vessels covered by the flag of the other power.

[35] *Source:* ANOM, FM, 1 CORR 124.

DOCUMENT 36. POLIGNAC TO ROTHSAY (Paris, 12 June 1830)

Your Excellency informed me on May 5th last that you were charged by your Court with protesting, in the interest of abolishing piracy and the slave trade, against the facilities afforded ships sailing in the Antilles and off the west coast of Africa for changing their nationality.[36]

Your Excellency's letter was accompanied by a report from Monsieur the Admiral Fleming, containing allegations tending to impute to the King's government the continuation of a traffic that he has opposed openly and effectively to the present by the most determined and rigorous measures.

Since Your Excellency abstained from repeating these allegations, I must limit myself to expressing my regret at seeing the agents of the government manifesting and communicating suspicions which show a lack of reflection on the causes which maintain the commerce in blacks.

The surveillance that the King's government has recommended, in the ports of both France and its colonies, has made it impossible there to outfit ships for this odious traffic. The most well-known facts, as well as Monsieur the Admiral Fleming himself, recognize that most of the ships outfitted at Martinique and Guadeloupe, ultimately destined for the trade, most of which are American, are obliged, in order to evade the legal action to which they would infallibly be exposed in these colonies, to go to St. Thomas to obtain permission to equip themselves and obtain their cargos.

As for the trade which takes place on the coast of Africa, the exactitude with which the French naval station in those waters fulfills the service entrusted to it is proven by the care that slave-ship captains take to disguise themselves in its presence with a foreign nationality by means of sea papers obtained in the Danish, Spanish, or Swedish islands. It is thus obvious that the King's officials have nothing to do with the facilities the guilty speculators still find to help them continue the trade.

The King's government regrets, Monsieur ambassador, to find itself in the impossibility of adopting new measures against this traffic. It has taken, as its actions clearly show, all those necessary to render it impossible for his own subjects to pursue, but it has neither the mission nor the power to prevent the subjects of foreign powers from engaging in it.

[36] *Source:* TNA, FO 84 110.

DOCUMENT 37. FLEMING TO CROKER (Spithead, 1 July 1830)

Be pleased to acquaint My Lords Commissioners of the Admiralty that the two men named in the margin [Thomas George, James Patterson], the former a free black of Sierra Leone, the husband of the free black Woman Sarah, detained in the Island of Guadeloupe, and the other of the Kroo Nation, both of good homes, were in His Majesty's Ship Eden, and are victims to that atrocious piracy committed by the Crew of the "Niersee" or "Estafette" as I have already had the honor of stating to their Lordships, having heard that a Ship is fitting out at Plymouth for the coast of Africa, have applied to me to procure permission for their return to their Country in her.[37]

It is with infinite regret I have to acquaint their Lordships, that notwith-standing my reiterated applications, the Governor of Guadeloupe, Rear Admiral the Baron des Rotours, obstinately and pertinaciously avoided do-ing justice to this unfortunate female, or returning a single Negro of those landed from that vessel; notwithstanding that I had ascertained, and made known to him where she was; and offered to send persons to point the place out. The unfortunate husband's distress on this occasion, it would be difficult to describe; but affords a very striking example of the good effects of freedom and mild treatment, in the amelioration of the best of human feelings in that unfortunate race.

The French Government could not have a better opportunity of shew-ing their good faith in putting down this inhuman traffic, than by visiting the Baron des Rotours with their displeasure for the open protection he has thus afforded to it; and if that Government does not promptly take some measures to repress the almost unlimited introduction of Blacks from the Coast, the safety of all the neighboring Islands will be endangered, for they do not possess the means of repressing what will inevitably take place at no very distant period throughout the whole of the West India Slave Colonies, unless speedy measures are taken for gradual emancipation, and milder treatment; for to such an extent is the discontent in the Island of Marti-nique that not only the desertion of the Negroes from there are constant, many perishing at sea in small canoes; but the use of poison has become so general, that in the years 1826 and 1827 it was thought necessary to establish provost courts with extensive powers, but the executions ordered by them; and the contempt of death and tortures shewn by the Negroes, rather increased the evil; and I have been informed they are discontinued.

[37]*Source:* TNA, ADM 1 283.

PART IV

THE QUESTIONS

TIME, SPACE, AND TECHNOLOGY

1. In 1829 long-distance communications traveled no faster than ships, coaches, and horses. How did this influence the unfolding of the *Neirsée* affair and its diplomatic aftermath?

2. How do you think the story would have been different if the protagonists had had access to modern communication technologies (radio, internet, etc.)?

3. How do you suppose the slow speed of communication affected the broader colonial endeavors of the European powers?

4. What do you think the transatlantic slave trade would have been like by the late nineteenth century if the British had not launched their campaign to end it? How would late-nineteenth-century technologies have changed the slave trade?

IDENTITIES

1. Examine the documents carefully. In what different ways are the individuals they reference characterized? Why are they described in certain ways at certain times and in other ways at others?

2. Where do you find racism in the events of the *Neirsée* affair and the documents it generated? Are there any points at which you expected to find racism, but did not?

3. Race was a major factor in defining the identities of the people involved in the *Neirsée* affair. But race was not the only factor. What were some of the other factors? Give examples of how they played a role in the story.

4. Chose one of these factors. What does the *Neirsée* affair, as related in the graphic history and documents, reveal about that factor in the 1820s Atlantic world?

5. How did the different markers of identity interact with, reinforce, contradict, or modify each other in the story? Is it possible to rank these factors in order of importance? If so, provide your ranking and explain it. If not, explain why it is not possible to do so.

6. How did attitudes, policies, and practices relative to the transatlantic slave trade contribute to the formation of collective identities in the Atlantic world?

7. Some historians have spoken of different national Atlantics—an African Atlantic, a British Atlantic, a French Atlantic, etc. Having read the graphic history and the documents, do you agree with this way of understanding the Atlantic world? If so, why? If not, how would you prefer to parse the Atlantic space and why?

AGENCY

1. Historians studying groups that have generally been excluded from traditional historical narratives have been concerned in recent years about highlighting the ways those groups have actually managed to exercise agency—that is, to shape the course of history. Drawing upon the graphic history and documents, can you give examples of people from such groups exercising agency?

2. Discuss the pros and cons of emphasizing agency over victimhood. Is there a way of reconciling the two aspects of the historical experience? How might you do so in the case of the *Neirsée* affair?

3. How can one visually depict the experience of enslavement without (a) dehumanizing the people you are portraying and (b) glossing over the terrible predicament they are in?

4. Given that the documents mostly provide the point of view of high-ranking European officials, how can one recover the perspective of those people (captives, seamen, Sierra Leonean craftsmen, Sarah) who rarely, if ever, got a chance to leave a firsthand account of their experiences?

THE TRANSATLANTIC SLAVE TRADE DATABASE

(http://www.slavevoyages.org/tast/index.faces)

1. How does the *Neirsée* slave-trading expedition compare to other illicit voyages undertaken by French-flagged vessels in 1828? Take into account factors such as the number of captives, their age and gender, the nationality of the slave-trading vessel, its destination, etc. Explain why you chose the parameters you selected for your discussion.

2. Describe the characteristics of the typical illicit slave-trading voyage undertaken in 1828. Consider a range of factors and explain why you chose these parameters.

3. How typical was the *Neirsée* slave-trading expedition compared to other illicit voyages attempted in 1828 in (a) Biafra, (b) the Gulf of Guinea, and/or (c) the entire transatlantic slave trade? Consider a range of factors and explain why you chose these parameters.

4. Compare and contrast the *Neirsée* slave-trading expedition with those undertaken in 1788 from (a) Biafra, (b) the Gulf of Guinea, and/or (c) the entire transatlantic slave trade. Consider a range of factors and explain why you chose these parameters.

5. Compare and contrast the *Neirsée* slave-trading expedition with those undertaken in 1818 from (a) Biafra, (b) the Gulf of Guinea, and/or (c) the entire transatlantic slave trade. Consider a range of factors and explain why you chose these parameters.

6. Compare and contrast the *Neirsée* slave-trading expedition with those undertaken in 1838 from (a) Biafra, (b) the Gulf of Guinea, and/or (c) the entire transatlantic slave trade. Consider a range of factors and explain why you chose these parameters.

PRIMARY SOURCE DOCUMENTS

1. Was there a British view of the *Neirsée* affair? What was it? Were there differences among the principal British officials involved?

2. Was there a French view of the *Neirsée* affair? What was it? Were there differences of opinion between the principal French officials involved?

3. Why do you think the documents are so relatively silent on the African captives of the *Neirsée*'s original cargo?

4. During the recapture of the *Neirsée* by the slavers, what do you think the Sierra Leoneans were doing? Explain your answer.

5. How do you think the slavers were able to regain control of the *Neirsée*? What do you think about the notion that they bribed the prize crew members and got them drunk? Why?

6. Compare and contrast Fleming's and Rotours' dispatches. How are they similar? How are they different? What are the facts and opinions in the two sets of documents? Are there statements that you cannot easily fit into either category? What are they?

7. Read the depositions against each other and compare and contrast them. How do they agree? How do they differ? Pay attention not just to their words but also to their organization and emphases.

8. Compare and contrast the way British and French naval and colonial officials (Owen, Nicolay, Fleming, Deare, Rotours, and Hyde de Neuville) viewed the *Neirsée* incident with the way the British and French diplomatic officials (Aberdeen, Rothsay, Portalis, Polignac) did. Was there a naval/colonial perspective distinct from a diplomatic one? Why?

9. Compare and contrast the character and behavior of the two principal British naval officers in the story, Owen and Fleming. Who was the better officer and why?

MAKING THE GRAPHIC HISTORY

1. Use the documents to write a graphic narrative of the *Neirsée* affair as I did. You can focus on just one incident or take on the entire story. You can do it in the form of an outline, an essay, or Cell/Image/Text Type/Text Box. You have examples of this format in part 4, "The Making of *Inhuman Traffick*."

2. Critique the way we've done the script and artwork. What are their biases and weaknesses?

3. How did we portray the inexpressible feelings and trauma associated with the experience of enslavement? How would you do so?

VALUES

1. Is it acceptable to violate the sovereignty of another country in order to achieve a higher moral aim?

2. Analyze Owen's argument about flagging (Documents 32, 33, and 34). Is it convincing or not? Why?

3. Can you speak of the friction between Britain and France in the narrative as a clash between virtue and honor? Discuss, using examples ranging from the individual to the national levels.

4. What kind of activities did naval officers engage in? What qualities did they need to do their job well?

GAPS AND SILENCES

1. The archival documents on which the graphic narrative is based convey very little information about many of the things the illustrator needed to know to make visual images. What are some of these things?

2. The documents have many gaps and silences. To make this graphic narrative, I had to use my knowledge and imagination to make educated guesses about key events the documents pass over in silence. Some of these are:
   (a) Why Feraud shot the *Kent*'s mate and how he eluded Badgeley's surveillance.
   (b) What exactly happened when the slavers retook control of the *Neirsée*.
   (c) The *Neirsée*'s Middle Passage to Guadeloupe.
   (d) What happened to Sarah?
   (e) What happened to the Sierra Leoneans and Krumen upon their return to Africa?

(f) What the *Neirsée* was doing before the narrative begins and what became of it afterward.

(g) Duke Ephraim's perspective on the specific incidents involved in this narrative (the shooting of the *Kent*'s mate, his attitude toward Feraud, his reasons for tipping off Owen that Feraud had returned, etc.).

3. Do you agree with my guess as to what happened at any or all of these junctures? What are some plausible alternatives? Which version to you prefer?

TIMELINE OF THE TRANSATLANTIC SLAVE TRADE

1440

1425

1450 —————— **1440s** Beginning of transatlantic slave trade

1475

1500

1550

1600

1625 —————— **1635** First French colonists settle on Guadeloupe

1650

1675 —————— **1671** Guadeloupe becomes colony of French Crown

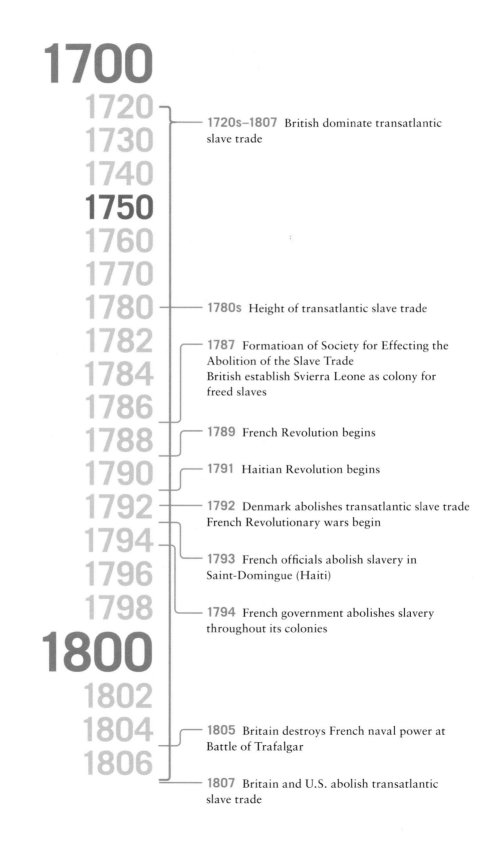

1700

1720
1730
1740
1750
1760
1770
1780
1782
1784
1786
1788
1790
1792
1794
1796
1798
1800
1802
1804
1806

1720s–1807 British dominate transatlantic slave trade

1780s Height of transatlantic slave trade

1787 Formatioan of Society for Effecting the Abolition of the Slave Trade
British establish Svierra Leone as colony for freed slaves

1789 French Revolution begins

1791 Haitian Revolution begins

1792 Denmark abolishes transatlantic slave trade
French Revolutionary wars begin

1793 French officials abolish slavery in Saint-Domingue (Haiti)

1794 French government abolishes slavery throughout its colonies

1805 Britain destroys French naval power at Battle of Trafalgar

1807 Britain and U.S. abolish transatlantic slave trade

1808
1810
1812
1814
1816
1818
1820
1822
1824
1826
1828
1830
1832
1834
1836
1838
1840
1842
1844
1846
1848
1850

1812 Beginning of War of 1812 between Britain and U.S.

1815 End of Napoleonic Wars and War of 1812

1815 Congress of Vienna issues proclamation condemning slave trade

1817 Netherlands, Spain, and Portugal sign anti–slave trade treaties with Britain

1819 Court of Mixed Commission opens in Sierra Leone

1819 First permanent West African Squadron begins operations

1822 Brazil declares independence from Portugal

1826 Brazil signs anti–slave trade treaty with Britain but does not enforce it

1827 British make establishment on Fernando Po

1828–1829 *Neirsée* incident

1830 Louis Philippe made king of France by July Revolution; he is an abolitionist

1831 France signs anti–slave trade convention

1833 Britain ends slavery in its colonies

1845 Brazil repudiates 1826 anti–slave trade treaty

1848 France ends slavery in its colonies

1850 Britain forces Brazil to end transatlantic slave trade

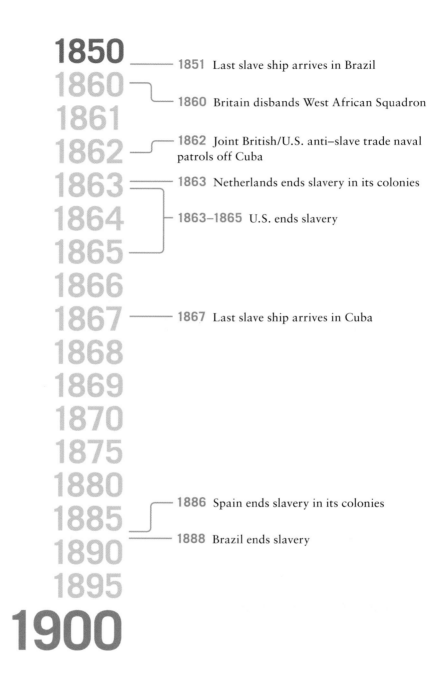

1850 —————— 1851 Last slave ship arrives in Brazil

1860 —————— 1860 Britain disbands West African Squadron

1861

1862 —————— 1862 Joint British/U.S. anti–slave trade naval
patrols off Cuba

1863 —————— 1863 Netherlands ends slavery in its colonies

1864 —————— 1863–1865 U.S. ends slavery

1865

1866

1867 —————— 1867 Last slave ship arrives in Cuba

1868

1869

1870

1875

1880

1885 —————— 1886 Spain ends slavery in its colonies

1890 —————— 1888 Brazil ends slavery

1895

1900

BIBLIOGRAPHY

PRIMARY SOURCES

THE BRITISH NATIONAL ARCHIVES
Admiralty (ADM) 1
- 280–283 Correspondence, Commander, West Indies Station
- 1682–85 Alphabetical Captains' Correspondence
- 2272–74 Alphabetical Captains' Correspondence
- 4243–44 Correspondence, Secretaries of State to Admiralty

ADM 2
- 1329 Orders to Commanders-in-Chief
- 1589 Military Orders

Colonial Office (CO) 71
- 67, 68 Dominica

CO 81
- 1 Fernando Po

CO 267
- 98–100 Sierra Leone

Foreign Office (FO) 84
- 73, 87, 89, 94, 96, 97, 110, 123 Slave Trade (Courts of Mixed Commission)

FO 146
- 105, 107 France (Slave Trade)

ARCHIVES DES AFFAIRES ÉTRANGÈRES
Affaires Diverses Politiques (ADP)
- 30 Slave Trade

Correspondance Politique (CP), Angleterre
- 627 Diplomatic Correspondence with British Government

ARCHIVES NATIONALES D'OUTRE-MER
Fonds Ministériel (FM), 1 Correspondence (CORR)
- 118, 120, 121, 124 Correspondence of Minister of Colonies

FM, Série Géographique (SG), Guadeloupe Correspondence (GUA/COR)
- 78, 79 Governor to Minister of Colonies

FM, SG, Martinique Correspondence (MAR/COR)
  • 65, 66 Governor to Minister of Colonies

SECONDARY SOURCES

THE ANTI-SLAVERY PATROLS
Edwards, Bernard. *The Royal Navy versus the Slave Traders: Enforcing Abolition at Sea, 1808–1898*. Barnsley, UK: Pen and Sword, 2008.
Lloyd, Christopher. *The Navy and the Slave Trade: The Suppression of the African Slave Trade in the Nineteenth Century*. London: Cass, 1968.
Rees, Siân. *Sweet Water and Bitter: The Ships That Stopped the Slave Trade*. Lebanon, NH: University Press of New England, 2011.
Ward, W. E. F. *The Royal Navy and the Slavers: The Suppression of the Atlantic Slave Trade*. New York: Pantheon Books, 1969.

THE EXPERIENCE OF ENSLAVEMENT AND THE MIDDLE PASSAGE
Behrendt, Stephen D., David Eltis, and David Richardson. "The Costs of Coercion: African Agency in the Pre-Modern Atlantic World." *Economic History Review* 54, n.s., no. 3 (August 2001): 454–476.
Christopher, Emma. *Slave Ship Sailors and Their Captive Cargoes, 1730–1807*. Cambridge: Cambridge University Press, 2006.
Falola, Toyin, and Amanda Warnock. *Encyclopedia of the Middle Passage*. Westport, CT: Greenwood, 2007.
Rediker, Marcus. *The Slave Ship: A Human History*. New York: Viking, 2007.
Smallwood, Stephanie. *Saltwater Slavery: A Middle Passage from Africa to American Diaspora*. Cambridge, MA: Harvard University Press, 2007.

ORIGINS AND EFFECTS OF ABOLITIONISM
Bender, Thomas, ed. *The Antislavery Debate: Capitalism and Abolitionism as a Problem in Historical Interpretation*. Berkeley: University of California Press, 1992.
Blackburn, Robin. *The Overthrow of Colonial Slavery, 1776–1848*. London: Verso, 1988.
Brown, Christopher Leslie. *Moral Capital: Foundations of British Abolitionism*. Chapel Hill: University of North Carolina Press, 2006.
Davis, David Brion. *The Problem of Slavery in the Age of Revolution, 1770–1823*. Ithaca, NY: Cornell University Press, 1975.
Drescher, Seymour. *Capitalism and Antislavery: British Mobilization in Comparative Perspective*. Basingstoke, UK: Macmillan, 1986.
———. *The Mighty Experiment: Free Labor versus Slavery in British Emancipation*. Oxford: Oxford University Press, 2002.
———. *Abolition: A History of Slavery and Antislavery*. Cambridge: Cambridge University Press, 2009.
Eltis, David. *Economic Growth and the Ending of the Transatlantic Slave Trade*. New York and Oxford: Oxford University Press, 1987.
Fradera, Josep M., and Christopher Schmidt-Nowara, eds. *Slavery and Anti-Slavery in Spain's Atlantic Empire*. New York: Berghan, 2013.
Jennings, Lawrence C. *French Anti-Slavery: The Movement for the Abolition of Slavery in France, 1802–1848*. Cambridge: Cambridge University Press, 2000.
Kielstra, Paul Michael. *The Politics of Slave Trade Suppression in Britain and France, 1814–48: Diplomacy, Morality and Economics*. Basingstoke, UK: Macmillan, 2000.

Miers, Suzanne. *Britain and the Ending of the Slave Trade*. London: Longman, 1975.

Mulligan, William, and Maurice Bric, eds. *A Global History of Anti-Slavery Politics in the Nineteenth Century*. Basingstoke, UK: Palgrave Macmillan, 2013.

Murray, David R. *Odious Commerce: Spain and the Abolition of the Cuban Slave Trade*. Cambridge: Cambridge University Press, 2002.

Oldfield, J. R. *Popular Politics and British Anti-Slavery: The Mobilisation of Public Opinion against the Slave Trade, 1787–1807*. Manchester, UK: Manchester University Press, 1995.

Ryden, David. *West Indian Slavery and British Abolition, 1783–1807*. Cambridge: Cambridge University Press, 2009.

OVERVIEWS

"Abolishing the Slave Trades: Ironies and Reverberations." Special issue. *William and Mary Quarterly* 66, 3rd series, no. 4 (October 2009).

Davis, David Brion. *Inhuman Bondage: The Rise and Fall of Slavery in the New World*. Oxford: Oxford University Press, 2006.

Eltis, David, and David Richardson. "A New Assessment of the Transatlantic Slave Trade." In *Extending the Frontiers: Essays on the New Transatlantic Slave Trade Database*, edited by David Eltis and David Richardson, 1–60. New Haven: Yale University Press, 2008.

———. *Atlas of the Transatlantic Slave Trade*. New Haven: Yale University Press, 2010.

Eltis, David, and Stanley L. Engerman, eds. *The Cambridge World History of Slavery*. Vol. 3, *AD 1420–AD 1804*. Cambridge: Cambridge University Press, 2011.

Klein, Herbert S. *The Atlantic Slave Trade*. Cambridge: Cambridge University Press, 1999.

Klein, Martin A., ed. *Breaking the Chains: Slavery, Bondage, and Emancipation in Modern Africa and Asia*. Madison: University of Wisconsin Press, 1993.

"New Perspectives on the Transatlantic Slave Trade." Special issue. *William and Mary Quarterly* 58, 3rd series, no.1: (January 2001).

Slavery & Abolition: A Journal of Slave and Post-Slave Studies. Many articles in numerous issues.

Tomich, Dale W. *Through the Prism of Slavery: Labor, Capital, and the World Economy*. Lanham, MD: Rowman & Littlefield, 2003.

REPRESENTING SLAVERY AND THE SLAVE TRADE

Wood, Marcus. *Blind Memory: Visual Representations of Slavery in England and America, 1780–1865*. New York: Routledge, 2000.

———. *Slavery, Empathy, and Pornography*. Oxford: Oxford University Press, 2002.

———. *The Horrible Gift of Freedom: Atlantic Slavery and the Representation of Emancipation*. Athens: University of Georgia Press, 2010.

SIERRA LEONE

Fyfe, Christopher. *A History of Sierra Leone*. Oxford: Oxford University Press, 1962.

Peterson, John. *Province of Freedom: A History of Sierra Leone, 1787–1870*. Evanston, IL: Northwestern University Press, 1969.

SLAVERY IN AFRICA

Diouf, Sylviane A., ed. *Fighting the Slave Trade: West African Strategies*. Athens: Ohio University Press, 2003.

Getz, Trevor R. *Slavery and Reform in West Africa: Toward Emancipation in Nineteenth-Century Senegal and the Gold Coast.* Athens: Ohio University Press, 2004.

Klein, Martin A. *Slavery and Colonial Rule in French West Africa.* Cambridge: Cambridge University Press, 1998.

Lawrance, Benjamin N., and Richard L. Roberts, eds. *Trafficking in Slavery's Wake: Law and the Experience of Women and Children in Africa.* Athens: Ohio University Press, 2012.

Lovejoy, Paul E. *Transformations in Slavery: A History of Slavery in Africa.* 3rd ed. Cambridge: Cambridge University Press, 2011.

Miers, Suzanne, and Igor Kopytoff, eds. *Slavery in Africa: Historical and Anthropological Perspectives.* Madison: University of Wisconsin Press, 1977.

Miers, Suzanne, and Richard Roberts. *The End of Slavery in Africa.* Madison: University of Wisconsin Press, 1988.

Miller, Joseph C. *Way of Death: Merchant Capitalism and the Angolan Slave Trade, 1730–1830.* Madison: University of Wisconsin Press, 1988.

Nwokeji, G. Ugo. *The Slave Trade and Culture in the Bight of Biafra: An African Society in the Atlantic World.* Cambridge: Cambridge University Press, 2010.

Shumway, Rebecca. *The Fante and the Transatlantic Slave Trade.* Rochester, NY: University of Rochester Press, 2011.

Sparks, Randy J. *The Two Princes of Calabar: An Eighteenth-Century Atlantic Odyssey.* Cambridge, MA: Harvard University Press, 2009.

SLAVERY IN AMERICA

Bethel, Leslie. *The Abolition of the Brazilian Slave Trade: Britain, Brazil and the Slave Trade Question, 1807–1869.* Cambridge: Cambridge University Press, 1970.

Brown, Vincent. *The Reaper's Garden: Death and Power in the World of Atlantic Slavery.* Cambridge, MA: Harvard University Press, 2010.

Eltis, David, Frank D. Lewis, and Kenneth L. Sokoloff, eds. *Slavery in the Development of the Americas.* Cambridge: Cambridge University Press, 2004.

Fehrenbacher, Don E. *The Slaveholding Republic: An Account of the United States Government's Relations to Slavery.* Oxford: Oxford University Press, 2001.

Marques, João Pedro. *The Sounds of Silence: Nineteenth-Century Portugal and the Abolition of the Slave Trade.* Trans. Richard Wall. New York: Berghan, 2006.

Schmidt-Nowara, Christopher. *Slavery, Freedom, and Abolition in Latin America and the Atlantic World.* Albuquerque: University of New Mexico Press, 2011.

Tomich, Dale W. *Slavery in the Circuit of Sugar: Martinique and the World Economy, 1830–1848.* Baltimore: Johns Hopkins University Press, 1990.

GLOSSARY

APPRENTICESHIP: A labor arrangement in which a beginning worker serves under an experienced master to learn a trade; used euphemistically to maintain former slaves as bound laborers.

COASTING: The period of time during which slave ships lingered off the African coast, gradually accumulating their human cargoes.

CONGRESS OF VIENNA: The European peace conference that followed the Napoleonic Wars.

COURTS OF MIXED COMMISSION: International tribunals established by treaty to judge cases of illegal slave trading.

DEBT PEONAGE: A type of bondage in which a person is required to perform unpaid labor in order to pay off an enormous, essentially unpayable debt.

ENLIGHTENMENT: The liberal intellectual movement that swept through much of Europe and parts of the Atlantic world during the eighteenth century.

EURAFRICAN: People of mixed African and European descent who often played key mercantile roles on the West African coast.

INDENTURE: A labor arrangement in which a worker agrees to serve out a long contract in order to repay a loan; used euphemistically to maintain former slaves as bound laborers.

KRU; KRUMEN: A group in West Africa whose members made money by serving as sailors on European vessels, frequently those of the Royal Navy.

MATRILINEAL: A form of family structure based around the female line.

MATRILOCAL: A type of residential structure in which the husband lives with his wife's family.

PRIVATEERS: Private warships licensed by belligerent powers to raid their enemy's seaborne commerce.

PRIZE CREW: Sailors placed on board a captured vessel to take charge of it.

QUAKERS: A British Protestant denomination known as the Society of Friends, which was one of the earliest, most outspoken opponents of the slave trade.

RECAPTIVES: African captives liberated from slave ships by the Royal Navy.

SHARECROPPING: A form of land tenure by which a landlord concedes a piece of land to a tenant in exchange for an annual share of the harvest.

The Runner's Edge

Stephen J. McGregor, PhD
Matt Fitzgerald

Human Kinetics

gress Cataloging-in-Publication Data

The runner's edge / Stephen J. McGregor, Matt Fitzgerald.
    p. cm.
  Includes bibliographical references and index.
  ISBN-13: 978-0-7360-8115-3 (soft cover)
  ISBN-10: 0-7360-8115-1 (soft cover)
  1. Running--Training. 2. Running--Physiological aspects. I.
Fitzgerald, Matt. II. Title.
  GV1061.5.M345 2010
  796.42--dc22

                        2009026622

ISBN-10: 0-7360-8115-1 (print)   ISBN-10: 0-7360-8611-0 (Adobe PDF)
ISBN-13: 978-0-7360-8115-3 (print)   ISBN-13: 978-0-7360-8611-0 (Adobe PDF)

The Web addresses cited in this text were current as of September 2009, unless otherwise noted.

Acquisitions Editor: Laurel Plotzke; **Developmental Editor:** Cynthia McEntire; **Assistant Editor:** Scott Hawkins; **Copyeditor:** Jan Feeney; **Indexer:** Dan Connolly; **Permission Manager:** Martha Gullo; **Graphic Designer:** Joe Buck; **Graphic Artist:** Tara Welsch; **Cover Designer:** Keith Blomberg; **Photographer (cover):** Erik Palmer/Fotstock/age fotostock; **Photo Asset Manager:** Laura Fitch; **Photo Production Manager:** Jason Allen; **Art Manager and Illustrator:** Kelly Hendren; **Printer:** United Graphics

Human Kinetics books are available at special discounts for bulk purchase. Special editions or book excerpts can also be created to specification. For details, contact the Special Sales Manager at Human Kinetics.

Printed in the United States of America   10   9   8   7   6   5   4   3   2   1

The paper in this book is certified under a sustainable forestry program.

Human Kinetics
Web site: www.HumanKinetics.com

United States: Human Kinetics
P.O. Box 5076
Champaign, IL 61825-5076
800-747-4457
e-mail: humank@hkusa.com

Canada: Human Kinetics
475 Devonshire Road Unit 100
Windsor, ON N8Y 2L5
800-465-7301 (in Canada only)
e-mail: info@hkcanada.com

Europe: Human Kinetics
107 Bradford Road
Stanningley
Leeds LS28 6AT, United Kingdom
+44 (0) 113 255 5665
e-mail: hk@hkeurope.com

Australia: Human Kinetics
57A Price Avenue
Lower Mitcham, South Australia 5062
08 8372 0999
e-mail: info@hkaustralia.com

New Zealand: Human Kinetics
Division of Sports Distributors NZ Ltd.
P.O. Box 300 226 Albany
North Shore City
Auckland
0064 9 448 1207
e-mail: info@humankinetics.co.nz

E4735